D1487915

796.32364 F875
Freedman, Lew.
The 50 greatest plays in
Chicago Bears football ...

MID-CONTINENT PUBLIC LIBRARY
Colbern Road Branch
1000 N.E. Colbern Road
Lee's Summit, MO 64086 **CR**

THE 50 GREATEST PLAYS
in CHICAGO BEARS
Football History

THE 50 GREATEST PLAYS
in CHICAGO BEARS
Football History

LEW FREEDMAN

TRIUMPH
BOOKS

MID-CONTINENT PUBLIC LIBRARY
Colbern Road Branch
1000 N.E. Colbern Road
Lee's Summit, MO 64086
CR

MID-CONTINENT PUBLIC LIBRARY

3 0000 13135697 8

Copyright © 2008 by Lew Freedman

No part of this publication may be reproduced, stored in a retrieval system, or transmitted in any form by any means, electronic, mechanical, photocopying, or otherwise, without the prior written permission of the publisher, Triumph Books, 542 South Dearborn Street, Suite 750, Chicago, Illinois 60605.

Triumph Books and colophon are registered trademarks of Random House, Inc.

Library of Congress Cataloging-in-Publication Data

Freedman, Lew.
 The 50 greatest plays in Chicago Bears football history / Lew Freedman.
    p. cm.
 Includes bibliographical references.
 ISBN-13: 978-1-60078-122-3
 ISBN-10: 1-60078-122-5
 1. Chicago Bears (Football team)—History. I. Title. II. Title: Fifty greatest plays in Chicago Bears football history.
 GV956.C5F7313 2008
 796.323'640977311—dc22

                    2008012089

This book is available in quantity at special discounts for your group or organization. For further information, contact:

Triumph Books
542 South Dearborn Street
Suite 750
Chicago, Illinois 60605
(312) 939–3330
Fax (312) 663–3557

Printed in U.S.A.
ISBN: 978-1-60078-122-3
Design by Sue Knopf
Page production by Patricia Frey
Photos courtesy of Getty Images unless otherwise indicated.

I dedicate this book to the 1963 Chicago Bears championship team, an underrated and overlooked squad on the long list of great Bears teams.

CONTENTS

FOREWORD

When someone mentions the Chicago Bears to me, the first thing that jumps into my mind is George Halas. I can see him back at the beginning when the National Football League was forming, sitting in that car showroom with the other owners, and then later in Decatur, Illinois, where he was putting the club together.

George Halas was always ahead of the game, and he was always thinking about the future of the game. When I retired as a linebacker with the Bears in 1979, I remember asking him, "What are the Chicago Bears worth?" He said, "Oh, I don't know kid, $20 million or $30 million, something like that. But I got to tell you, down the road TV is going to make a big difference in what we do."

He was right. Now the Bears are worth close to $1 billion. Of course, no way George would have sold them at any price. This team was his love.

The Bears have had a long and glorious history, and won a lot of championships. Of course, there have been many great plays along the way. My all-time favorite play with the Bears occurred on December 16, 1979. We were playing against the St. Louis Cardinals.

We had to beat St. Louis to get into the playoffs. But that wasn't all. We had to win by 32 points, and the Dallas Cowboys had to beat the Washington Redskins. An impossible set of circumstances, right? Well, it happened.

My favorite play was a fake punt. I was playing fullback and Bob Parsons was punting. We knew we had to try everything to get points. I said, "Bob, let's go for it. Let's fake it." The Cardinals rushed the punter and it was almost like a screen pass. I picked up the guy coming in on a block and then slid off. Bob passed out to the flat and we got a first down. I gained 20 or 30 yards on the play, but the guy who knocked me out of bounds almost killed me.

We needed to keep the drive going. Think about it: we had to win by 30 points. We pulled everything out in that game. That play sticks out in my mind because of why we needed to do it. This was good, old-fashioned backyard football. Fake a punt. It wasn't really even a play call. It was, "Bobby, hit me with the ball, will you?"

It all worked out. Dallas beat Washington, and we won the game 42–6 to go to the playoffs.

I have seen quite a few Bears plays that were exciting. I blocked for Gale Sayers when he was returning punts and kicks. Dick Butkus and I blocked, and we knew if we could get somebody out of the way, look out. I watch Devin Hester and I think the same thing: give him an inch and he's going to take it all.

Those guys create excitement, and it's even more exciting when you are part of it. I was starting as a linebacker, but I'd volunteer to be part of the blocking wedge. We took it seriously.

I played eight years with Dick Butkus and six years with Sayers. And then I had five years with Walter Payton. I saw so many Hall of Famers. You don't hear as much about the great defensive guys besides Butkus. Guys like Bill George and Doug Atkins. Atkins was a terrible practice player, but when he suited up on Sunday, he was great. I knew as soon as I saw Dan Hampton that he was going to be a Hall of Famer. We had other great defenders who didn't even get into the Hall, like Joe Fortunato, Gary Fencik, and Doug Plank. They were outstanding.

When I tell someone I played linebacker for the Chicago Bears for 14 years, and someone else says they played for Tampa Bay, it's not the same. There's a little more pride in your voice when you're a Chicago Bear.

One way or another, as a player and as a sports broadcaster, I have been around the Bears for 42 years, and I have seen a lot of great players making great plays.

Something that is very special about the Bears is the team's link to the community. They are more a part of the community than other teams, and I think George Halas instilled that, and it's never left. For the fans, it became something you were part of. Even in the bad years—and I played during a lot of them—back at Wrigley Field, the fans made you feel as if you were playing in championship games. They loved the physical play. That's one thing about Chicago. The fans always looked at the defense and looked at the middle linebacker and looked at the running game. It's inherited.

The Bears stand for something. When you think of the Chicago Bears, a vision of George Halas pops up, a vision of the old days and Bronko Nagurski. Then you work your way up to Gale Sayers and Walter Payton. The Bears have always had somebody special who is the face of the team. Right now it's Brian Urlacher.

When you are working in radio, you always get the question, "Is Chicago a Bears town? Is it a Cubs town? Is it a White Sox town?" There's no question what it is. Chicago is a Bears town.

—Doug Buffone

ACKNOWLEDGMENTS

A special thank-you to the always-terrific research staff at the Pro Football Hall of Fame Library, who went above and beyond the call with its help this time.

Thanks also to the Chicago Bears' public relations staff for their assistance, and to Bill Wade, quarterback of the 1963 title team.

INTRODUCTION

The Chicago Bears are one of the most storied franchises in the National Football League. The Bears, once known as the Decatur Staleys, were there at the beginning when league organizers jump-started the creation of professional football that led to the game we have today.

Bears founder, owner, coach, and player George Halas was there at the beginning, too, as were some of the greatest players in professional football history. The Bears date back to 1920, and over time they built themselves into a Chicago institution and the pride of the city.

The Bears contributed heavily in authorship as the early history of the league was written, and the oldest of fans, with the longest of memories, can remember when Red Grange, the Galloping Ghost, first took the field for the Bears, or when Bronko Nagurski, the human battering ram, powered through defensive lines.

When the first meaningful professional indoor football game was played, the Bears were part of it. When the largest margin in a pro football game was recorded, the Bears were part of that. When an icy field determined the results of a championship game, the Bears were part of that, too.

Whether it was winning championships, establishing milestones, or introducing some of the most exciting and talented players to NFL lore, the Bears were omnipresent.

With such a long and glorious history, it was not easy to determine—in order—the 50 greatest plays in the annals of the team. That is less than one per season. No such list could be compiled without some controversy, so positioning in the ranking is bound to be debatable.

Some general criteria helped contribute to the list's final order. If a single play's execution won a championship game, that was considered extremely significant. If a play was part of a record-setting performance, that raised its value. If a play was flat-out spectacular and meaningful within the context of a game, that was good for bonus points. The record book was studied. The offbeat was examined. Sheer flashiness on the excitement meter was considered.

Many of these plays occurred before many of today's fans were born. Some were never recorded on film. Even newspaper accounts of the day did not always focus on explaining exactly how a key play unfolded, and quotes from players in years past were an afterthought rather than commonplace, as they are now. In some cases I wish more details were available pertaining to specific plays. Alas, many of those who participated in them passed away many years ago.

I was present and accounted for in Soldier Field to witness several plays on the list. One day, if he stays healthy, perhaps there will be a *Devin Hester Chronicles* featuring 50 of his best plays. I was in attendance when Mike Brown intercepted two passes to win overtime games in two consecutive weeks. Surreal moments, times two.

Some of the 50 plays are engraved in Bears fans' minds. Some plays may have been forgotten. Some plays may be symbolic of great moments. But it is neither accident nor coincidence that the names most familiar to Bears fans played key roles in pivotal moments over the years.

Red Grange, Bronko Nagurski, George Halas, Sid Luckman, Gale Sayers, Dick Butkus, Mike Ditka, Walter Payton, Rick Casares, Harlon Hill, Kevin Butler, Jim McMahon, William Perry, Brian Urlacher, and Devin Hester are only some of the Bears stars who immortalized themselves in a stop-the-clock, freeze-the-frame moment.

Much thought and a lot of opinion went into compiling this list. It wasn't just a matter of throwing darts. There are bound to be favorites overlooked, and there are bound to be disagreements with the final ranking. But that's what talking sports is all about.

December 7, 1980

50 DESTROYING ENEMY MORALE

Bears Massacre Green Bay 61–7

The Chicago Bears–Green Bay Packers rivalry dates back to the beginnings of the National Football League. It is the most intense, longstanding rivalry in pro football and is one of the most anticipated and respected rivalries in all of sports.

The teams are located in the neighboring states of Illinois and Wisconsin and although the state line is barely 50 miles north of Chicago, it is a very tangible rooting interest divider. If you live south of the boundary, you are a Bears fan; if you live north of the boundary, you are a Packers fan.

Year after year the battles play out. The cast of characters, great players, and famous coaches comes and goes. From Curly Lambeau and George Halas to Mike Ditka and Forrest Gregg, the men in charge have always known there is something special about the two dates on the calendar each autumn.

Bears fans hated Brett Favre, not because of the type of player he was (that they admire), but because he regularly beat their team for 16 years. There have been ups and downs in the rivalry with trends of dominance in various decades. But

one game stands out as the most lopsided wipeout of all.

Late in the 1980 season, the Bears laid the most nasty, vicious, take-'em-to-the-woodshed beating imaginable on the Packers. The 61–7 thumping was a Bears fan's fantasy come to life, a game appreciated as much for its excitement as it was for its unexpectedness.

The Bears made the playoffs in 1979 and were optimistic heading into the 1980 season. When the Packers bested the Bears 12–6 in overtime in the season opener, it was a hint that things might not go so smoothly. As the season unfolded, it turned out the Bears were not particularly good in 1980 (they finished 7–9). But for one day, they became the best team on the planet.

There was a bit of controversy, too, as Packers coach Bart Starr hinted that the Bears were trying to run up the score. And it was suggested later that the Bears were so successful in stymieing the Packers' offense because they had been stealing Green Bay's signals. The Packers left the field humiliated and angry.

Walter Payton rushed for three touchdowns in a 61–7 rout of the Green Bay Packers in 1980. *(Photo courtesy of WireImages)*

In sheer magnitude, the score rivaled the Bears' 73–0 mashing of the Washington Redskins in the 1940 NFL Championship Game—and it occurred 40 years minus one day of the anniversary of that mauling. In pure meaning, however, it was well... meaningless. During the rout the Bears learned they had been eliminated from playoff contention. One reason was that they didn't play with this same level of vigor all year and juggled quarterbacks (three of them) like a circus performer.

The Bears led 28–7 at the half but didn't feel safe because only a month earlier, a 35–0 first-half lead turned into a close game in the second half. Against the Packers, though, the Bears ran up touchdowns like pinball points before 57,176 gleeful fans at Soldier Field. On

a demoralizing day for Green Bay, the Bears scored every which way. Backups scored touchdowns. Lenny Walterscheid, enjoying his best year in the secondary, stole a pass and ran it back for a touchdown.

Vince Evans had a free-and-easy day at quarterback, completing 18 of 22 passes for 316 yards and three touchdowns. Running back Walter Payton, who rushed for three touchdowns and 130 yards to take over the league lead, became the focus of Packer ire late in the game. He retired to the sideline four plays into the fourth quarter, but as it turned out, he was only taking a breather.

At one point the Bears had backup quarterback Mike Phipps filling in for Evans, and Willie McClendon and John Skibinski in the game replacing Payton and Roland

PARTNERS ON AND OFF THE FIELD

Rarely do friendships in the locker room fit so neatly together and transcend football, as well.

The tandem of Bears fullback Matt Suhey and halfback Walter Payton in the 1980s did. The men were best friends away from the game and close, working cogs on the field. Payton was the glamour player, always in the public spotlight, gaining most of the yards and making most of the All-Pro teams.

Yet while overshadowed, Suhey was blessed to play on a running football team that had room in its offensive plans for more than one ball carrier. In 1981, Payton was the workhorse with 1,222 yards gained, but Suhey added 521 yards of his own. In 1983, Payton rushed for 1,421 yards and Suhey added

> **H**e wants that rushing title.
> —LINEMAN NOAH JACKSON ON WALTER PAYTON

681 yards. Any time teammates rush for more than 2,000 yards in an NFL season it is regarded as superb production.

Suhey and Payton socialized off the field, joked around together (Payton did a lot of joking), and in the final days of Payton's life as he was dying from side effects of his liver disease, the men shared private thoughts.

Running back Walter Payton and fullback Matt Suhey were a winning combination both on and off the field. *(Photo courtesy of WireImages)*

GAME DETAILS

Bears 61 • Packers 7

Location: Soldier Field, Chicago

Attendance: 57,176

Why did I put [Payton] back in? He wanted to run the ball a few more times.

—BEARS HEAD COACH NEILL ARMSTRONG

Box Score:

Packers	0	7	0	0	**7**
Bears	0	28	13	20	**61**

Scoring:

CHI Payton 1-yard run (Thomas PAT)

CHI Payton 3-yard run (Thomas PAT)

CHI Harper 1-yard run (Thomas PAT)

GB Lofton 15-yard pass from Dickey (Stenerud PAT)

CHI Baschnagel 4-yard pass from Evans (Thomas PAT)

CHI Earl 9-yard pass from Evans (PAT blocked)

CHI Watts 53-yard pass from Evans (Thomas PAT)

CHI Payton 14-yard run (Thomas PAT)

CHI Walterscheid 36-yard interception return (Thomas PAT)

CHI McClendon 1-yard run (PAT failed)

Harper. But on the Bears possession after Walterscheid's return, with the score 55–7, Payton trotted back onto the field.

Payton's mere presence had the feel of rubbing it in, though Bears coach Neill Armstrong later defended the move by saying while he wanted to rest Payton for the remainder of the game, Payton insisted on going back in.

Although another coach might have refused to listen, Payton had earned the right to tell a coach to put him back in. Who wanted to discourage Walter Payton from playing?

As for Payton's motivation, who could blame him? Payton was a sparkling star on a mediocre team. He had to find ways to psyche himself up week to week.

Armstrong actually said afterward, "I'm not one to run up the score."

Of course, during his three-season tenure to date, that hadn't been the Bears' biggest problem. They were just happy to win, never mind score so many points they would be badmouthed. Some Packers would talk about the notion that the Bears were perhaps running up the tally a bit.

"When you see guys like him (Payton) come back in with the score that lopsided, it kind of sticks in your mind," said Green Bay defensive back Estus Hood.

The game meant nothing in the standings, but the thoroughness of the beating, the size of the point differential, is fondly remembered by Bears fans. When the cheeseheads come to town or Bears fans venture north a few hours to visit Lambeau Field, the 61–7 score is a trump card in most discussions.

It may not have been a pretty game. It may not have been the most meaningful win. But heck, the Chicago Bears beat the Green Bay Packers 61–7 in a genuine game. That is not something forgotten easily. It was a day when Walter Payton was at the top of his game and he didn't want to quit early. He wanted in on all 60 minutes of football and he was Walter Payton.

November 15, 1931

Talk About Being on a Roll

Joe Lintzenich's 94-Yard Punt

It is a general belief in football that punters should be seen and not heard.

Mostly because anything you hear about them typically involves bad news. If you hear about a punter, it normally means A) he had a punt blocked, or B) he shanked a short one. Once in a great while there are reports of good news, such as a punter hitting one high and deep for great distance, or of regularly pinning the enemy deep in his territory.

Other than that, most punts are an afterthought. The team is coming off a downer of a possession where it failed to make a first down and had to give the ball away. The punter's role is to catch the long snap cleanly and boot the ball out of harm's way. All mistakes are greatly magnified.

Once in a great while a punter smacking one deep will elicit oohs and ahhs from fans and then be quickly forgotten as the action resumes. And once in a great, great while, a punt will roll and roll and be remembered forever.

Such was the 94-yard boot that came off the foot of Bears punter Joe Lintzenich in a 12–6 victory over the New York Giants in 1931. The sheer audacity of the number is hard to fathom. The ball was a bit rounder in those days and more subject to rolling than the aerodynamic football of the modern game. But to travel 94 yards, it seemed as if the ball might need the properties of one of those toy superballs.

Lintzenich was not a big guy at 5'11" and 187 pounds and this was well before the age of specialization, so he was listed on the Bears' roster as a running back. He came out of St. Louis University and joined the Bears in 1930. His NFL career lasted only two seasons, but his name has remained in the Chicago record book for 77 years.

Lintzenich's kick did not figure into the scoring (and was not even mentioned by famed columnist Westbrook Pegler in his commentary on the game) but was nonetheless an impressive feat. The punt trapped the Giants with their backs to their own end zone and hindered their offense for a series. No safety followed, though, and the Giants escaped the predicament with their own punt. So the kick was not a game-turner, merely an eyebrow-raiser of a play during the course of the game.

When in doubt, punt.
—LEGENDARY HEAD COACH JOHN HEISMAN

The game was played on a Sunday afternoon at the Polo Grounds in New York. The Giants scored first and held the lead into the second half. The Bears began their comeback in the third quarter and Lintzenich played a key role. On a halfback option play he threw a 25-yard touchdown pass to Luke Johnsos. The extra point was blocked and the game was deadlocked at 6–6.

Although the Bears drove down to the 1-yard line in the fourth quarter, they were repelled. The Giants appeared to escape with a tie. However, an interception by Chicago's Roy Lyman followed, setting up the Bears for a final crack at the end zone from the New York 30.

The Bears notched the winning touchdown on a pass from quarterback Carl Brumbaugh to Garland Grange, the younger brother of the famous Red Grange, who also spent a few years with the Bears.

During a 1920 game, Joe Guyon of the Canton Bulldogs was credited with a 95-yard punt. And during a 1923 game, Pete Henry, also of Canton, was credited with a 94-yard punt. When performances were examined more carefully, however, neither of those was recognized as an official record. Lintzenich's 1931 boot was adopted as

Head coach Ralph Jones and the Bears used a 94-yard punt by Joe Lintzenich to beat the Giants in 1931. *(Photo courtesy of the estate of Richard Whittingham)*

ONLY NOTICED WHEN THINGS GO WRONG

The best punters are invisible. They are brought onto the field as an admission of failure. It is fourth down and hopeless. It is fourth down and the team just can't make that first down, so get the team out of trouble.

The ball is snapped. The punter kicks. The ball soars high in the air. The ball lands downfield. The punter trots off the field again and is forgotten.

Punters are rarely noticed unless they drop the snap, kick the ball off the side of their foot out of bounds, have the boot blocked, or even worse, when their punt is being returned in the open field and they are the last man standing who can possibly make a touchdown-saving tackle.

If you saw a 94-yard punt like Joe Lintzenich's you would remember it. There are probably not many people alive, if any, who did see the 1931 kick.

Perhaps some Bears fans do remember Dave Finzer's 87-yard punt against New Orleans in 1984 or Bob Parsons's 81-yard kick against New England in 1982, other exceptionally long team punts. But few probably have vivid recollection of other individual punts among Parsons's 884 career team-record total.

Bears punter Joe Lintzenich's 94-yard punt was the longest in NFL history until the Jets' Steve O'Neal booted a 98-yard punt in 1969.

Game Details

Bears 12 • Giants 6

Location: Polo Grounds, New York

Attendance: 20,000

Box Score:

Bears	0	0	6	6	**12**
Giants	0	6	0	0	**6**

Scoring:
NY Friedman 1-yard run (PAT failed)
CHI Johnsos 15-yard pass from Lintzenich (PAT failed)
CHI G. Grange 28-yard pass from Brumbaugh (PAT failed)

Punt returns will kill you quicker than a minnow can swim a dipper.

—FORMER TEXAS COACH DARRELL ROYAL

the official league record and it was not eclipsed until Steve O'Neal of the New York Jets recorded a 98-yard punt against the Denver Broncos on September 21, 1969.

Talk about catching a good roll. Official placement of the ball in the plays sandwiching O'Neal's punt meant he kicked from his own 1-yard line to the Broncos' 1-yard line. While it is difficult to see how the record can officially be broken since the NFL doesn't deal in inches, the official college record is 99 yards.

Lintzenich did not have a very long professional football career. He appeared in 24 games in his two seasons, throwing for two touchdowns and scoring two touchdowns. Yet 10 years after his departure from the Bears, when coach George Halas was asked to name his all-time Chicago team, he placed Lintzenich at halfback.

After leaving pro football, Lintzenich became a beverage distributor and during World War II served as a lieutenant aboard a battleship in the South Pacific. Although his pro career was short, Lintzenich's alma mater, St. Louis, inducted him into its athletic Hall of Fame in 1976 for his football achievements there.

And his name still stands out in the Bears' record book. Under the category of "Punting" there is a small section labeled "Long." Joe Lintzenich's name is atop that list for his one-time, miraculous 94-yard punt. The word "Long" is the perfect summary of the play.

September 19, 1971

Sending the Fans Home Happy

Kent Nix Touchdown Pass Wins It for Bears in Soldier Field Opener

From the moment the Decatur Staleys moved to Chicago and officially became the Bears in 1922, the city's National Football League team played its home games at Wrigley Field.

It was fitting. The big Bears and the little Cubs called the same park home. Bears owner George Halas had good relations with the Cubs organization, but as the NFL grew in popularity the league demanded larger stadiums.

Soldier Field held more than double the number of fans as Wrigley for certain events, on occasion putting more than 100,000 spectators in the stadium. It was never contemplated that the huge stadium located next to Lake Michigan would become another Los Angeles Coliseum with crowds hitting six figures for Bears games, but the seating capacity was definitely going to be much larger.

When it came time to move forward, Halas seemed content. He especially liked the artificial turf on the playing surface at Soldier Field. The city invested $770,000 in improvements and renovations to make

Soldier Field NFL-ready, so this was no minor switch.

Halas, who was known as a tough salary negotiator with his players, did not relish his rent negotiations with Chicago Mayor Richard J. Daley. In the months leading up to the change, Halas agreed to pay the Chicago Park District 10 percent of his gross receipts as a rental fee. However, on the eve of the opening of the NFL season, Daley demanded more, and Halas ultimately acceded and agreed to pay 12 percent.

The initial plan—at least in Halas's mind—was for the Bears to play at Soldier Field for three seasons while a new stadium was considered and built somewhere nearby. Some 37 years later, Soldier Field is still the home of the Bears. And it underwent another major renovation, this time costing in the millions. No alternative stadium or plan is on the horizon as a new home for the Bears in the immediate future.

Before the start of the 1971 season, the Bears had a dry run at Soldier Field, hosting an exhibition game against the Denver Broncos. More than 47,000 people

I just asked Kent how he felt and told him we needed two touchdowns.

—JIM DOOLEY

Quarterback Kent Nix hooked up with receiver George Farmer for the winning score in the Bears' Soldier Field debut in 1971.

attended and saw the Bears pull off a late comeback for the victory. The game also marked the return to action of star running back Gale Sayers, who was in the recuperative stages of one of his unfortunate but necessary knee surgeries. Sayers appeared only briefly, but that was planned.

The Bears officially christened Soldier Field on September 19, 1971, in a game against the Pittsburgh Steelers. The fresh location, coupled with the additional seats and the excitement of the season opener, combined to attract a Bears home record crowd of 55,049. That sellout number became the standard attendance figure for home games throughout the season.

What started as a festive occasion, however, appeared to be spoiled during the afternoon as the Steelers outplayed the Bears. Deep in the fourth quarter, with less than four minutes remaining, Chicago trailed Pittsburgh 15–3. Those happy-to-be-there fans began glumly filing out of Soldier Field, chalking up the loss and a 0–1 start to the season.

Only nobody told the Bears the game was lost. It was definitely an it's-never-over-till-it's-over day.

The Steelers certainly seemed to be in control of the outcome. With the clock winding down, Pittsburgh's strategy was simply to run out the clock. The idea of throwing a pass never even flitted across any Steeler's mind. The handoff from quarterback Terry Bradshaw went to 6'4", 235-pound fullback Warren Bankston. Bankston was on the field because Pittsburgh starter John Fuqua had been shaken up earlier in the game.

A nice, simple, safe play, good for maybe a few yards and good for wasting important seconds. Only Bears defensive end Ed O'Bradovich put all his force and power into a devastating hit on Bankston. The tackle was so hard that Bankston might have been temporarily transported back to the last century. In any case, he was separated from the football and Bears linebacker Ross Brupbacher collected the bouncing ball, tucked it away, and ran 30 yards into the end zone for a Chicago touchdown.

The score brought the Bears closer, but it also gave the ball back to the Steelers. Once again, the Steelers had no intention of passing. Bankston appeared to redeem himself with a 13-yard gain.

Defensive coordinator Abe Gibron frantically flipped through ideas that might throw the Steelers off balance. He decided on a middle linebacker blitz by Dick Butkus. Butkus, who like his partner Sayers was coming off

A New Home

After two years headquartered in Decatur, the Staleys moved to Chicago and became the Bears. Halas chose Bears as the team nickname because he was a Chicago Cubs baseball fan and the kinship was obvious.

Looking for the proper stadium to play in, Halas cut a deal with the operators of Wrigley Field, which was called Cubs Park. Although the confines were not friendly because of the configuration, and sometimes players fell down dugout steps or ran into brick walls, Halas probably never would have abandoned Wrigley Field for a renovated Soldier Field if the NFL had not outgrown its roots.

At one time a stadium that held 40,000 people was more than enough for a Bears game. Then the league sought stadiums with 50,000-seat minimums. Soldier Field, remodeled again in 2002, now holds more than 62,000.

The popularity of the Bears, however, is great enough that if the opportunity ever arises to play in a stadium that holds 80,000 fans, the team could routinely fill it.

GAME DETAILS

Bears 17 • Steelers 15

Location: Soldier Field, Chicago

Attendance: 55,049

It was the hardest I ever hit anybody in my life.

—ED O'BRADOVICH

Box Score:

Steelers	0	6	6	3	**15**
Bears	0	3	0	14	**17**

Scoring:

PIT Pearson fumble recovery in end zone (PAT failed)
CHI Percival 33-yard field goal
PIT Gerela 32-yard field goal

PIT Gerela 29-yard field goal
PIT Gerela 42-yard field goal
CHI Brupbacher 30-yard fumble return (Percival PAT)
CHI Farmer 8-yard pass from Nix (Percival PAT)

---

off-season knee surgery, was back to full strength. Picking his spots, shedding would-be blockers, Butkus exploded into the Pittsburgh backfield and steamrolled the sad victim Bankston once again. The ball popped loose for a second time and this time O'Bradovich recovered.

The Bears had an improbable first down at the Steelers' 17-yard line with less than two minutes remaining. After three periods of offensive stagnation, Bears head coach Jim Dooley had replaced starting quarterback Jack Concannon, showered with boos, with backup Kent Nix at the beginning of the fourth quarter.

Nix, a rangy, 6'2" thrower out of Texas Christian, had been a member of the Steelers before joining the Bears in 1970. He appeared in only one game that season, but this game heralded the fact he would see a bit more playing time in 1971.

Nix was a career backup who spent just those two seasons with the Bears. He was, however, about to make his enduring Chicago mark. Nix threw two incompletions, but on a keeper dashed 14 yards to the three. First-and-goal.

The Steelers defense clawed back, dropping Nix for a one-yard loss and then pinning fullback Jim Grabowski for a four-yard loss. Wide receiver George Farmer, in his second year out of UCLA, was beginning his most productive NFL season (he ended up with 46 catches in 1971). He was never smoother than on the next play. Farmer ran a down-and-out pattern, fooling the defender and then took the ball into the end zone after Nix's pump fake. The eight-yard catch with 44 seconds remaining won the game and completed the comeback.

Dooley looked like a whiz for bringing Nix into the game when he did, but said he whispered nothing particularly inspirational into the quarterback's ear. In fact, their brief conversation sounded as fundamental as it can get along the sideline: go score.

If it were so easy to order two touchdowns on demand every time he wished, Dooley would have been acclaimed the greatest coach of all time. But one thing was for sure: Nix felt just fine after orchestrating the rally.

December 17, 1967

47 A BITTERSWEET VICTORY

George Halas's Last Game as Bears Coach

The Bears won. Chicago beat the Atlanta Falcons 23–14.

In a season that ended 7–6–1, the Bears also recorded a winning record.

They didn't make the playoffs, finishing second in the NFC Central Division, but those other facts were important. They won and they posted a winning record. They were important because the game in Atlanta was George Halas's last game on the sideline and the season was George Halas's last one supervising the play-by-play of the team he founded in 1920 and spent a lifetime operating.

It was too bad that the last game of the season wasn't in Chicago at Wrigley Field, the Bears' home in the Windy City from the start. Halas did not let on that he was finished. He had become frailer, didn't have the go-get-'em to run up and down the sideline screaming at referees as he always had. He said he didn't have the old zip. So he believed it was time to retreat full-time into the front office.

However, Halas made no announcement to his players or the fans going into the game, nor immediately after, so it appeared to be a simple wrap-up of a season with some hope, just not the overall results hoped for. It was nobody's greatest season, but it did have memorable moments, including a 103-yard kickoff return for a touchdown by halfback Gale Sayers.

Looking back at the final game, as many people did later, it seemed appropriate that Sayers's plays were the most memorable. He was always one of Halas's favorites and they held a tremendous respect and affection for one another.

The Bears had begun the season poorly, losing five of their first seven games, so there was considerable satisfaction for Halas to walk away a winner. Mac Percival kicked three field goals and Sayers scored on a 32-yard touchdown pass and a 51-yard run.

The victory gave Halas a 324–151–31 coaching record, the winningest of all time until Don Shula surpassed him in 1993.

The Bears got their win and their winning season, at the time their 40th in their 48 years of existence. The players scattered for the winter and Halas returned to his office in downtown Chicago doing business—it seemed—as usual.

Things were quiet on the Bears' front for several months. Then Halas called a news conference. On May 27, 1968, the 73-year-old Bears patriarch announced that he was retiring from coaching. He had stepped aside three other times to leave the team in different coaching hands, but always with plans to return to the bench. This time it was clear that he would not return. The audience of reporters had no inkling this would be the subject of the meeting and the gathering was shocked.

"There was a strong temptation to continue for another season," Halas said. "But looking at practical realities, I am stepping aside now because I can no longer keep up with the physical demands of coaching the team on Sunday afternoons. I have always followed the ball, and the officials, up and down the field."

Halas chiefly blamed arthritis in his hip for slowing him down. It was half funny, half sad when Halas said that he had set out in anger to chase down an official during a game the preceding season and couldn't catch him.

Truly, Halas had kept a lid on his intentions. He did not tell his assistant coaches, players, or even the front office staff that he planned to retire. As he always had, he did it his way.

Halas on the Bears' sideline had been as familiar a sight as the

George Halas was victorious in his final game as Bears head coach in 1967.

No Regrets

Given his stubbornness and success, it is possible that if someone asked George Halas if he had any regrets, he would probably say "no." Even if he recognized he had made a mistake he would likely look at it in the context of the big picture and let it stand as such.

Papa Bear was a titan of the NFL. He was bedside at its birth, helped guide it with fresh ideas and force of personality as a toddler when it was just learning to walk, and he was the pillar of one of the league's cornerstone franchises. The man's calling was pro football and his Chicago Bears, and nearly 90 years after its founding, it is remarkable that the team remains in the control of his family.

For all his gruffness and merciless style on the field, Halas was sensitive to the common good in the game and supported changes that opened up the style of play, initiated the draft, and strengthened the league's commitment to television.

Halas was right on all the big issues.

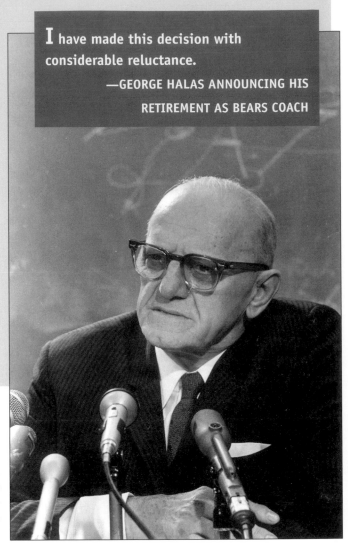

I have made this decision with considerable reluctance.

—GEORGE HALAS ANNOUNCING HIS RETIREMENT AS BEARS COACH

Though he announced his retirement at a press conference in 1968, George Halas would continue to be a driving force behind the Bears for years to come. *(Photo courtesy of AP Images)*

Tribune Tower, the Water Tower, or any other Chicago institution. His fedora was as much a head-gear symbol of the Bears as the team helmet. And Halas's overcoat was as recognizable as the blue-and-orange team jerseys.

His bark was loud and his bite was fierce. Halas battled for his Bears on every occasion and he fought equally hard to establish the National Football League in the minds of the public as a big-time sporting venture. He nourished feuds with Curly Lambeau in Green Bay and held grudges against former assistant coach George Allen and players who violated his sense of loyalty.

GAME DETAILS

Bears 23 • Falcons 14

Location: Fulton County Stadium, Atlanta

Attendance: 54,107

Box Score:

Bears	7	10	3	3	**23**
Falcons	7	0	0	7	**14**

Scoring:

ATL Coffey 6-yard pass from Johnson (Traynham PAT)
CHI Sayers 32-yard pass from Concannon (Percival PAT)
CHI Sayers 51-yard run (Percival PAT)

CHI Percival 48-yard field goal
CHI Percival 47-yard field goal
CHI Percival 19-yard field goal
ATL Coffey 3-yard run (Traynham PAT)

> **H**e was the boss, period.
>
> —MIKE DITKA ON GEORGE HALAS

Yet when Halas was aging and ill, he reached out to prodigal son Mike Ditka to come back to the Bears as coach and rebuild the Monsters of the Midway in his image. Ditka did so and won the most-publicized Bears championship in team history.

Through more than a half century's worth of operating the Bears, young George Halas matured into Papa Bear George Halas. Halas grew up with the Bears and nurtured the team and the NFL through their own growing pains of the 1920s and the hardships of the Depression-era years of the 1930s.

Critics called him cheap, and Ditka's own description of his money battles with Halas contained one of the most vivid salary negotiation lines ever uttered in sports when Iron Mike said Halas "threw nickels around like manhole covers."

"My first impression of George Halas," said Ditka, who was drafted by the Bears in 1961, "was that he was the leader. What he said, went."

That was a very accurate perception. It was the Halas Way or no way with the Bears. And although Halas made many behind-the-scenes overtures to help former players or their families in need, he was sure to do it out of the limelight. Publicly he cultivated the gruffness with which he came across and seemed to hate any softening of his image.

In retrospect, even if Halas knew, even if he was sure, during that Atlanta Falcons game that he planned to retire, it was very much in character for him to maintain the secret. He would never have been comfortable with a showering of flowers and affection.

Besides, he was only walking away from the sideline; this was Halas's last game on the field only. He had another good 15 years in him with the Bears, another 15 years of life in football.

October 8, 1961

THE LONGEST PASS PLAY OF ALL

Bill Wade's 98-Yard Touchdown Throw to Bo Farrington

The Bears of 1961 were coming off a lean year. Coach George Halas was trying to rebuild his team to contend with the resurgent Green Bay Packers and the improving Detroit Lions at a time when the Western Conference was top-heavy in power.

These were the Packers of Bart Starr, Paul Hornung, and Vince Lombardi. These were the Lions of Joe Schmidt, Alex Karras, and Nick Pietrosante. It was the fourth week of the NFL season and the Bears were 1–2, fresh off a 24–0 thrashing by the Packers. Another loss and they would be out of the picture for the playoffs before mid-October. If that happened, autumn would just get colder and colder.

The game took place in Detroit and things did not begin well for the Bears. The Lions took a 10–0 lead in the first half and clung to it. Detroit was constructing its own reputation for good defense and the Lions were controlling Chicago's offense this day. The Bears tied it 17–17 and quarterback Bill Wade scored on one of his famous keepers to take the lead. Then halfback Willie

Galimore exploded for a 52-yard run and Chicago won going away 31–17.

But the play everyone talked about was Chicago's first touchdown. At a time when the Bears could have been swamped, they stayed close with a momentum-busting big play that shocked Detroit.

Stuck on their own 2-yard line, the Bears were facing the likelihood of punting from their own end zone and providing the Lions with good field position. But on a daring play, Wade faded back and passed to wide receiver John "Bo" Farrington.

Farrington was a sturdy, 6'2", 217-pound split end who joined the team in 1960. He never blossomed into a big stat guy during his four seasons with the Bears, but did make some key catches and brought down 21 receptions in limited duty in two different seasons.

On this play Farrington gathered in Wade's toss, broke free, and scampered 98 yards for a touchdown down the left sideline. The longest pass reception in Bears history has stood as the team record for 47 years. And it is a play that Wade, living

After being acquired from the Los Angeles Rams, Bill Wade would go on to quarterback the 1963 Bears to the NFL championship.

in retirement in Nashville, Tennessee, remembers fondly.

"Farrington was a slow-starting runner, but once he got going it seemed like he could run," Wade said. "He had a huge gait. Once he got going he was hard to catch."

Wade remembers standing behind the line of scrimmage and just watching Farrington go. The end had a distinctive step and he ate up ground.

"Farrington's was just a real long stride," Wade said. "It was more of a galloping stride."

He galloped all the way into the end zone.

Farrington was born in 1936 in DeWalt, Texas. He attended high school in Houston and then enrolled at Prairie View A&M, one of the historically black colleges that provided a good education and football opportunity for African Americans when they were shut out of many of the largest schools in the country.

Farrington was one of those throw-at-the-dartboard, take-a-chance draft picks. The Bears took him in the 16th round in 1960, and he didn't catch a pass that season while appearing briefly in six games. But the next season, when he made this memorable play, Farrington played in all but three games, caught 21 balls, and scored four touchdowns.

In the 1963 championship season, Farrington was a notable contributor, again catching 21 passes. It was felt Farrington was coming into his prime and that he would become a major player in the 1964 season.

Instead, Farrington and Galimore, another potential star at halfback, were the victims in one of the greatest tragedies in Bears team history.

One late July evening after practice on the campus of St. Joseph's College in Rensselaer, Indiana, where the Bears held their training camp, Galimore and Farrington went out for some relaxation. Returning to their dormitory to make the 11:00 PM curfew, Galimore, at the wheel of his Volkswagen with Farrington in the passenger seat, apparently missed a curve in the road. A highway sign on the site marking the spot as an "S" curve was downed. Not traveling at high speed, the vehicle nonetheless soared off the road and crashed into a ditch and rolled over, killing both players.

A maintenance worker at a nearby factory was out and witnessed the crash 1.4 miles west of town. The accident took place at about 10:25 PM on July 26. At

LOOKING FOR WIDE RECEIVER HEAVEN

The Bears have always cultivated the image of a smash-mouth football team, a team that would run, run, run.

Certainly there have been occasions when for a few seasons a wide receiver has played a critical role in the offense. Bill Hewitt was a Hall of Fame player. Johnny Morris had some great seasons. Marty Booker turned in some exceptional work. Willie Gault was the prototype speedburner. But over the long haul, year after year, the Bears always seem to be looking for a fresh face with a long stride, sure hands, and stop-watch-challenging speed.

Current coach Lovie Smith is looking at game-breaking return man Devin Hester to transform himself into the same type of game-breaking wide receiver. If such a position shift works out, the Bears might find themselves in the unlikely position of having the most exciting receiver in football on their side.

GAME DETAILS

Bears 31 • Lions 17

Location: Tiger Stadium, Detroit

Attendance: 50,521

Box Score:

> **I** don't think anybody thought it would work.
>
> —BILL WADE OF HIS 98-YARD TOUCHDOWN PASS TO BO FARRINGTON

Bears	0	7	3	21	**31**
Lions	10	0	7	0	**17**

Scoring:

DET Martin 32-yard field goal

DET Barr 61-yard pass from Morrall (Walker PAT)

CHI Farrington 98-yard pass from Wade (Leclerc PAT)

CHI Leclerc 50-yard field goal

DET Studstill 100-yard kickoff return (Walker PAT)

CHI Ditka 37-yard pass from Wade (Leclerc PAT)

CHI Wade 1-yard run (Leclerc PAT)

CHI Galimore 53-yard run (Leclerc PAT)

> **T**his was the saddest day in Bears history.
>
> —GEORGE HALAS COMMENTING ON THE DEATHS OF BO FARRINGTON AND WILLIE GALIMORE

practice the next day, Bears players cried and reacted with disbelief and horror.

"Both were tremendously popular with their teammates," Halas said.

Wade called for a minute of silent prayer and reflection.

Future Hall of Fame defensive end Doug Atkins participated in the identification of the bodies and said neither Galimore nor Farrington was battered. Neither man was wearing a seat belt. Galimore was 29 years old, Farrington 28.

The Bears of 1964 were shaken by the loss of their teammates and played more erratically that season. They never came close to defending their title and slipped completely out of the race, finishing 5–9.

"The tragedy blotted out enthusiasm carried over from our 1963 championship," Halas said. "For the Bears, the season was over before it began. 1964 was a painful season."

October 20, 1968

BEARS GET A KICK OUT OF MAC

Mac Percival Boots Five Field Goals

Mac Percival looked like an athlete. He stood 6'4" and weighed 220 pounds. In the eyes of his Chicago Bears teammates, he had the build of a real football player, not just an ordinary kicker. That was good for his credibility when he joined the team in 1967.

Rookie kickers come and go and often aren't really part of the team until they prove themselves in the clutch. Percival replaced Roger Leclerc that season and did well enough to be invited back. But no one—not Percival, not the coaches, not the other players—expected the 1968 season to evolve into the Percival Weekly Miracle Show.

Percival came out of Texas Tech and walked into a sensitive role in Chicago. George Blanda had been a reliable kicker for the Bears throughout much of the 1950s, but he was treated shabbily by owner George Halas and let go. The fans never quite took to his replacement, Leclerc, who performed some mighty impressive feats. (Leclerc once kicked five field goals in a game for Chicago, and during the 1965 season he connected on all 52 of his extra-point tries.)

Leclerc, though, could not live down missing a 20-yard field goal that would have won a game against the Detroit Lions. He was often booed unmercifully. Percival was the replacement and he hit 13 out of 26 attempts as a rookie. In today's NFL that is viewed as a pathetic rate of success; in the 1960s it was good enough for him to keep the kicking job for another season.

Percival was an improved kicker his second year and solidified his new standing in the fifth game of the season at Philadelphia. The Bears outlasted the Eagles 29–16, helped dramatically by Percival's toe. Mac the Knife kicked five field goals—equaling Leclerc at his best with a record that still stands for the Bears.

It was a game that included the first start at quarterback by Virgil Carter in a very hostile atmosphere where Eagles fans took turns booing the Bears and their own team that was on its way to a 0–6 start. Percival was the steadying foot in this one.

In a game where all points were useful, if not critical, Percival kicked field goals of 39, 31, 28, 15, and 14 yards. He also kicked two extra points and thus accounted

Mac Percival kicked the Bears to victory against the Eagles in 1968.
(Photo courtesy of WireImages)

for 17 of Chicago's points. By coincidence, the only Philadelphia touchdown was scored by Mike Ditka, in his intermediate stop between playing for the Bears and finishing his career with the Cowboys.

It was Mac's day as much as Carter's, and with the increased value placed on field-goal kicking in the National Football League over the ensuing years, it is surprising to note that 40 years later Percival's (and Leclerc's) feat by foot is comfortably leading the list in the Bears' record book.

Percival always had fans among the Bears' coaching staff. Coaches kept telling anyone who would listen that Percival possessed the strongest leg in the league. What Percival lacked was field-goal kicking experience. Percival grew up in Texas and played high school football but had only handled extra points and kickoffs, not field goals.

By enrolling at Texas Tech, Percival chose a school where football is *the* game. But Percival concentrated on basketball, not football, again aging a few years

before he ever attempted a field goal in competition. After college, as a lark, he and a friend tried out for the team in a Dallas Cowboys kicking caravan search. Percival won the competition and gained some respect and attention. The Cowboys wanted to see how far he could take it.

Percival was the object of some one-on-one focus from former kicker Ben Agajanian, who sought to teach him the finer points of field-goal kicking, but eventually Percival was cut by the Cowboys. When he tried out for the Bears his lack of experience was at first ridiculed.

But things changed rapidly in 1968.

The week after Percival kicked his five field goals against Philadelphia, the Bears trailed the Minnesota Vikings 24–23 late in the fourth quarter at Wrigley Field after surrendering what seemed to be the decisive points on a drive kept alive by major Chicago penalties. With little optimism in the stands, the Bears started at their own 41-yard line with less than 30 seconds to go

1968: A Very Weird Year

America was changing all around the Bears. It was the era of student protests and rising indignation against the war in Vietnam. And it was a time when African Americans grew more outspoken in their push for civil rights.

The Bears featured a healthy Gale Sayers, who rushed for 856 yards on 6.2 yards per attempt, but as was so often the trademark of the team during that era, the struggle to find the right quarterback was as

elusive as finding harmony in the streets of the United States.

The Bears switched back and forth between one-time Boston College star Jack Concannon, emerging Virgil Carter, and even Larry Rakestraw. None offered the long-term answer and in 1969 things only got worse, with Chicago finishing 1–13. They weren't great for the Democrats, either, who were looking at four more years of Richard Nixon in the White House.

GAME DETAILS

Bears 29 • Eagles 16

Location: Franklin Field, Philadelphia

Attendance: 60,858

Box Score:

Bears	7	6	3	13	**29**
Eagles	3	10	3	0	**16**

Scoring:

PHI Baker 30-yard field goal

CHI Turner 11-yard pass from Carter (Percival PAT)

PHI Baker 27-yard field goal

CHI Percival 39-yard field goal

PHI Ditka 2-yard pass from Snead (Baker PAT)

CHI Percival 31-yard field goal

CHI Percival 28-yard field goal

PHI Baker 44-yard field goal

CHI Percival 15-yard field goal

CHI Taylor 96-yard interception return (Percival PAT)

CHI Percival 14-yard field goal

We never tried a field goal in high school.

—MAC PERCIVAL

and dragged the ball over midfield before turning their prospects over to Percival.

At the time that didn't sound like such a bad thing. A week earlier he had kicked five field goals, and during this game he had already succeeded in booting three more. Center Mike Pyle snapped the ball to holder Rich Petitbon and Percival booted a 47-yard field goal with three seconds remaining to give Chicago a 26–24 victory. It was Percival's ninth straight connection. As the ball landed, players erupted with joy, ran onto the field, and mobbed Percival. He was a football player now.

The crowd of more than 46,000 stood on its feet shouting. The Vikings were stunned. The Bears were thrilled.

"I'm a guy who can psyche himself out and I just tried to make my mind a blank," Percival said about preparing for the kick.

Percival said the play unfolded perfectly and he felt his foot hit the ball solidly. But when he raised his head and saw the ball sailing, he feared it was veering off to the left and would be no good.

Kickers are supposed to watch what they're doing, meaning that instead of looking at the stands, the goal posts, and the opposing defense, their task is to look down at the ground, where the ball is placed, and coordinate their foot with the position. Percival said he had to fight an inclination to look up, but Petitbon began reminding him not to.

"I have a bad habit of looking up," he said. "But since Richie has been telling me that just as I kick, I've hit nine in a row."

To complete a trifecta, a week later Percival boomed a 43-yard field goal with 23 seconds left to best the Green Bay Packers 13–10. He didn't look up that time, either.

A New Formation on Defense

Bill George Invents the Middle Linebacker Position

When people think of the Chicago Bears, they often think of the team's glorious history of producing Hall of Fame middle linebackers. But until Bill George came along as a 1951 second-round draft pick out of Wake Forest, nobody used the job description.

George, one of the Bears' fiercest hitters in a long line of tough-guy players, was a George Halas favorite for his hard-nosed style and his generally upbeat mood off the field. When George first joined the team in 1952, the Bears played the standard defense that other NFL teams played. Teams employed a five-man front on defense—two defensive ends, two defensive tackles, and a nose guard over the center. There were two linebackers—one for the left and one for the right. There was no middle linebacker.

The tobacco-chewing George, who grew up in Pennsylvania where high school football is king, became pals with George Connor, the 6'3", 240-pound wrecking ball of a linebacker who (like George) would one day be elected to the Pro Football Hall of Fame in Canton, Ohio.

In a game during the 1954 season, George complained to Connor that he didn't like the way the opposing team was moving the ball. As the nose guard, George was expected to line up over the center and put a hit on him before reacting to the play. When George rushed forward, he vacated the spot right over the middle behind the line of scrimmage, and the Bears were repeatedly getting burned by short passes into that zone.

In a moment of disgust, George vented to Connor, saying, "Hell, I could break up those passes if I didn't have to hit that offensive center first."

Connor, the defensive captain, gave George approval to break with the formation

> **I**'m thrilled to death.
> —BILL GEORGE, UPON HEARING HE WAS ELECTED TO THE PRO FOOTBALL HALL OF FAME

Bill George changed NFL defenses forever by moving to the middle linebacker position in 1954. *(Photo courtesy of WireImages)*

George Invents the Middle Linebacker

Bill George was a stalwart of the Bears defense during the 1950s and 1960s. He routinely lined up at middle guard, in the middle of the team's five-man defensive front. It was George's responsibility to rush toward the passer after the ball was snapped. However, George realized that opposing quarterbacks were dumping passes over the middle into the precise area he kept vacating. Frustrated, George came up with the idea of faking his rush before dropping back into coverage. He immediately began intercepting passes and disrupting offenses. As a result, the middle linebacker position was created and teams shifted to four-man defensive fronts.

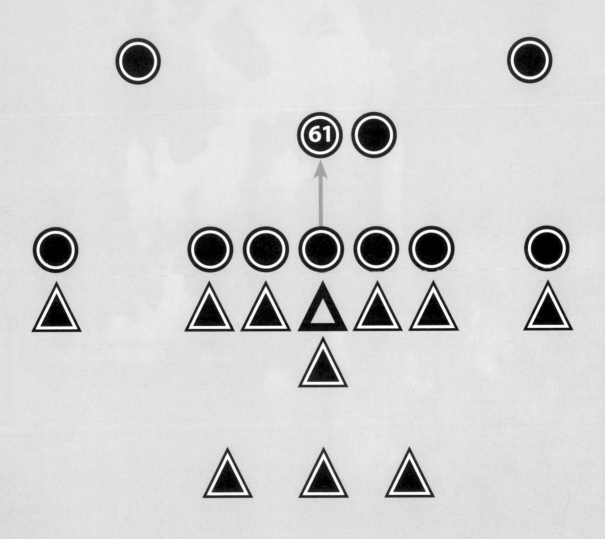

and try something different. "What are you hitting him for then?" Connor said. "Why don't you go for the ball?"

In later years, Connor, who became a Bears broadcaster, made it sound as if it was his idea for George to move back. Connor said the Bears had experimented with some defensive lineups that had three linebackers before, but they were always linked to a 5–3, with five men still up front.

The next time the circumstances on the field were right, George backed up instead of rushing forward. The move was so unexpected that the quarterback threw anyway, and George was so surprised the ball hit him in the chest and bounced away. Apparently chalking the situation up to a fluke, the quarterback refused to give up on what had been such a successful play. So he tried the play again, and this time George intercepted the pass.

Although the specifics of how George came to change the way he lined up and the conversation with Connor are unknown, most accounts attribute these events to taking place during a 1954 game against the Philadelphia Eagles. However, the Bears did not play the Eagles that season.

Teams had been catching up to the old five-man front with more innovative offensive formations. In a stroke of inspiration, George had eliminated the built-in disadvantage of the five-man front. Teams gravitated to 4-3 defensive formations and within a couple seasons the nose guard position had disappeared and use of the middle linebacker had taken hold in football strategy.

While George made the move to middle linebacker spontaneously, unforeseen was the long-term effect. The 4-3 became the defense teams preferred because the middle linebacker was a free agent—sometimes rushing, sometimes covering receivers, and sometimes pursuing ball carriers when they broke through the line. Middle linebackers became the glamour players of the defense. They had to be nearly as big and strong as linemen and nearly as fast as defensive backs because their job involved doing a little bit of everything.

From Sam Huff , Joe Schmidt, Chuck Bednarik, and Ray Nitschke to Dick Butkus, Mike Singletary, and Brian Urlacher, the middle linebacker role has morphed into a place where the meanest tacklers go to star and where defenders rise from anonymity. No team has had more great ones than the Bears, and it all started with George.

George spent all but his final season in the league in a Bears uniform. He wanted to play one more year than the Bears wanted him.

"The game gets in your system," George said.

After a single season with the Rams, he finished his career with 18 interceptions. George played 15 years in the NFL and was chosen for the Hall of Fame in 1974.

When George retired from playing, he returned to Chicago and became a Bears assistant coach. His life was sadly and unexpectedly cut short in 1982 when the car he was driving was slammed by a truck.

Bill George was the first great middle linebacker. He brought all the romance and charisma to the position.

— BEARS HEAD COACH ABE GIBRON

October 31, 1954

HILL RUNS PAST THE 49ERS

Harlon Hill's 214 Yards Receiving

It is difficult to find photographs of Harlon Hill where his hair doesn't look like it was just cut by a drill sergeant. Maybe they don't exist.

Certainly there were no long hairs where Hill came from—small-town Alabama in the 1940s and 1950s. But there was no one else around who could run like the wind, either, and not just a slight breeze but a full-scale howler of a tornado.

It is often lamented that football and all other sports have grown up too much, that the children who play the games for their schools are not left alone long enough to be children. Too often they are trained to be specialists in a game, hyped and rated just when they are reaching their teens.

On the other hand, in days gone by it was almost impossible for athletes to be discovered and to be selected for a scholarship if they lived in an out-of-the-way place. In an era before high school coaches and parents could make home videos to send to college coaches and post on the Internet, scouting was done by word-of-mouth and it was important to have the right contacts.

Young Harlon Hill was a phenomenal athlete in Rogersville, Alabama, but not many people knew where Rogersville was. (Most still don't.) Hill went the small-college route and enrolled in Florence State Teachers College. This was definitely not Wide Receiver U. The college put more of a premium on turning out math instructors than pro football players. Much later, the school changed its name to the University of North Alabama and won small-college national championships.

Bears owner George Halas had cultivated a cadre of sources around the nation and one of them whispered in his ear about Hill. The young man was an antelope, and his 6'2" height and good hands on a 200-pound frame enhanced his stellar ability. Halas never saw Hill play in person, but he liked what he heard and in the end he obtained some grainy footage of Hill's college action. Hill stood out enough to be invited to play in a postseason college all-star game, no mean feat for a small-college player.

The NFL Draft was quite different a half-century ago. There was no around-the-clock newspaper or television analysis in the days leading up to it. And teams received 30 picks, not the current eight. With almost no investment in scouting, teams were winging it after a certain point, or picking players from nearby teams because they had heard of them, picking cousins of present players because a lineman dropped a word of praise. Reviewing the list of names of players chosen by the Bears in later rounds during the 1950s is like reading a membership list in Football Players Anonymous.

Against that backdrop the Bears chose Hill in the 15th round in 1954. Not exactly a big risk. With that low level of enthusiasm it appeared the Bears did not even expect Hill to make the 33-man roster. But one thing could be said in Halas's favor: once he realized Hill's true talents, he rushed him into the starting lineup as a rookie and took full advantage of them.

For a guy some said had a prejudice against playing rookies, Hill's selection and use quieted all Halas doubters. And the dividends were immense. In a 12-game season, four less than are played now, Hill caught 45 passes. Pretty good considering the Bears were in their quarterback juggling phase. Hill caught 12 touchdown passes. Very good. And he accumulated 1,124 yards through the air, for an average of 25.0 yards gained per catch. Absolutely unbelievable.

Hill was a secret weapon unleashed on NFL teams. Only once before in the

Bears receiver Harlon Hill racked up 214 receiving yards against the 49ers in 1954. *(Photo courtesy of WireImages)*

nearly 90 years of Bears history, when Ken Kavanaugh averaged 25.6 yards a catch in 1947, has Hill's average been exceeded. And only one other time, by Hill himself in 1956, when he averaged 24 yards a grab, was the mark approached.

Hill had a knack for getting open, he had a knack for catching the ball, and he had a knack for outrunning defenders after he caught the ball. Throw the ball to Harlon Hill and the Bears had a first down.

Hill made an impact on the Bears offense from the start, but he established himself for all time in the sixth game of the season. The Bears struggled at the start of the year. They

HARLON HILL'S BIG DAY

Bears receiver Harlon Hill's fourth touchdown catch of the day proved to be the game-winning score when Chicago beat the San Francisco 49ers in 1954. With just 34 seconds left in the fourth quarter, quarterback George Blanda took the snap and pitched the ball to rookie backup quarterback Ed Brown, who was lined up in the backfield. Hill lined up on the left, then broke toward the middle of the field before cutting back up the left sideline. Brown's pass hit Hill in stride, and the receiver took it to the end zone for a 31–27 Bears victory.

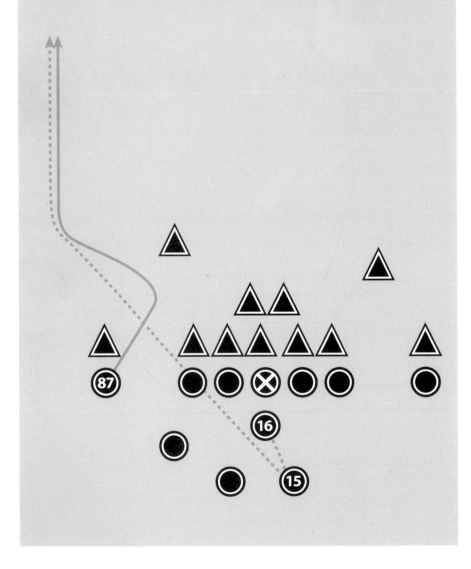

were 2–3 and already had lost once to the San Francisco 49ers in a close game at Wrigley Field.

The second showdown with the 49ers in San Francisco had the makings of a make-it-or-break-it game for the season. And that's exactly what the game turned out to be. The 49ers were favored by 11 points, but the Bears were hardly quaking after a 31–24 loss just two weeks earlier.

San Francisco was undefeated and took the first lead. Often it seemed as if the 49ers were on the verge of pulling away, but each time the Bears retaliated to stay close. Starting quarterback George Blanda found a streaking Hill just open enough for touchdown passes in the first and third quarters. In the type of all-around clutch play demonstrated many times later in his career with the Houston Oilers and Oakland Raiders, Blanda also kicked a field goal from the 15-yard line and threw another touchdown pass to Hill to tie the game at 24–24.

However, when San Francisco's Gordie Soltau kicked a field goal for a 27–24 lead with 45 seconds remaining, the Bears seemed finished. More than 49,000 fans were at Kezar Stadium—a park with no lights—cheering for the 49ers to close out Chicago before it got completely dark. Lights could be seen flickering on in buildings outside the stadium.

GAME DETAILS

Bears 31 • 49ers 27

Location: Kezar Stadium, San Francisco

Attendance: 49,833

Let's give this kid a look.

—GEORGE HALAS
ABOUT HARLON HILL ON DRAFT DAY

Box Score:

Bears	7	0	7	17	**31**
49ers	7	14	0	6	**27**

Scoring:

SF Wilson 32-yard pass from Tittle (Soltau PAT)

CHI Hill 47-yard pass from Blanda (Blanda PAT)

SF Johnson 38-yard run (Soltau PAT)

SF McElhenny 16-yard run (Soltau PAT)

CHI Hill 20-yard pass from Blanda (Blanda PAT)

CHI Blanda 15-yard field goal

SF Soltau 16-yard field goal

CHI Hill 11-yard pass from Brown (Blanda PAT)

SF Soltau 17-yard field goal

CHI Hill 66-yard pass from Brown (Blanda PAT)

Soltau kicked off into the wind and the ball did not travel well. Ed Sprinkle caught the short boot and stepped out of bounds at the Chicago 34-yard line. Decent field position, but still the Bears had just 35 seconds to travel 66 yards to reach the San Francisco end zone.

There was no time to work the ball downfield—the Bears had to go for broke. Halas called a trick play. The snap went to Blanda, who pitched the ball to rookie backup quarterback Ed Brown, a graduate of the nearby University of San Francisco.

Hill had lined up on the left side and when the play began, he darted toward the center of the field at an angle. He straightened for a few steps and then ran toward the left sideline. Brown faded back to his own 25-yard line and flung the ball 50 yards in the air to Hill, who took it in stride at the 49ers' 25 and raced into the end zone for the winning touchdown.

The Bears won 31–27 and went on to complete an 8–4 season. Hill finished with four touchdowns and 214 yards in pass receptions that day, still a Bears record. He says it is his favorite game of his nine-year NFL career.

"When you're in a game like that," Hill said, "you don't think about the game, or what you're doing at what time. At the end, when you're trying to win the game, all you do is get in a hurry-up offense."

The Bears hurried up and won it.

Coach Halas generally didn't think rookies were ready to play. He had a different opinion of me, I reckon.

—HARLON HILL

LOSING AND WINNING THE SAME DAY

Mark Carrier Grabs Three Interceptions in One Game

Occasionally defensive backs who are magnets for the ball come along. They seem to get their hands on thrown passes almost as often as the intended receiver, and they intercept more than their fair share of shaky throws.

They are ballhawks, defenders whose eyes gleam at the opportunity to pluck a wounded duck out of the air, who covet the ball as much as the wide receiver silly enough to venture into their territory. They watch quarterbacks' eyes and with some special instinct they sense when a ball is going to be thrown and then react if the ball is coming their way.

Men throughout NFL history like Paul Krause, Emlen Tunnell, and Dick "Night Train" Lane had this built-in radar. It is not something that can be quantified on a scouting report, yet it was something seen on the field.

When it came time to draft Mark Carrier out of the University of Southern California with their first-round pick in 1990, the Bears thought they sniffed that singular trait. They understood Carrier had a nose for the ball that transcended most others'.

He had flashed that sixth sense enough in college to make everyone believe he was a can't-miss pro.

Carrier showed his stuff in training camp and he jumped right into the starting lineup. And from day one the 6'1", 192-pound safety was a hit. He terrorized quarterbacks with his speed and sharp play.

Playing both ways in 1948, quarterback Johnny Lujack grabbed eight interceptions. Pretty good rookie production. In 1963, during the Bears' title run, defensive back Rosey Taylor intercepted nine passes and that was the subsequent team record.

As a rookie, Carrier intercepted 10 passes. He set the new Bears record in 1990, which has only once again been approached, when Nathan Vasher stole eight passes in 2005. Carrier played in every game, made his share of tackles, and stole more passes than any Bears player ever had.

The team record for the most interceptions in a game is three. It was set by Bob Margarita in 1945 and tied by Lujack in 1948, Richie Petitbon in 1967, Curtis Gentry in 1967, and Ross Brupbacher in 1976. Carrier got a piece of that record, too.

Safety Mark Carrier's three interceptions against Washington in 1990 tied a Bears record.

He intercepted three passes against the Washington Redskins in December of 1990.

Turnovers usually decide the outcome of games. The unusual aspect of Carrier's record-equaling day, and the reason it was not generally celebrated, is because the Bears managed to lose the game 10–9. No cakes with chocolate frosting or sips of champagne for Carrier that day.

Reporters surrounded Carrier at his locker after the Redskins game, probing for words about the spectacular performance. All around them gloom and doom pervaded the locker room. It would have been unseemly for Carrier to yuk it up and he did not.

"Look, you guys," he said to the sportswriters, "the day I had really doesn't matter. I didn't do enough. We lost. I should've got four interceptions. Then maybe we win. I know I could have had one more and I didn't make it."

Carrier's three interceptions came off Redskins quarterback Mark Rypien. The Bears intercepted two other passes, as well. It was almost as if the Chicago secondary was in the Washington huddle hearing the plays called or reading Rypien's mind. Five interceptions, yet they still didn't win the game.

Carrier's first interception could have been the most important. Rypien's pass was tossed into the end zone, intended for wide receiver Gary Clark. Carrier and Clark jumped and wrestled for the ball. Carrier won the tussle. Carrier's second interception was opportunistic. The pass hit receiver Ricky Sanders in the hands and bounced in the air. The third interception represented Bears teamwork. Chicago linebacker Ron Cox pressured Rypien and forced a hurried throw. Carrier caught it.

"We used a lot of man-to-man and zone," Carrier said of the confusing coverages the Bears presented to Washington. "That kind of threw them off a little bit."

Unfortunately for Chicago, not even five thefts could give the offense enough of a boost. The Bears stalled as badly as the Redskins offensively.

What was most remarkable about the game and the season was how seamlessly Carrier fit into the lineup as a rookie and made things happen. Often rookie safeties get burned on touchdown bombs. It's part of the learning process. Carrier arrived fully developed, impressing everyone with his know-how and the ability to adapt to professional football without growing pains.

MEMORY IS A FUNNY THING

On the greatest day of his professional football career, Mark Carrier couldn't celebrate. His team lost the game.

In many ways the 1990 season is an overlooked one in Bears history. It followed by a respectable interval the glory of the 1985–86 Super Bowl championship and it preceded some hard times. But the Bears finished 11–5 that year, won the NFC Central Division, and after handling the New Orleans Saints in the opening round of the playoffs, seemed genuine contenders to reach the Super Bowl again.

Unfortunately they were swallowed up 31–3 by the Giants in the next round and everyone figured it was best to forget about the whole thing. After all, there was always next near. Next year's regular-season record was the same, but the playoffs were over in a week. And not until 2001, a decade later, did things go so well again on the field.

GAME DETAILS

Bears 9 • Redskins 10

Location: RFK Stadium, Washington, D.C.

Attendance: 53,920

Box Score:

Bears	3	6	0	0	**9**
Redskins	0	0	7	3	**10**

Scoring:

CHI Butler 29-yard field goal

CHI Butler 23-yard field goal

CHI Butler 46-yard field goal

WAS Clark 8-yard pass from Rypien (Lohmiller PAT)

WAS Lohmiller 35-yard field goal

> **So I had three interceptions. Big deal.**
>
> —MARK CARRIER

"Mark Carrier is playing as good a free safety as anybody in the league right now," coach Mike Ditka said, "including the guys who are the honchos."

A week after the Redskins game, Carrier intercepted another pass to tie Taylor's record. He finished the year with 10 takeaways as the Bears completed the regular season an upbeat 11–5 and advanced to the second round of the playoffs. Carrier was involved in 122 tackles and was selected as the NFL Defensive Rookie of the Year. One of the reasons things worked out so well for Carrier immediately was his partnership with the other Bears safety, Shaun Gayle, who was nearly as good.

What happened next was a natural progression, though a frustrating one for Carrier. Quarterbacks began to avoid his side of the field. He hurt too many of them too fast and they stopped throwing into his zone. He got to cover decoys instead of swiping passes.

In August 1991, almost presciently, Carrier spoke about improving his all-around game, not just his pass-coverage skills.

During Carrier's second season he intercepted two passes. And over the course of his 11-year NFL career, he ended up with 32. He never again approached the glory of his first season. The glory was brief, but the numbers were lasting.

> **The interceptions are what you read and hear about, but knowing the game and being able to anticipate are important.**
>
> —MARK CARRIER

October 30, 1977

A RECORD DAY IN THE BACKFIELD

Walter Payton Rushes for 205 Yards

As the Bears entered their seventh game of the 1977 season, they were a tightrope act. Coming off a 7–7 record in 1976 under head coach Jack Pardee, there was a feeling that the Bears were on the upswing, that they had finally turned a corner in development and could make a run at the playoffs.

But then they began the season 2–4. As the Bears journeyed to Green Bay to play their favorite rivals, there was a sense that this was a pivotal game. If they lost they would be 2–5 and the season would devolve into hopelessness. A win? Well, that could turn things around.

"No one took the Bears seriously last year," linebacker Doug Buffone said in 1977. "We could sneak up on people. But I'll tell you how they are preparing for us now. Their coaches are saying, 'They've got Walter Payton. They've got the potential to blow you out of the water.'"

The Bears got the game they wanted, making Buffone sound like a crystal ball genius. They crushed the Packers 26–0, recording their first shutout in five years, and star running back Walter Payton produced his greatest game to date, rushing for 205 yards. The yardage precisely equaled the previous one-game record set by Gale Sayers.

Payton had displayed a stunning array of moves. He slithered between tacklers. He pirouetted around charging defenders. He outran slower tacklers. Once in a while Payton leaped over fallen would-be tacklers. Sometimes an enemy tackler caught him and Payton dragged him a few yards on his back. He put on a show that left fans agape. It was the kind of performance that demoralizes a defense, as well. When a defender believes he has put his best lick on a guy and the guy keeps on going, it plants doubt.

"Payton just breaks those tackles when you think you have him nailed," said Packers defensive end Bob Barber. "You think you have both arms wrapped around Payton and he still gets away. He's a great runner."

The Bears had established such firm control of the game that Pardee removed Payton from the lineup during the fourth quarter, trying to preserve his diamond untarnished for future games. Then word came from those statisticians in the press box upstairs that Payton's game total was 197 yards.

Payton liked the sound of rushing for 200 yards in one game, so he asked Pardee to be put back in the lineup. Quarterback Bob Avellini, immediately recognizing that his bread-and-butter in the offense had returned for a reason, handed off to Payton. He gained eight yards, good enough to tie Sayers's 1968 record. Pardee removed Payton from the game again and kept him on the sideline for good.

"I didn't want to break Sayers's record because Sayers is a super guy," Payton said of equaling it. "What's a record? I just wanted to win the game. I didn't do anything. I'm trying to figure out all the attention."

Bears players wanted to see Payton break the record. They felt he was playing in such a zone that day the runner could have racked up as many yards as he wanted. It was easy enough to see why. Payton had rushed for 117 yards in the first quarter. The biggest single gainer of the game was a 58-yard burst in the first period where Payton saw an opening on the left on a play designed to go right.

The game itself turned out to be a season-maker. Subsequently the Bears went on a hot streak, finishing 9–5 and advancing

Walter Payton's 205 rushing yards against the rival Green Bay Packers was one of his career highlights.

PAYTON BREAKS AWAY

On October 30, 1977, Walter Payton broke 200 yards in a game for the first time and tied the Bears single-game mark of 205 yards set by Gale Sayers. Payton picked up most of his yards in short and mid-range bursts, but he had one long gainer in the first quarter that was good for 58 yards. The play was intended to be a simple off-tackle run to the right side, but after quarterback Bob Avellini handed him the ball, Payton saw a hole developing between the guard and tackle. Seizing the opportunity, Payton changed direction, cut left at the line of scrimmage, ripped through the Green Bay defense, and sped away down the left sideline.

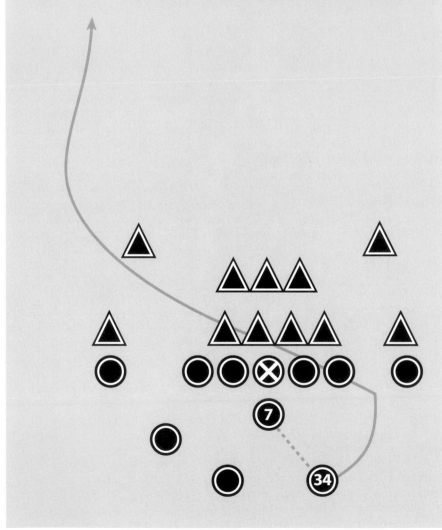

to the playoffs. The discussion over Payton's 205-yard game proved moot. Only three games later he set the new National Football League mark with a 275-yard day.

Payton was indeed a runner for the ages. He was one of the greatest rushers in NFL history and his 13-season career proved it. The numbers he put up in separate Bears games, the 275 and the 205, remain at the top of the list in the Bears record book.

What no one could imagine at the time, with Payton early in his career and in his prime, is that he would not live to old age and that the records he set coming out of the backfield would long outlast him.

Almost 22 years after the 205-yard game, Payton, nicknamed "Sweetness," died of cancer stemming from complications from a rare liver disease. In February 1999, Payton went public, announcing that he had a disease of the bile ducts and that he was waiting for a liver transplant. He said he was fighting the illness like an injury, trying to make his body whole again so it could perform as expected. It was surprising to see such a strong man made weak, but nobody anticipated an early death. During the following months, cancer moved in and attacked Payton's system very quickly and in early November surprise became shock became grief.

GAME DETAILS

Bears 26 • Packers 0

Location: Lambeau Field, Green Bay

Attendance: 56,267

Box Score:

Bears	13	3	0	10	**26**
Packers	0	0	0	0	**0**

Scoring:
CHI Musso 3-yard run (run failed)
CHI Payton 6-yard run (Thomas PAT)

CHI Thomas 47-yard field goal
CHI Payton 1-yard run (Thomas PAT)
CHI Thomas 20-yard field goal

He could have gained 300 yards.

—SAFETY GARY FENCIK

Payton was only 45 years old.

In his last days, surrounded by his family, including his son Jarrett, who also became a college and pro running back, and some teammates such as close friends Matt Suhey and Mike Singletary, Payton was said to be serene.

When Mike Ditka, who coached Payton during the Super Bowl era, heard his star had died, he proclaimed Payton "the greatest Bear of all."

Payton was such a popular figure in Chicago that a memorial service was conducted at Soldier Field, with an estimated 15,000 or so in attendance. The Reverend Jesse Jackson spoke at the 1½-hour service. Fans held up signs, as if they were attending a football game, but rather than offering sentiments of encouragement to win, they offered sentiments of love.

The huge men who opened holes for Payton to run through and who shared good times in victory brushed away tears and spoke of what a special man he was. Connie Payton, Walter's widow, spoke eloquently for Payton, whose brother Eddie was also a professional football player.

"I thank the city of Chicago for loving Walter as much as my family and I did," she said.

And it was true.

Ballet's loss is football's gain.

—*CHICAGO TRIBUNE* FOOTBALL WRITER DON PIERSON
AFTER WALTER PAYTON'S 205-YARD GAME

October 7, 2001

BRIAN URLACHER
RUINS FALCONS

Linebacker Fills Up the Stat Sheet

A few years ago Brian Urlacher was asked to name his favorite game as a member of the Chicago Bears. It was stressed he should pick a game that highlighted his personal play, not a team victory, and the question was popped before the 2006 Bears advanced to the Super Bowl, anyway.

The star middle linebacker, who will go down in history as one of the Bears' best and most popular players, willingly jumped in the wayback machine and stopped it on a game during his second NFL season.

A rookie in 2000, Urlacher, the one-time defensive back who retained the speed to play that position and the power and size at nearly 260 pounds to move into the linebacker slot, was a superstar by 2001. Urlacher recorded 148 tackles, six sacks, and three interceptions that year. He was chosen NFL Defensive Player of the Year by *Football Digest* and, in a reflection of respect rarely afforded defensive players, finished fifth in the league's Most Valuable Player voting.

Defensive players are always at a disadvantage when their performances are weighed against offensive stars. There are no defensive statistics that can help compare a player like Urlacher to the Patriots' Tom Brady, who threw 50 touchdown passes in 2007, or Chargers running back LaDainian Tomlinson, who set a league record for points scored in 2006. So to even be considered among the league's all-around elite, a defensive player must build the reputation of being someone who can control a game.

By his second season in the league, Urlacher was that feared among opponents. When Urlacher thinks back to October 2001 when the Bears crushed the Atlanta Falcons 31–3 in the Georgia Dome, he jokingly says, "I filled up every category [on the stat sheet]."

Make that half-jokingly. That day Urlacher was in on eight tackles, collected an interception, forced a fumble, recovered a fumble, and scored a touchdown. He was not *on* the stat sheet; he *was* the stat sheet.

This was a pleasurable breakout season for the Bears. Picked to place last in the NFC Central, they ended up winning the division and finished the regular season 13–3. The

Linebacker Brian Urlacher terrorized the Atlanta Falcons during a 31–3 victory in 2001.

Falcons contest was a statement game. The Bears scored their 31 points in the last 32 minutes and it marked the first time in three seasons they had scored as many as 31 points in a game.

The Bears defense, starting to construct a born-again reputation as Monsters of the Midway, sacked the Falcons' quarterbacks seven times. Chris Chandler was forced out of the game with a concussion on one of those sacks. Although Atlanta substituted the mobile Michael Vick, it did little to slow the Bears' pass rush—Vick was sacked six times.

The Bears were ahead 17–0 in the fourth quarter when Urlacher contributed his most memorable play. Defensive end Phillip Daniels forced a fumble, and Urlacher scooped it up and ran 90 yards for a touchdown. He did it pretty quickly, too, even though he didn't have Jim Thorpe chasing him the way George Halas did so many years before.

The Bears' showing was very liberating. It demonstrated potential and provided confidence. The team won seven of its next eight games. If opponents hadn't feared the Bears defense before, all they had to do was listen to defensive end Bryan Robinson to be quaking in their Nikes.

"You've got some animals on this team that have always been caged and have always backed down," Robinson said, "and now we're coming out of the cage and we're going for people. We're absolutely sick of losing. We don't want to be that caged animal anymore."

Although everyone already recognized that Urlacher was a special player, in a way his complete domination of the Falcons was a coming out party. He showed off everything he could do, all in one game. He was chosen NFL Defensive Player of the Week. Smart move, or Urlacher might have come out of that cage after some of those voters.

Urlacher also knew that defense was not a one-man job. He could lead the unit of 11, but there was plenty going on in a game spread around the field that he couldn't reach. What he wanted to see was the Bears defense as a whole return to the glory of old.

"We just got to make plays," Urlacher said. "That's what it comes down to. We know there [have been] a lot of good defenses here in the past, and we feel like we're one of those teams."

When the Bears reached the Super Bowl in 2006 only to fall to the Indianapolis Colts, they were one of those defenses, surrendering only 255 points and outscoring teams in each quarter.

The Bears flooded the NFC Pro Bowl roster that season, and Urlacher said the selection of his teammates was well deserved after the year they had.

THOSE OTHER LINEBACKERS

The Bears' tradition of fielding great middle linebackers has overshadowed the fact that those middle linebackers have frequently had help from other great linebackers on their right and left.

Brian Urlacher's partner in defense is Lance Briggs, a three-time NFL All-Pro himself.

Mike Singletary was the man in the middle for the Super Bowl XX Bears, but he was flanked by Wilber Marshall and Otis Wilson. Opponents running around end knew nothing good could come out of an encounter with either of them.

Doug Buffone was good company for Dick Butkus. And so was Joe Fortunato, at the end of his career, after being Bill George's primary sidekick. Of all the Bears "other" linebackers who didn't play the middle, Fortunato was the best. He was a five-time All-Pro who is not in the Hall of Fame probably because so many Bears middle linebackers are.

GAME DETAILS

Bears 31 • Falcons 3

Location: Georgia Dome, Atlanta

Attendance: 46,483

Box Score:

Bears	0	10	0	21	**31**
Falcons	0	0	0	3	**3**

Scoring:

CHI Robinson 34-yard pass from Booker (Edinger PAT)

CHI Edinger 42-yard field goal

CHI Booker 63-yard pass from Miller (Edinger PAT)

CHI Urlacher 90-yard fumble return (Edinger PAT)

ATL Feely 44-yard field goal

CHI Thomas 32-yard run (Edinger PAT)

> **W**e know about that [defensive] tradition here and all that good stuff.
>
> —BRIAN URLACHER

"We've got some good, young talent on this team, and it's nice to see they got recognized for their play," he said, "because they're not the biggest names. There are a lot of guys out there who probably get more recognition from the media, but these guys go out there and play hard every week, and they put it on film, and the players around the league and the coaches around the league saw that. That's why they're going."

In 2005 Urlacher was chosen NFL Defensive Player of the Year, and in 2006 he led the Bears with 185 tackles. He was on his way to becoming one of the greatest defensive players in National Football League history, a player headed for Hall of Fame enshrinement.

However, in 2007 Urlacher hit a speed bump. He began complaining of back pain and there were suggestions that he suffered from arthritis that could eventually terminate his career. After the season Urlacher underwent neck surgery.

The two ailments combined created significant worry about Urlacher's future with the Bears and whether or not he would be able to continue playing at his usual superstar level. The prospect was alarming since Urlacher was in the middle of a nine-year contract and was only 30 years old. Urlacher stayed mum on the topic, and every official pronouncement from the Bears was encouraging.

Indications were that Urlacher would be ready to resume knocking the teeth out of opposing offenses in the fall of 2008.

> **P**ersonally, that was my best game of that season.
>
> —BRIAN URLACHER

October 13, 1963

MIKE DITKA'S GREATEST GAME

Tight End Nabs Four Touchdown Passes

The funny thing about Mike Ditka's best day as a professional football player was that it began poorly. Mike Ditka dropped the first pass that Bears quarterback Bill Wade threw to him.

It was coach George Halas's theory that the mistake made Ditka mad and that he stampeded through the Los Angeles Rams secondary for the rest of the day to make up for the miscue. The Bears crushed Los Angeles 52–14 in a game that illustrated just how powerful Chicago might be that season.

Ditka caught nine passes for 110 yards and four touchdowns. The All-Pro tight end who elevated the position to a new level with his pass-catching ability and his fearless blocking said it was the best performance he turned in on an NFL field.

Ditka would never rate the pass-catching extravaganza over winning a title as a player and another as a coach. The 6'2", 230-pound Ditka had many accomplishments on the football field. He was a key cog on the 1963 team that won the NFL crown. And as a head coach he led the 1985 Bears to a Super Bowl championship. But for play-for-play

excellence, Ditka was never better than in this game.

Ditka caught three touchdowns from Wade and one from Rudy Bukich. The four touchdown receptions equaled the team record set by Harlon Hill in 1954 that remains intact today.

If anything, the Bears defense was more dominating than the offense, intercepting six Rams passes and forcing five fumbles, three of which were recovered. The decisive triumph marked the Bears' fifth straight win to start the season and showed that they might be kings of the NFL's Western Division.

One touchdown pass to Ditka started the Bears' scoring at the end of the first period, and he was still plucking passes out of the air into the fourth quarter.

At that time the Bears were gaining a belief in themselves, making it easy for Bears fans who had been shut out of rooting for a championship since 1946 to think this might be a special team. Halas was trying to keep the excitement under control so the Bears didn't get swelled heads.

After the overwhelming victory, Halas was already being asked if this Bears edition was his best team of all time. No one could blame him for being in a hold-your-horses mode given the great Bears teams of the past that had already won championships. Memories of prior accomplishments had indeed dimmed.

"No, they are not the greatest in Bear history," Halas said. "Just a helluva good team on five days so far this year. You can't judge a team until it has played 14 games. Then you can only do it in retrospect. But they are a good team. They are building up a great deal of pride."

Actually, whether it was the hype or just the law of averages catching up to the Bears, Chicago went out and lost the next week. But that was the only defeat of the regular season. Chicago finished 11–1–2 and won the NFL title by beating the Giants. The 1963 group may not have been Halas's best team ever, but especially after the long wait it was one of his most satisfying champions.

"We were a better defensive team than offensive team that year," Ditka said.

Indeed, the Ditka-fueled mashing of the Rams was the only major explosion the Bears posted offensively that season. They did not break 40 points in any other game.

Ditka the offensive player caught 56 passes as a rookie in 1961, 58 the next year, and 59 during the championship season. His best season, however, was in 1964 when he hauled in 75 passes, unheard-of then for a tight end.

Ditka was a tough, tough player. Doug Buffone, soon to be a teammate but at the time a member of the College All-Star team, said he first met Ditka when he lined up against him and the Bears in that summer's exhibition game.

Tight end Mike Ditka hauled in four touchdown passes against the Los Angeles Rams in 1963.

"The guy was beating me to death," Buffone said.

Ditka was so strong and rugged to play against, Buffone actually questioned his own future in the NFL at the time, as if just maybe he had made the wrong career choice.

ONCE A BEAR, ALWAYS A BEAR

Mike Ditka surprised George "Papa Bear" Halas with a heartfelt letter just as Halas was about to search for a new Bears coach. Ditka, Halas's wayward "son" and an assistant coach with the Dallas Cowboys, said he was a true Bear at heart. Halas agreed and brought Ditka in to coach the Bears in 1982.

It was the perfect match between man and moment. Just how different would Bears history and Chicago itself be if Halas had gone in another direction for his final important franchise hire?

> **I felt it was the greatest game I ever played in.**
>
> —MIKE DITKA

The Bears probably would not have won the franchise-defining Super Bowl Ditka led them to after the 1985 season. Ditka would not have become a Chicago hero for life. Ditka is at least as well known as Mayor Richard M. Daley and more admired.

A man who grew up in western Pennsylvania has in many ways become the symbol of the city, a tough tell-it-like-it-is guy who preached hard work, who burned to win, and who lends his name to many charities. Ditka was right that he was born to coach the Chicago Bears. And most football fans probably barely remember that he actually coached the New Orleans Saints for a short, unhappy period after the Bears let him go.

In Chicago, Mike Ditka is "Da Coach" forever.

Mike Ditka and George Halas formed a bond that would eventually lead the Bears back to the Super Bowl in 1986.

GAME DETAILS

Bears 52 • Rams 14

Location: Los Angeles Coliseum, Los Angeles

Attendance: 40,476

If you didn't hustle, he would get on your tail.

—GALE SAYERS ON MIKE DITKA

Box Score:

Bears	7	21	3	21	**52**
Rams	0	7	0	7	**14**

Scoring:

CHI Ditka 13-yard pass from Wade (Jencks PAT)

CHI McRae 35-yard interception return (Jencks PAT)

LA Phillips 10-yard pass from Bratkowski (Villaneuva PAT)

CHI Ditka 25-yard pass from Wade (Jencks PAT)

CHI Ditka 2-yard pass from Wade (Jencks PAT)

CHI Leclerc 31-yard field goal

LA Bass 4-yard run (Villaneuva PAT)

CHI Ditka 14-yard pass from Bukich (Jencks PAT)

CHI Galimore 2-yard run (Jencks PAT)

CHI Farrington 17-yard pass from Bukich (Jencks PAT)

Ditka predated Gale Sayers on the Bears by a few years, but Sayers said Ditka established new levels for dedication and toughness on the practice field. He was almost like an additional coach, yelling at players if he didn't feel they practiced hard enough. It was good practice for later, as it turned out, when Ditka was coach in name as well as demeanor.

Although Ditka was a natural-bred Bear, he and Halas clashed over money matters. For those who understood both strong-willed men, it was not a major surprise that they had disagreements. There was some surprise, however, when Ditka was exiled to another team and finished his playing days with the Dallas Cowboys in 1972.

Ditka caught 427 passes during his playing career for a 13.6-yard-per-catch average. And then he went into coaching, again surprising some who didn't picture him as an assistant coach to Tom Landry in Dallas.

Halas had his favorites during his long career, but he also held grudges. He loved George Allen, but treated Allen's move to Los Angeles to become a head coach as a breach of loyalty. From then on, Allen might as well have been Benedict Arnold in Halas's eyes. Ditka pretty much fit into the same category of out of sight, out of mind—out of the Bears lineup, out of Halas's.

But Ditka wrote a conciliatory letter to Halas at the right time in 1982, when the Bears patriarch was getting older and the Bears needed a coach to replace Neill Armstrong. Ditka pronounced himself a true Bear, and Halas believed him. One of Halas's last major acts in Bears management before his 1983 death was to anoint Ditka as the coach of the future.

Halas did not live to see Ditka lead the Bears to a Super Bowl championship, but he set the wheels in motion for it to happen.

October 4, 1992 and September 23, 1991

GOOD NEWS, BAD NEWS

Jim Harbaugh Wins Big Against the Jets, Gets Hammered Against the Vikings

Jim Harbaugh comes from a football family. The one-time Bears quarterback is now head coach at Stanford University. His father, Jack, was a long-time coach and his brother, John, was named the coach of the Baltimore Ravens in 2008.

As a player, Harbaugh, who starred at the University of Michigan, endured a love-hate relationship with another coach—Mike Ditka. One minute Ditka was in his corner, counting on Harbaugh to light up the skies with passes. The next minute Ditka was fuming on the sideline because the quarterback made a mistake. Iron Mike Ditka sometimes seemed to be Schizo Mike Ditka around Harbaugh.

During his seven seasons with the Bears between 1987 and 1993—in the post-Jim McMahon era and before he became an All-Pro with the Indianapolis Colts—Harbaugh had some terrific, memorable moments and some lousy, unforgettable moments. Somehow the tiffs with Ditka became more magnified than the results on the field.

Nothing quite matched the Ditka blowup during a 1992 game. The Bears were ahead 20–0 in the fourth quarter but blew the game, losing 21–20 to the Minnesota Vikings. The infamous incident that grew out of the bitter disappointment was Ditka dressing down quarterback Harbaugh for an audible called at the line of scrimmage that went awry. The following poor throw was a nightmare, igniting the Vikings' rally with a 35-yard Todd Scott touchdown return.

The original play called for running back Neal Anderson to run a deep fly pattern. When Harbaugh saw the Vikings defense line up, he switched the play. That changed Anderson's responsibility. He was supposed to run a six-yard stop-and-hitch pattern. But Anderson didn't hear the change in the notoriously loud Metrodome.

"Because of the noise, or whatever reason, I didn't get it," Anderson said.

When Harbaugh returned to the sideline Ditka let him have it, screaming in his face, gesturing wildly, and clearly berating him for screwing up. Metrodome fans were treated to a special video of the performance on the stadium scoreboard. Ditka told Harbaugh if he ever called another audible he would be benched, though that was an unrealistic comment and was a policy later rescinded in a clearer-thinking moment.

Apparently the Bears had discussed the likelihood of a sound problem in the Metrodome in practice all week leading up to the game. The general message was to steer clear of audibles if possible. The audible was called. The execution was off. And the result was incendiary.

If Ditka came off as a bully, so be it. If he threatened to destroy his quarterback's standing on the team, so be it. It was an embarrassing reaction to a frustrating situation, but Ditka did not back down or apologize.

"There is nothing to regret," he said a day later. "I am a man of very few regrets. I don't care. I can't help it. I'm only me. You don't audible on the other team's turf when half the team can't hear. That I won't back off on. That's the last thing I told him Saturday night."

That was the lowest moment of Harbaugh's Bears career and is remembered as well among Bears fans as any of the good things he did on the field. The best among those plus-side events occurred against the Jets.

The Jets game is Harbaugh's favorite among those he played for Chicago. The Bears seemed dead in the water during the *Monday Night Football* game as the seconds rapidly ticked by in the fourth quarter at Soldier Field.

Chicago trailed 13–6, but Harbaugh directed a late drive that looked likely to tie the game and send it into overtime. The Bears advanced to the Jets' 2-yard line, but could not penetrate the end zone and had to turn the ball over on downs. It seemed the Bears were doomed.

The relationship between head coach Mike Ditka and quarterback Jim Harbaugh was often volatile.

The Jets worked the clock and methodically moved the ball safely away from their own goal line to about the 40-yard line. Then the Bears got a break. A Jets fumble gave Chicago a final chance. Harbaugh came back on the field and on a critical play hit receiver Tom Waddle with an 18-yard strike on fourth down to keep the ball. With seven seconds to go, Harbaugh whipped a pass to Anderson in the end zone for a five-yard touchdown. Overtime.

In the extra period, Harbaugh ran a bootleg and threw to Cap Boso, who struggled inside the 1-yard line. Officials raised their hands signifying a touchdown. Bears win! Only upon further review, even as the Bears jogged off the field, the touchdown was negated and the ball was placed near the goal line. Do over. Harbaugh kept the ball himself on the next call, bulling in on the quarterback sneak. The final score was Bears 19, Jets 13. It was an unexpected and satisfying victory.

Harbaugh had some difficult times with Ditka and he had some difficult times during stretches when he was sacked three and four times in a game. But in 1991 he also completed 275 passes and threw for more than 3,100 yards.

The Bears suffered a six-game losing streak in 1992, and of all people, Harbaugh publicly defended Ditka against his critics.

"I think it is frustrating for him right now because he can't walk across those lines and play football," Harbaugh said. "Coach Ditka is the guy who gets blamed a lot and has people throwing stuff on him, screaming and yelling obscenities at him. And he is probably the last person to blame at this point."

By 1993 Ditka was gone, and by 1994 Harbaugh was the quarterback for the Colts, leading the team to so many late-game victories he was nicknamed "Captain Comeback."

But although life has taken him far from Chicago and he has been out of the Bears' lineup for years, Harbaugh admits that he has only warm feelings for the place, that Chicago remains his favorite big city in the country.

MY WAY OR THE HIGHWAY

As a coach Mike Ditka cared and agonized so much about the Bears winning and playing right that he had a heart attack during a season. If a player didn't go along with his program, he might dress him down in front of the world or simply trade him away.

But the older he gets, the more sides of Mike Ditka's personality become public. Starting in about 2006, Ditka became very publicly aligned with the cause of older NFL players whose pensions were not taking care of them as they aged and suffered from various ailments. Ditka spoke out repeatedly against what he saw as the injustice of the Players Association not coming up with better benefits. He testified before Congress. He organized fund-raisers. And he donated the proceeds from the sale of his own memorabilia to the retired players.

Ditka might have his spats, but no one doubts his heart is in the right place. In the city of big shoulders, it sometimes seems that Mike Ditka has the broadest shoulders of all. As a guest football commentator, as a purveyor of fine wines, and as a potential candidate for the U.S. Senate from Illinois, Ditka is never very long out of the news in Chicago and his name remains golden in the community.

GAME DETAILS

Bears 20 • Vikings 21

Location: Metrodome, Minneapolis

Attendance: 60,992

Box Score:

Bears	3	10	7	0	**20**
Vikings	0	0	0	21	**21**

Scoring:
CHI Butler 50-yard field goal
CHI Butler 37-yard field goal
CHI Waddle 28-yard pass from Harbaugh (Butler PAT)

CHI Harbaugh 6-yard run (Butler PAT)
MIN Scott 35-yard interception return (Reveiz PAT)
MIN Carter 16-yard pass from Gannon (Reveiz PAT)
MIN Craig 1-yard run (Reveiz PAT)

> **H**e was dead wrong.
> —MIKE DITKA ON HARBAUGH'S AUDIBLE

GAME DETAILS

Bears 19 • Jets 13

Location: Soldier Field, Chicago

Attendance: 65,255

Box Score:

Jets	3	3	7	0	**13**
Bears	3	0	10	6	**19**

Scoring:
CHI Butler 33-yard field goal
NY Leahy 19-yard field goal
NY Leahy 34-yard field goal

NY Baxter 1-yard run (Leahy PAT)
CHI Butler 44-yard field goal
CHI Anderson 5-yard pass from Harbaugh (Butler PAT)
CHI Harbaugh 1-yard run

> **B**ad call, bad throw.
> —JIM HARBAUGH
> ON HIS OWN AUDIBLE AND INTERCEPTION

37

MAKE IT...OR ELSE

Kevin Butler Kicks the Bears Over the Packers

Kevin Butler possessed a very confident toe. In high school, in college, and from the moment he arrived at the Chicago Bears' training camp in 1985 as a fourth-round draft pick out of the University of Georgia, he believed in the power of his foot.

He needed the faith.

Butler was a rookie trying to break in with a veteran team that was chock full of strong personalities and had the Super Bowl on its mind. There would be no tolerance for a rookie who needed a learning curve. The Bears already had a solid kicker in Bob Thomas, who had scored 101 points in 1984. What did they need with a newcomer like Butler?

But Butler had special talents. He won the kicker's job and although it did take him a little while to win the hearts and minds of the position players, he had an attitude that left him mostly impervious to coach Mike Ditka's rants. That helped as Butler ended up scoring a league-leading 144 points that season.

During that rookie season Butler never missed an extra point, making 51 out of 51 tries and adding 31 field goals. When Ditka got in his face, Butler yelled back, earning more respect from his teammates. Ditka

definitely did not want a shrinking violet kicker around whose confidence would be shattered by his snarling. With Butler he did not have to worry about that. Kickers were supposed to have ice water in their veins and short memories. They had to know they were going to make the kick when the team put them in range and the coach counted on them to earn their salary.

During the successful Super Bowl run, Butler, as the most visible face of special teams, merely represented another meshing, smooth-operating facet of the game. The Bears were so dominant, however, they didn't need to be bailed out by too many last-minute kicks. It's possible Butler showed his true worth a little bit later in his career when the Bears were still good but involved in more close games.

One game that stands out when Butler's foot came to the rescue was a 1987 midseason encounter with the Packers in Green Bay.

During the 1987 season, a labor-action year that disrupted the schedule, the Bears were making their way to an 11–4, first-place NFC Central Division title. The game came at a pivotal moment in the season— the Bears were 6–1, but a loss might have sent them tumbling in the wrong direction.

Kicker Kevin Butler
came through in
the clutch to beat
Green Bay in 1987.

The game was a classic with each team trading the lead and more than once seeming to lay claim to the win. In the fourth quarter Green Bay edged out to a 21–13 lead, but the Bears embarked on an 80-yard drive for a touchdown. It was a two-score game for the Bears, but Chicago took the risk of going for the six points first on a one-yard leap by Walter Payton instead of kicking the safe field goal. Butler added the extra point and the Bears trailed 21–20.

Chicago's defense held and the Bears drove again. This time the Jim McMahon-steered rush to the end zone stalled and Butler trotted out to kick a 24-yard field goal. The boot gave Chicago a 23–21 lead with 3:59 left.

Things were looking good for the Bears, but on this day the defense couldn't hold. The Packers roared back and got their own field-goal kicker within range. Al Del Greco hit a 47-yarder and the Packers led again 24–23. This time the Packers looked safe.

The Bears took the kickoff deep in their own territory and McMahon sought to hustle them into something passing for Butler's long-distance range. A few sideline patterns, a mix of plays, and the Bears were barely at midfield and just about out of time. The Packers had to be feeling pretty good with four seconds to go and the Bears contemplating the odds of a 52-yard field-goal attempt.

It is standard procedure around the National Football League for opponents to call timeout at such moments to "ice" the kicker. The idea is to disrupt his rhythm, to upset his thinking, to make him worry about the pressure during the lull in the action.

Packers fans were howling. Packers players made snide remarks. But Butler didn't listen to any of it and he didn't allow his thoughts to run away under the pressure. Instead he formulated a quick game plan to take advantage of the torn-up turf on a less-than-perfect field. The Packers had hoped to make Butler nervous. He used the time to adjust to the circumstances.

Butler surveyed the spot on the field where the snap would be placed and realized there were holes all around. So during the timeout, he bent over and

KICKERS ARE FOOTBALL PLAYERS, TOO

For decades kickers on pro football teams were regular members of the offense or defense who took time out from their regular duties to try a field goal or kick an extra point when the occasion warranted it.

There were no specialists on the gridiron, and the phrase "special teams" for kicking units and kick coverage units hadn't been invented. When the first kicking specialists were employed in the 1960s, they were initially resented because they took someone else's job.

In the macho football world guys who manned the offensive or defensive line had little respect for puny guys who trotted on the field periodically and used their toes rather than their biceps and pecs to decide games.

Kickers are better accepted now than they were since the preponderance of the evidence shows how important their presence is to winning and losing, but at one level a certain prejudice prevails. There is only one pure place-kicker—Jan Stenerud—in the Pro Football Hall of Fame.

GAME DETAILS

Bears 26 • Packers 24

Location: Lambeau Field, Green Bay

Attendance: 53,320

Box Score:

Bears	7	6	0	13	**26**
Packers	14	7	0	3	**24**

Scoring:

CHI Anderson 59-yard pass from McMahon (Butler PAT)
GB West 27-yard pass from Wright (Del Greco PAT)
GB Fullwood 2-yard run (Del Greco PAT)
CHI Butler 27-yard field goal
CHI Butler 29-yard field goal

GB Epps 26-yard pass from Wright (Del Greco PAT)
CHI Payton 1-yard run (Butler PAT)
CHI Butler 24-yard field goal
GB Del Greco 47-yard field goal
CHI Butler 52-yard field goal

> **T**hank God for Butthead.
>
> —JIM MCMAHON
> PRAISING BUTLER AFTER THE WINNING KICK

smoothed out the ground. That allowed the hold to be placed on conveniently flat ground.

When the Bears lined up, the ball was hiked cleanly, placed cleanly, and the clock ticked down to zero as Butler kicked cleanly, 52 yards for the winning points in a 26–24 game. A buzzer shot to beat the Packers.

"So, actually, that timeout helped me," Butler said, rubbing it in, though truthfully, on the Packers' backfired strategy. "I built up a nice little mound and smoothed it out and had me a clean spot to kick from before it was time to kick. Only thing I didn't get to do was tee the ball up, but it was almost the same thing."

McMahon was praised for leading the team downfield, but he deflected the compliments Butler's way. "Winning drive?" McMahon said. "Never mind what I did."

The kick, which equaled Butler's longest boot in the pros to that date, was a critical one in more than one way. He was in a slump at the time and needed the mental boost. And Ditka had cornered him on the sideline and said, "You better make this one."

That was the real pressure on Butler. Ditka's was no idle threat. Butler really did feel like missing the kick might have put him on the waiver wire. Instead, he added just a little bit more to Bears lore.

December 27, 1987

36 When He Hit, It Hurt

Richard Dent Sacks the Known World

The great thing about Richard Dent's name is that it is the same as what he did. He put dents into quarterbacks. Sometimes they didn't let it show. Sometimes they rubbed the bruises. Sometimes they had to soothe themselves in whirlpools on their days off after the games against the Bears. But Dent always let them know he was there.

In the past few years Dent has been a finalist for enshrinement in the Pro Football Hall of Fame, but he keeps missing out. He collected 137½ sacks during an NFL career that began in 1983 and lasted until 1997. He still owns the Bears' record in that category.

Apparently those voting for the Hall have not interviewed quarterbacks who were hit by Dent. That's if they can still talk or have stopped crying yet. When Dent was under a full head of steam his 6'6", 265-pound physique was a registered weapon. Quarterbacks could run, but they couldn't hide. And if they couldn't run far enough or fast enough without dumping the ball off, Dent caught up to them.

Dent, originally from Atlanta, attended Tennessee State, and before he was drafted in the eighth round by the Bears in 1983 he was already a sack king, collecting a school record 39.

One of Dent's greatest games in the NFL occurred during the interrupted 1987 season, when the Bears entered the final regular season game against the then-Los Angeles Raiders needing a victory to host a game in the first round of the playoffs. The game was played in Los Angeles and more than 78,000 fans attended.

The way the game played out was boring for many, except lovers of defense. Defense ruled all day long and the Bears defense was led by Dent. The Bears won 6–3 in an all-field-goal encounter to finish 11–4, and the Bears had more quarterback sacks—eight—than points.

"He was a scared puppy all day," Bears defensive back Dave Duerson said of Raiders quarterback Marc Wilson.

The Bears were credited with eight sacks of Wilson, but when the films were reviewed, the math was revisited and Dent was given another sack. That equaled his team record of 4½ in a game, a mark that still stands. It's possible that Dent chased the Raiders all the way back to Oakland by himself, never mind owner Al Davis's pursuit of the best deal.

In 12 regular season games that year, Dent collected 12½ sacks. When quarterbacks saw Dent's No. 95 bearing down on

Defensive end
Richard Dent
notched 4½ sacks
in a game against
the Raiders in
1987.

them their first thought was, "Duck!" The game was the final regular-season event for retiring halfback Walter Payton and Payton was almost the goat with an inconvenient fumble. The Raiders almost, maybe, sort of, could have reached good enough field position for their kicker, Chris Bahr, to tie the game with his foot. However, one of Dent's handy-dandy sacks came along to push the Raiders back a key five yards and cause a wasted down.

As time passed and Dent became the old man on what had possibly been the greatest defense of all time in 1985, he was occasionally criticized for taking plays off. He angrily denied it and said sometimes it only looked that way because he was trying to recoup energy.

"We are not the Energizer [bunny]" Dent said. "You can't put a battery in us and have us run, run, run all the time. We are not those kinds of people. I put my pants on like any other guy and I get tired like any other guy. But I make plays and that's what it's all about. As a defensive player, you have to believe in yourself and you have to produce."

Boy, oh boy, did Richard Dent make plays. He was a bonebreaker and a heartbreaker all rolled into one when he bowled over those quarterbacks.

Near the end of his playing days, Dent and the Bears went separate ways for a while, but then Dent re-signed to play for the team in 1995.

"Families sometimes split, but they always get back together," Dent said.

Dent actually did play another two seasons in other towns before coming back to Chicago for good and spending a year as an assistant coach for the Bears.

THE FEAR OF GOD DEFENSE

The whole Monsters-of-the-Midway business was not only a great marketing strategy, but also a tremendous psychological advantage for the Bears. Dating back to when Bronko Nagurski was an unleashed, heat-seeking missile who always found the ball carrier and nearly always came close to dismembering him, the Bears loved to portray themselves as the toughest guys on the block.

When teams played Chicago, the Bears wanted them to think that they were venturing into a bad neighborhood where they might be mugged. George Halas fostered the idea that the Bears defense was populated by players who chewed nails rather than licorice. And the players reveled in the descriptions.

The Bears wanted opposing blockers, runners, and quarterbacks to bring a little fear with them into the games, wanted them to worry a little bit, wanted them to hesitate a little bit.

A story Mike Ditka told once illustrates the persona of Bears defensive players. According to Ditka, when he first became head coach he and his wife went out to dinner. The waiter informed him some of his players wanted to buy the couple a round of drinks. Ditka found Steve McMichael, Mike Hartenstine, and Dan Hampton in the bar downing shots of tequila. The next morning all three were on time and ready for practice.

"They were throwbacks to the old years I had with the Bears as a player," Ditka said.

GAME DETAILS

Bears 6 • Raiders 3

Location: Los Angeles Coliseum, Los Angeles

Attendance: 78,019

Box Score:

Bears	0	3	0	3	**6**
Raiders	3	0	0	0	**3**

Scoring:
LA Bahr 48-yard field goal
CHI Butler 38-yard field goal
CHI Butler 30-yard field goal

> **H**e'll go down in history as one of the best defensive ends.
>
> —ALONZO SPELLMAN ON DENT

Inevitably during his sojourns with other clubs, Dent had to play a game or two against Chicago. When facing old teammates it was like going up against members of his own fan club.

Before Dent even retired from the Bears, he began establishing community-based programs to help the needy. In 1992 Dent raised money to help rehabilitate a hospital and renovate it into a housing option for the homeless. And after he retired Dent stayed in the Chicago area and threw himself into other worthy projects.

"Chicago has given me a great opportunity as a player," Dent said when he announced his commitment to the first project. "This is something I can do for Chicago."

There was no truth to the rumor that Dent was going to build another kind of housing project—an old folk's home for worn-down quarterbacks.

December 9, 1962

THE FIELD WAS WIDE OPEN

Richie Petitbon Returns an Interception 101 Yards

It has been almost 40 years since Richie Petitbon roamed the Bears' defensive secondary, but his name is still prominent in the team's record book for his prowess in catching other squads' thrown footballs.

Petitbon, who joined the Bears in 1959 out of Tulane, was one of the premier thieves of his time. During a career that continued through 1972, Petitbon intercepted 48 passes. Of those steals, 37 were recorded for the Bears, one shy of the team record.

Petitbon accounts for many of the Bears' interception-related records. He owns the record for most yards returned with interceptions in a career at 643. He owns the record for most yards returned with interceptions in a season with 212. He returned three interceptions for touchdowns for the Bears.

And in the single most-electrifying regular season interception of Petitbon's career, he set the record for the longest interception runback in Bears history—a 101-yard return against the Los Angeles Rams in 1962.

That was during the Bears' 9–5 season, a few weeks after they edged the Cowboys by a single point in Dallas. In this game the Bears clobbered the Rams 30–14 on a day when the temperature at Wrigley Field was 13 degrees at kickoff and dropped throughout the contest.

The pass Petitbon intercepted was thrown by L.A. quarterback Zeke Bratkowski, a former Bear.

"The Rams were driving toward what was home plate at Wrigley Field," Petitbon recalled. "We doubled the wide receiver and I don't know if Bratkowski just didn't see it or what."

Bratkowski threw the ball into the end zone, but Petitbon stepped in front of the receiver and snatched it. Many times defensive backs kneel down for a touchback in the end zone and permit the ball to be placed at the 20-yard line.

It is much more unusual for them to quickly survey the field, realize they are not immediately covered or surrounded, and attempt to make a return so deep in their own territory. Playing it safe often rules. Not

Richie Petitbon returned an interception 101 yards for a touchdown in 1962—still a team record.
(Photo courtesy of WireImages)

The first 50 yards I was worried that someone was going to catch me and the last 50 yards I was afraid they weren't going to catch me.

—RICHIE PETITBON

only was Petitbon in no immediate danger, he saw clear sailing ahead. With his long legs churning, the strong safety burst out of the end zone and swiftly outran the out-of-balance Rams. Petitbon didn't have to do much zigging and zagging. He hugged the sideline. Most of the run was in the open field, with no Rams player able to run Petitbon down from behind.

Petitbon was 6'3" and 206 pounds, not one of those lumbering linemen who find themselves in a once-in-a-career position where they have to run 100 yards and almost collapse gasping for air before they hit pay dirt. In many ways the return was no sweat after making the initial grab.

"I think the only reason it is remembered is just the length," Petitbon said. "It's going to be hard to beat."

Petitbon underestimated the importance of the play in some ways, however. The Bears had the upper hand in the game's early going, but Rams head coach Harland Svare made superb defensive adjustments at halftime. In the second half the Bears offense was stifled and they recorded just one first down. Without the assistance of the defensive touchdown, the Bears might have been in bigger trouble. Petitbon's interception came in the fourth quarter with the Rams closing in on the end zone and not only did the play stop the drive cold, it also reversed the momentum abruptly and shockingly, putting six points on the board for Chicago. At least in the context of the game, if not the big picture of the season, the interception was more important than Petitbon lets on.

DEE-FENSE!

The more a football fan studies the history of the Chicago Bears, the more one comes to think that the franchise invented defense. While that is not entirely true, the preponderance of the fame accumulated by the Monsters of the Midway is on the defensive side of the ball.

Throughout the decades the Bears have featured some signature offensive stars, from Red Grange and Bronko Nagurski (both of whom played defense full-time) to Sid Luckman, Gale Sayers, and Walter Payton. But whether the Bears would be merely successful or regularly contend for a championship has depended upon the defense.

Richie Petitbon was a devastating hitter and a ballhawk in the Bears' defensive backfield, and he also had good company in the secondary, notably Rosey Taylor. During the 1963 season, Taylor pilfered nine passes, still second on the team's record list. Tied for third on that list was a man better known for throwing the ball rather than catching it: Johnny Lujack, who intercepted eight passes during the 1948 season.

GAME DETAILS

Bears 30 • Rams 14

Location: Wrigley Field, Chicago

Attendance: 38,685

It really was an easy thing.

—RICHIE PETITBON

Box Score:

Rams	7	0	0	7	**14**	
Bears	13	10	0	7	**30**	

Scoring:

LA Bass 17-yard run (Villaneuva PAT)

CHI Wade 1-yard run (PAT failed)

CHI Ditka 20-yard pass from Wade (Leclerc PAT)

CHI Leclerc 41-yard field goal

CHI Taylor 11-yard blocked punt return (Leclerc PAT)

CHI Petitbon 101-yard interception return (Leclerc PAT)

LA Pardee 32-yard fumble return (Villaneuva PAT)

Still, to Petitbon and other Bears of the time, he made a more meaningful interception, even if it was not attached to such a flashy return. At the end of the 1963 world championship game against the Giants, New York was threatening. A field goal would not rescue the Giants, but a touchdown would.

As the game wound down to 14 seconds on the clock and the Bears' dominant defense tried to protect a four-point lead, New York quarterback Y.A. Tittle faded back and threw into the end zone, hoping for the game-changing touchdown. Instead, he completed his pass to a gloveless Petitbon, who didn't want to jeopardize the genuine feel of hands on the ball, even in extreme cold. The interception clinched the Bears' title.

That was a very cold day with the temperature around 5 degrees, and Petitbon remembers the heaters the players used by the bench not being quite hot enough to warm them up without standing very close. Linebacker Joe Fortunato was so close to the heater, when Petitbon looked down once he exclaimed, "'Joe, your blanking foot's on fire!' That's how cold it was. He could have burned his foot up."

After his stint with the Bears from 1959 to 1968, Petitbon played for the Rams and the Redskins, each time brought in as voice of experience by George Allen, the ex-Bears' defensive coordinator turned head coach.

Petitbon was a long-time Washington assistant coach and served one year as head coach of the Redskins. Throughout his entire tenure in the NFL, as a player in three cities, as an assistant coach and a head coach, and now beyond in his retirement, Petitbon's signature 101-yard interception return has lasted in the Bears record book.

November 18, 1962

34 BEARS MUST-WIN OVER COWBOYS

Bill Wade Throws for 466 Yards

In some ways Bill Wade is probably the most overlooked successful Bears quarterback in history. Sid Luckman was the steady man at the helm throughout the 1940s and Jim McMahon was the flamboyant leader of the 1985 Super Bowl bunch.

But over the four decades in between, Wade was the only Bears quarterback to lead Chicago to a National Football League title. Wade was never the icon Luckman was in Chicago and was never the presence McMahon was in Chicago. But he got the job done for several years and he was a key figure in some of the team's most memorable games of the era.

Not only did Wade score the only two touchdowns for the Bears in their 14–10 win over the New York Giants in the 1963 title game, but he also had some spectacular throwing moments in games of less significance.

The Bears' 34–33 victory over the Dallas Cowboys was a special one during the team's 9–5 season of 1962, the year of success that set the Bears up for their 1963 championship run. It was a dramatic game and in a contest that featured many touchdowns Wade kept hauling the Bears down the field to the end zone.

In the end, Wade's arm shared the glory with Roger Leclerc's toe, but Leclerc's piece of anatomy wouldn't have been in the picture if not for Wade's throwing. When the Bears traveled to Texas for their 10th game of the season, their record was 5–4. This was a team on the cusp of jelling. But a loss would have been a setback of more than one game in the standings. It would have been a psychological blow. A team that felt it was a winner would retreat to .500 and likely be questioning itself.

The Cowboys were still a new franchise, only a few years removed from their 1960 expansion-year start-up and still a long way from being viewed as America's Team. The Cowboys' home field was still the venerable Cotton Bowl, the site of so many stirring New Year's college football matchups. Not only were the Cowboys not quite waking up the echoes, however, there were echoes in the big, old stadium that day when only

Quarterback Bill Wade threw for 466 yards to lead the Bears over the Cowboys in 1962.

> **I** thought Johnny Morris was a great football player. Without any question I felt there were times when he could get clear against anybody in the business.
>
> —BILL WADE

12,692 fans showed up. The other approximately 50,000 empty seats witnessed a great game.

It was a day of big plays and a day for big names in football history.

The Cowboys' usual starting quarterback, Eddie LeBaron, was out with an injury. He was replaced by Don Meredith. Meredith, the former Southern Methodist University All-American, gained even more fame later as an announcer on *Monday Night Football*.

In the seesaw game, when the Cowboys first scored in the second period, kicker Sam Baker's streak of hitting 33 consecutive extra points was ended by rushing Bears linebacker Joe Fortunato. Fortunato, a five-time All-Pro, blocked the kick and the single point would cost Dallas later.

The action started slowly, with a scoreless first quarter, but Wade showed he was going to be a hot pitcher soon enough. A 48-yard strike to Johnny Morris set up Chicago's first touchdown on a 16-yard catch by tight end Mike Ditka.

Wade and Iron Mike were clicking that day, accounting for seven completions. The second-quarter score might have been the most important, but in the closing minutes Wade also hit Ditka for a 36-yard gain that positioned the Bears on the Dallas 3-yard line for the winning field goal.

"A lot of people never threw to the tight end," Wade said of that period of NFL play.

When a team had a guy on their side who was reinventing the position week to week, there was definitely proof accumulating that it was a good play to call. Halfback Ronnie Bull, who had achieved college fame at nearby Baylor, also caught six of Wade's 28 completions that day. Ditka, Bull, and Morris combined for 23 catches.

The busiest Bears receiver was Morris, who caught 10 passes and gained 201 yards. That total, 46 years later, remains the second-best single-game mark for a Bears receiver. The running game was almost forgotten that day, a rarity in Bears annals, with the leading ground

THE BILL WADE BEARS

Perhaps because their championship year was sandwiched between the championship success of the Green Bay Packers, the Bears' 1963 title team often seems overlooked. When thoughts drift back to great Bears teams, they first alight on the 1985 Super Bowl bunch, then shift to the 1940s when the Monsters of the Midway first roamed.

The 1963 championship was the only Bears title won between 1946, near the end of the Luckman

era, and the Super Bowl Shuffle Bears of the mid-1980s.

Hall of Fame players like Bill George, Stan Jones, and Mike Ditka and stars like Joe Fortunato, Rick Casares, Johnny Morris, and Larry Morris helped create that glory. The last George Halas-coached championship team was an outstanding team, but it suffered in comparison with Vince Lombardi's Packers of the time.

GAME DETAILS

Bears 34 • Cowboys 33

Location: Cotton Bowl, Dallas

Attendance: 12,692

Box Score:

> **I** thought it was a pretty good play to call.
>
> —BILL WADE
>
> ON THROWING TO TIGHT END MIKE DITKA

Bears	0	10	7	17	**34**
Cowboys	0	13	13	7	**33**

Scoring:

DAL Bullocks 22-yard pass from Meredith (PAT blocked)
CHI Ditka 16-yard pass from Wade (Leclerc PAT)
DAL Folkins 15-yard pass from Meredith (Baker PAT)
CHI Leclerc 21-yard field goal
DAL Baker 36-yard field goal
CHI Marconi 1-yard run (Leclerc PAT)

DAL Baker 37-yard field goal
DAL Howton 26-yard pass from Meredith (Baker PAT)
CHI Wade 1-yard run (Leclerc PAT)
DAL Bullocks 73-yard run (Baker PAT)
CHI Morris 45-yard pass from Wade (Leclerc PAT)
CHI Leclerc 12-yard field goal

gainer being Bull with 43 yards. There have not been many occasions in Bears history when the passing game outgained the running game 10 to 1.

Meredith, who many contend retired his own arm too young in order to exercise his vocal cords on television, matched Wade drive for drive during the final three quarters, sometimes settling for field goals, sometimes throwing his own way into the end zone.

Wade's total of 466 yards remains the second highest total in a single game by a Bears quarterback, two yards behind Johnny Lujack's 468-yard game of 1949. Wade also ran for a one-yard touchdown, culminating a 61-yard touchdown drive, and threw one interception and two touchdown passes that day.

As the end of the game approached, the Cowboys led 33–31 (and had led 33–24). Wade and the Bears needed to use the clock shrewdly to complete their rally. On the final drive, Ditka's big grab brought the Bears inside the Cowboy 5-yard line. Leclerc kicked a 12-yard field goal for the winning points with nine seconds left.

Ordinarily with the way the game played out, the boot would have tied the game. But Fortunato's blocked extra point earlier gave the Bears and Leclerc the chance to win it. The kick ensured that Wade's greatest passing game was also a sweet day.

December 11, 1949

The Next Luckman Is the First Lujack

Johnny Lujack Throws for 468 Yards

When Bears fans think of the good old days of the best Bears teams, they ruminate over the 1940s and the inspired quarterback leadership of Sid Luckman. They hardly ever dwell on Luckman's successor, Johnny Lujack, even though Lujack turned in some of the greatest quarterback performances in team history.

Lujack is forgotten because he played and starred so briefly. It is not impossible that Lujack would have been remembered as one of the greatest football players of all time if he hadn't quit and/or been exiled from the game at age 27 and gone into private business.

Born in western Pennsylvania, Lujack was the first of the famous quarterbacks to emerge from that region of the country, the forerunner of Johnny Unitas, Joe Namath, and Joe Montana. Lujack attended Notre Dame and won the 1947 Heisman Trophy. He was the Bears' top draft pick and arrived in Chicago at a confusing time for Chicago quarterbacks.

Luckman was approaching retirement. Coach and owner George Halas was trying to find the right replacement. He drafted Lujack as well as George Blanda and Bobby Layne, both of whom eventually starred elsewhere. Lujack beat them out for the starting job and looked like the Bears' quarterback of the future as Luckman retired following the 1950 season. By then Luckman was Lujack's backup.

That reversed their roles of 1948, when Luckman was still the leader and Lujack appeared in nine games. By 1949, however, Lujack was starting and turned in the best season of any NFL quarterback. He was selected as an All-Pro after leading the league in touchdown passes (23), completions, attempts, and yards. Sid who?

That was the season of Lujack's greatest game. The Bears carried an 8–3 record into the final game of the regular season against their favorite opponent, the Chicago Cardinals, a team the Bears liked to beat as much as the Green Bay Packers.

More than 50,000 fans turned out for the season finale, and Lujack was at the helm for one of the Cardinals' worst all-time beatings. Throwing 40 times and completing 24, Lujack's passes gained 468 yards, a new NFL single-game record and 60 years later, still a Bears record. Lujack also threw six touchdown passes and capped his throwing day by kicking seven extra points to boot (no pun intended) as the Bears blasted the Cardinals 52–21 at Wrigley Field.

Lujack and the Bears came out throwing at a vulnerable Cardinals secondary, and on the second play from scrimmage the bombardier completed his first touchdown pass to George McAfee as the back zipped downfield behind the coverage to complete the 52-yard score.

A case can be made that the 6'0", 177-pound McAfee was the greatest all-around player in Bears history, and it would have been fun to see how he would have performed in a more recent era of the sport. He joined the team in 1940 and played with Chicago through 1950, except for World War II service. At various times McAfee ran the ball (4.9 yards per carry), caught the ball (16 yards per catch), ran back punts, and played in the defensive secondary (intercepting 25 passes). An All-American at Duke, McAfee returned a kickoff 97 yards for a touchdown in his first pro game. He also averaged 12.8 yards per return on punts. He did whatever the Bears asked and did it well enough to be selected for the Hall of Fame in 1966.

"The highest compliment you can pay a ball carrier is just to compare him to McAfee," Halas said.

Lujack's second touchdown pass, a 17-yarder, came only two minutes later

Johnny Lujack unleashed an aerial assault on the Chicago Cardinals in 1949 and set a team record in the process. *(Photo courtesy of WireImages)*

when Ken Kavanaugh made a jumping catch in the end zone. Other touchdown passes went to J.R. Boone and John Hoffman.

It seemed as if the fortunate Halas had found his quarterback of the future to succeed the aging Luckman. Lujack made a second All-Pro team, too, but he and Halas did not share the warm relationship of Halas and Luckman. Their personalities did

Bobby Layne, Johnny Lujack, and Sid Luckman remain three of the most talented quarterbacks in Bears history.

MY KINGDOM FOR A QUARTERBACK

Although Johnny Lujack was a Heisman Trophy winner for Notre Dame and the Bears' top draft pick in 1946, coach George Halas did not really know what he was getting.

As the career of future Hall of Fame player Sid Luckman wound down, Halas was in the market for a critical personnel hire. He played the draft like a whiz, acquiring Lujack, Bobby Layne, and George Blanda in a short period of time.

From afar, Halas seemed like a genius. However, his embarrassment of riches dwindled when he had a falling out over money with Lujack, when he dealt Layne to the Lions, and when he mostly relegated Blanda to the bench. Halas had a trio of all-time great quarterbacks under contract and none of them reached their potential with the Bears.

GAME DETAILS

Bears 52 • Cardinals 21

He [Lujack] gave them four damned good years and he did everything.

—CHICAGO SPORTSWRITER BILL GLEASON

Location: Wrigley Field, Chicago

Attendance: 50,101

Box Score:

Cardinals	7	0	7	7	**21**
Bears	14	17	7	14	**52**

Scoring:

CHI B McAfee 52-yard pass from Lujack (Lujack PAT)

CHI B Kavanaugh 17-yard pass from Lujack (Lujack PAT)

CHI C Trippi 3-yard pass from Christman (Harder PAT)

CHI B Kavanaugh 37-yard pass from Lujack (Lujack PAT)

CHI B Boone 18-yard pass from Lujack (Lujack PAT)

CHI B Blanda 25-yard field goal

CHI B Gulyanics 2-yard run (Lujack PAT)

CHI C Kutner 49-yard pass from Christman (Harder PAT)

CHI B Hoffman 6-yard pass from Lujack (Lujack PAT)

CHI B Hoffman 65-yard pass from Lujack (Lujack PAT)

CHI C Trippi 19-yard pass from Christman (Harder PAT)

not mesh. Lujack resented that he was not better paid, and actually used the word "cheated" to describe how Halas took advantage of him during negotiations. Halas, with the Depression and his near forfeiture of the Bears because of finances lodged firmly in his memory, was never known as Mr. Generosity for the salaries he paid.

Lujack stuck with the Bears for only four seasons. When he quit it was because of his personality conflict with Halas and their feud over money. The Bears announced that Lujack was leaving the game because of injury. Lujack did have a separated shoulder and had played with two injured shoulders for a time, but that was not the real reason he was no longer affiliated with the Bears. Lujack just didn't want to play for Halas anymore and by spreading the word that he was damaged goods, Halas prevented him from going anywhere else.

In an era with no free agency, Lujack couldn't easily hook up with another team. The reserve clause bound him to the Bears whether he played or not. The Los Angeles Rams and Chicago Cardinals each inquired about a trade for Lujack. On the first occasion Halas reportedly asked for four starters in return, ending that discussion. In the second case he asked the Cardinals for three starters. Both teams refused the demands, and Lujack, who went on to spend two years as an assistant coach at Notre Dame, never got any closer to playing again.

"You see," Lujack said, "that was his [Halas's] way of keeping me out of the league."

Despite every indication that he had plenty of football left in him, Lujack never threw another pro pass. While he developed his business interests through auto dealerships and other investments, Lujack never knew what he ultimately might have accomplished in pro football. And after disposing of Layne and Blanda in different manners, Halas spent the rest of his life trying to find a Bears quarterback who was Lujack's equal.

December 18, 1977

32 BOB THOMAS'S BOOT DOES THE TRICK

Bears Reach Playoffs after 14-Year Absence

Bears fans were used to great teams. Bears fans were used to championship teams. Being a fan of one of the National Football League's oldest, most storied franchises was ingrained from birth and the guarantee that all-knowing leader George Halas would provide winners was a birthright.

From the time the team was founded in the 1920s, throughout the 1930s, and beyond World War II, Bears fans never had to wait long for championship success. Regardless of long-term accomplishments there usually comes a downtime in a team's history when the glories fade and the glow of championship triumph, once almost taken for granted, dims.

After the regrouped Bears won the NFL title in 1946, with its players back from fighting in World War II, Chicago did not win another title until 1963. And then, despite the addition of Hall of Fame selections Gale Sayers and Dick Butkus in 1965, the

rest of the 1960s were also hard times. Fans today are used to a playoff system that rewards participation to many teams. But for many years there were no playoffs, only a championship game. A team had to win its conference to advance to the title game.

During the Bears' drought of the 1960s, when the NFL and AFL merged and created the Super Bowl, the Bears were on the outside looking in. They did not qualify for a conference or league championship contest and they did not make it into the new playoffs.

Halas retired from coaching following the 1967 season, and it wasn't until 1977 with Jack Pardee in charge for a third season that the Bears contended again. The Bears came into their final game of the 1977 regular season with an 8–5 record. They needed a victory over the New York Giants to squeeze into the playoffs.

Not so many weeks earlier such a scenario would have seemed preposterous.

> **H**e thinks he has to carry the Bears on his shoulders.
>
> —JACK PARDEE ON WALTER PAYTON

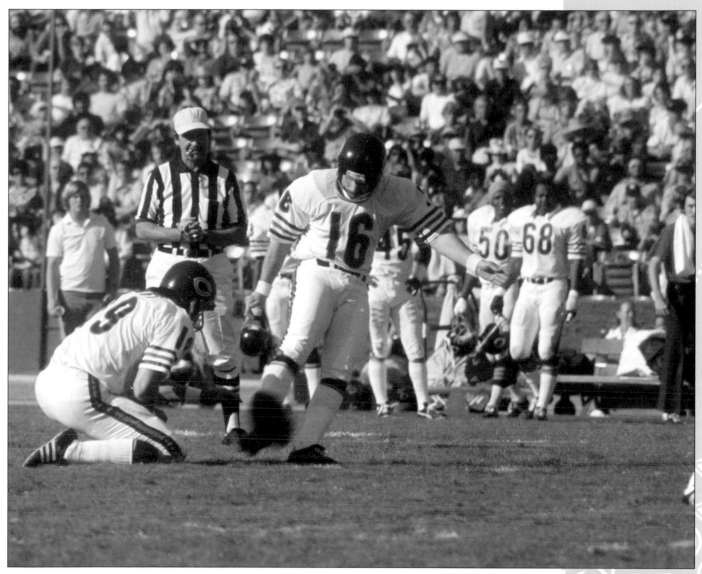

Kicker Bob Thomas helped end a long playoff drought for the Bears in 1977. *(Photo courtesy of WireImages)*

The Bears started 3–5 and appeared doomed to another season of mediocrity. Halfback Walter Payton was enjoying his greatest season and lifted the team on his back. He rushed for 1,852 yards that season, caught 27 passes, and scored 16 touchdowns. Without Payton the Bears had virtually no offense. If teams could stop Payton, they could beat the Bears. But Payton was so good other teams couldn't stop him.

That was the season when Payton set his NFL record of 275 yards rushing in a game—and still the Bears struggled to beat Minnesota 10–7. Many times Payton, taking handoff after handoff from quarterback Bob Avellini, carried Chicago into field-goal territory and then turned over the offense to kicker Bob Thomas. Thomas scored only 69 points with his toe that season, hitting just 14 of 27 field-goal tries. Accuracy was iffier 30 years ago compared to now when place-kickers make more than 80 percent of their field goals and nearly 100 percent of their extra points.

When the postseason was a single one-and-done game, teams could go a long time without participating. But when the playoffs were expanded, failures were only magnified. As the Bears readied for the last game of the 1977 season in New York to face the Giants, they had been absent from postseason play for 14 years. Entire careers came and went during that time. For sure, entire head coaching careers came and went for the Bears. Jim Dooley and Abe Gibron were in, then out, between Halas and Pardee.

It was a cold-weather day in New York and neither team moved the ball much or crossed the goal line often. It was 9–9, a field-goal bonanza, as the clock ticked down to :00 in the fourth quarter. Then the game moved on to overtime.

Weather conditions were ugly, with sleet and wind disrupting the kicking game. The Bears had botched a snap for one intended attempt and Thomas missed a try in OT that would have ended the game. The weather was more hostile than the Giants.

The overtime period was drawing to a close with nine seconds remaining when the Bears got within range to give Thomas another chance to win it in the nasty conditions. With the road to the playoffs either wide open or blocked depending on the kick, Thomas put his foot to the ball and made the 28-yard boot heard around the world. Or at least around the Midwest, where Bears fans went delirious.

KICKERS TO REMEMBER

It is possible that the greatest Chicago Bears kicker of all time will be Robbie Gould. A few more clutch kicks to win games and he will be rated with the best of them. All he seems to need is a little bit more longevity.

Although kickers like Roger Leclerc, Mac Percival, and Bob Thomas had their moments, their best years did not measure up to the best performances of Kevin Butler (who has to rate number one at the moment) or Gould.

Overall accuracy is the measuring stick. A modern place-kicker can go entire seasons without missing an extra point. And a modern place-kicker who misses more than five field-goal attempts in a season is ripe to be replaced. The straight-ahead place-kicker is like a dinosaur, a relic of the past, and the soccer-style kicker took over because the method proved more efficient.

The evolution of the place-kicker parallels the evolution of the high jumper. Until Dick Fosbury came along with his unique "Fosbury Flop" style, everyone ran straight at the bar. Fosbury's style was first adopted by the few, then the many. Now the old style is antiquated. The simple reason is that athletes jump higher using Fosbury's form.

In the case of place-kickers, they are all specialists now, too, rather than regulars who didn't have as much time to practice.

GAME DETAILS

Bears 12 • Giants 9

Location: Giants Stadium, East Rutherford, New Jersey

Attendance: 50,152

Box Score:

Bears	3	0	0	6	3	**12**
Giants	3	0	0	6	0	**9**

Scoring:

CHI Thomas 32-yard field goal

NY Danelo 38-yard field goal

NY Danelo 19-yard field goal

CHI Earl 4-yard run (PAT blocked)

NY Danelo 27-yard field goal

CHI Thomas 28-yard field goal

> **O**ld place-kickers never die. They just go on missing the point.
>
> **—HALL OF FAME KICKER LOU GROZA**

Chicago's 12–9 win was their sixth straight and gave the team a 9–5 record, good enough to advance the Bears into the playoffs against the Dallas Cowboys eight days later. Although the Bears were waxed 37–7 in that game, that dismal result was still in the future as fans celebrated the win over the Giants.

Trying to fly out of Newark, New Jersey, after the game, the Bears were delayed by icy conditions. While they sat, revelers massed at O'Hare International Airport in Chicago, building up to 3,000 strong. The frustrations of years of disappointment were wiped out. Fans partied, yelled, drank, and sang in support of their football team—and that was before the team arrived.

Predictably, the fans yelled, "We're No. 1." They also sang the "Bear Down, Chicago Bears" theme song. They probably sang a few other songs with more risqué lyrics that were not reported in the daily newspapers.

When the Bears landed, the crowd grew more enthusiastic and a detachment of police barely kept the fans under control. At one point, apparently operating under the theory that the star would soothe the crowd, a policeman asked Payton if he would speak. It was an idea, but that did not happen. As the fans overloaded the terminal, the Bears sought escape routes.

Payton weaved his way through some fans to get out of the building and he gave them a raised fist salute. The action spoke as loud as words. Payton, who was trying to find his wife, Connie, had to use more moves to hit the open field in the terminal than he did in the game and afterward joked of his airport play, "That was probably one of my better runs this year."

Thomas, who was an Academic All-American at Notre Dame, earned a law degree in 1981, ran for circuit court judge and won in 1988, and was sworn in as a justice on the Illinois Supreme Court in 2000 and as Chief Justice in 2006, finished his 12-year NFL career with 756 points.

31

JUST DOING HIS JOB–ALL SEASON

Marty Booker's 100th Reception

He was a first-down pro's pro, the guy quarterback Jim Miller looked for when the rushers were breathing down his neck. Miller knew Marty Booker would get free and bail him out if he could only get him the ball.

Booker was probably the Bears' least flashy great receiver of all time. He lacked the flamboyance of a Chad Johnson or Terrell Owens, yet produced similar results. For an organization that has spent half its existence trying to elevate the quality of its passing game, Booker was a find.

Standing 5'11" and weighing a sturdy 218 pounds, Booker came out of small-school Northeast Louisiana, drafted by the Bears in the third round in 1999. Booker's college numbers were very good—178 receptions averaging 15.6 yards per grab—but no one really knew how good he might be in the NFL because of the relatively low-key nature of his college schedule.

The arc of Booker's career was rising, however, after catching 75 passes as a senior, and the Bears thought he was worth the draft pick. As a rookie, Booker eased into the lineup with spot duty, appearing in nine games and making 19 catches. He wasn't making anyone forget Don Hutson, but Booker was starting to show he belonged.

By 2000, Booker was a more frequent target, catching 47 balls in 15 games. The apprenticeship was over. It was time to see if the Booker investment would pay off. He did and it did. During the Bears' surprise 13–3 2001 campaign, coming when nobody thought Chicago was a playoff-caliber team, Booker recorded the greatest single season ever by a Bears receiver.

The Bears' mainstay has always been the running game, the smash-mouth football style that the game grew up with. The Bears have often seemed a couple of years behind in the development of the passing game,

> **M**arty is a special receiver.
>
> —DICK JAURON

Marty Booker's 100 receptions during the 2001 season set an all-time Bears record.

reacting for decades as if it was a newfangled approach that would run its course.

The opposite has occurred with more emphasis on the passing game than ever, with more passers completing a higher percentage of their throws than ever, and with more receivers recording triple-digit pass-catching seasons.

Going into the 2001 season, the Bears record for single-season catches was 93 set by Johnny Morris in the 1964 season. Booker was growing into the role of a number one receiver, but he was hurried along under emergency conditions when deep threat Marcus Robinson went down for the season with a knee injury in the fifth game.

Rather than wilt, the Bears, under low-key coach Dick Jauron, fooled experts on a march to the playoffs, and Booker became the go-to receiver, the man with hands that seemed dipped in glue. He caught everything that came his way, including those he had to stretch out and dive for.

In a 27–24 Bears victory over Tampa Bay in November, Booker caught three touchdown passes. Booker's scores came on gains of 66, 44, and 28 yards. Overall, Booker caught seven passes during the game for 165 yards. Booker pointed out one attribute that he felt made him a dangerous receiver and something he'd heard criticism of in the past—an analysis that he wasn't fast enough. That was his biggest day of the season.

"I feel I have deceptive speed," Booker said.

Whether it was speed, shake–and–bake moves, meticulous route running, or a combination of all three, Booker got open, and that's what mattered most. All of Booker's maneuvers worked even better when foes tried to cover him one-on-one. Whether his athleticism was more subtle or not, Booker got the job done.

"He's caught the ball inside," Jauron said. "He's caught the ball when he got hit hard in the end zone."

The more Booker came through, the more the Bears relied on him. They were not getting it done with flash and dash, anyway, but with work ethic. Guys scrapped for every inch of territory during an unlikely series of wins.

This was the autumn of the 9/11 attacks on the World Trade Center and the Pentagon, and football took a sad holiday break at the start of the season. The game pushed the Bears' final regular-season game into early January.

The Bears crushed Jacksonville 33–13 on the road to the playoffs, with Booker catching six passes. The catches brought Booker's season total to exactly 100, a new team record and a notable milestone. Catching 100 passes in a season is a symbolic figure of enduring value that said

WHATEVER HAPPENED TO THE FULLBACK?

One reason more wide receivers now catch more passes than they used to is because the fullback is a forgotten man. More quick, short passes are completed to wide receivers now instead of using the fullback as a safety valve for quick, short passes.

And fullbacks almost never get to run the ball anymore. In most offenses in the 1950s, the fullback took a backseat to the halfback when it came to running, though not always. Jim Brown, the Cleveland Browns' battering ram and considered the greatest runner in NFL history by many, was a fullback. So was his chief running rival of the late 1950s and early 1960s, Green Bay's Jim Taylor.

Fullbacks were the tanks of the offense. In general, halfbacks were lighter, often weighing less than 200 pounds, shiftier, and speedier. If the fullback was not quite in the same league as Brown, he was expected to block as well as he ran.

Rick Casares was more in the mold of Brown and Taylor than a primarily blocking fullback. He could—and did—gain 1,000 yards in a season. In recent years all the carries have shifted to the halfback, who is now simply called a running back. The fullback has become just another lineman. Casares laments the change and said the modern-day fullback slot would not be the position for him.

Game Details

Bears 33 • Jaguars 13

Location: Soldier Field, Chicago

Attendance: 66,944

Box Score:

Jaguars	0	0	6	7	**13**
Bears	3	10	10	10	**33**

Scoring:

CHI Edinger 47-yard field goal

CHI Johnson 2-yard run (Edinger PAT)

CHI Edinger 23-yard field goal

CHI Terrell 9-yard pass from Miller (Edinger PAT)

JAX McCardell 15-yard pass from Brunell (PAT failed)

CHI Edinger 25-yard field goal

CHI Edinger 22-yard field goal

CHI Thomas 2-yard run (Edinger PAT)

JAX Smith 3-yard pass from Brunell (Holmes PAT)

> **A** lot of people have underestimated my speed.
>
> —MARTY BOOKER

something about a receiver the way 1,000 yards gained on the ground said something about a running back. The performance was also enhanced because opposing teams knew Booker was the main threat and covered him accordingly, often with two men.

In the Jacksonville game, Booker's most prominent in-the-flow catch was probably a 17-yard gain on a fourth-and-eight play. But the one he will remember best was his final grab of the day, made on a short sideline out-of-bounds play, an insignificant two-yard gain that was a gift from Miller.

Miller scrapped the called play with an audible. He knew that Booker was sitting on 99 catches and he wanted his partner to crack the 100-catch barrier. He set up the situation so Booker could make one of his easier catches of the season.

"The guy has worked extremely hard and nobody deserves it more than him," Miller said.

The team guy that he always was, Booker said the most important thing about the day was defeating the Jaguars. But he admitted he was happy that he was now a member of the exclusive 100-catch club.

"That kind of tops things," Booker said. "To get that 100 catches is pretty special."

Booker also knew he had been a mighty contributor to an NFC Central Division champion.

1985

30 Striking Fear Into the Hearts of Men

The 46 Defense

The name of the defense caught on. Fans might not know how it spread itself out on the field, but they had heard of the "46 defense" supervised by Bears defensive coordinator Buddy Ryan and named after No. 46 himself, safety Doug Plank.

Plank was so aggressive other teams cowered if he was in the neighborhood. But he took such a battering that he retired in 1982, well before the Super Bowl season. His fame lived on with the glory of the defense.

The 1985 Bears, including Mike Singletary, Richard Dent, Dan Hampton, Wilber Marshall, Otis Wilson, Steve McMichael, Dave Duerson, Leslie Frazier, and a few more of their friends, combined to make the Bears defense perhaps the greatest of all time.

The defenders intimidated, sacked the quarterback, squashed running backs, just about decapitated receivers, and above all

kept opponents out of the end zone. Any game played against the Bears of the mid-1980s very likely meant that those who came near the ball would need a soothing hot bath the next day if they could walk at all.

The Bears had the number one–rated defense in the league in 1984 and were better and certainly more respected the next season.

The Bears were equal-opportunity tacklers in 1985, with Gary Fencik's 118 leading the team, Singletary next with 113, and Marshall third with 78. Dent had 17 sacks, Wilson 10½, and McMichael 8. The Bears did not so much chase down and grind quarterbacks into the ground as they did hit them so hard they separated their rib cages. As a team the Bears scored 456 points, enough to post a 15–1 regular-season record, but as a defense the Bears

> **I** don't think I'm outspoken. Someone asks me a question and I answer it truthfully. Is that outspoken?
>
> —BUDDY RYAN

The Bears' legendary 46 defense overwhelmed opposing offenses in 1985, including the New England Patriots in Super Bowl XX.

allowed just 198 points. In nine games Chicago allowed one or fewer touchdowns, with two shutouts.

And the Bears only got better in the playoffs. The scores read Chicago 21, New York Giants 0; Chicago 24, Los Angeles Rams 0; and Chicago 46, New England Patriots 10. They crushed minds and bodies.

Plank attended Ohio State and spent eight seasons with the Bears, where he intercepted 15 passes. Buddy Ryan, a man with a nimble mind for innovation and an insatiable need for loyalty, bred fierceness and cohesion into his defenses. He nurtured a Bears-against-the-world mentality—even within the confines of the team. He and head coach Mike Ditka often clashed, and at halftime against Miami in 1985, the one game the Bears lost, players had to separate the two men from blows before the second half could commence.

It was Plank who uttered the candid and ultimate summation of what the 46 defense was all about.

"Its main purpose is to get to the quarterback and then let's see how good the second-string quarterback is," Plank said in his prime.

Plank said the 46 was about breaking free of a conservative defensive scheme and playing with more abandon. The Bears could do it, he said, because they had the right personnel. Ryan had been on the job as coordinator seven full years before the Bears reached the Super Bowl and made the 46 a household name. The scheme left a lot of room for blitzing. Sometimes there were eight men on the line. Sometimes it was a 5-1-5 set. And it all grew out of a standard 4-3 alignment.

San Francisco 49ers coach Bill Walsh, regarded as an offensive genius and credited with inventing the West Coast offense, admired Ryan's ingenuity on the other side of the ball. Walsh described the 46 as an "extreme defense" set up to avoid double-team blocking and to increase pressure on the quarterback. The defense was also supreme against the run. If there was vulnerability, it was in the secondary where the cornerbacks and Fencik at safety had to provide considerable one-on-one coverage. It was taking a risk that the quarterback couldn't complete the bomb for a touchdown. But the main part of the theory was that the quarterback would not have time to look downfield under pressure from the other eight guys.

Walsh said the Bears' success had spawned copycats around the NFL, but no one could pull the scheme off

It's in the Growl

In 1939 after the University of Chicago dropped its football program, the Bears scooped up the squad's nickname, the Monsters of the Midway. It was fate because it was a perfect nickname for a Chicago team with a certain meanness and fierceness.

Although the Bears defense under Buddy Ryan was popularized by its simple number, "46," other professional units' nicknames enhanced the image of their abilities.

The Los Angeles Rams had the "Fearsome Foursome" with its defensive front four. The Minnesota Vikings were famously known as "The Purple People Eaters" for a while. There has also been a "Doomsday Defense" and a "No-Name Defense." The Washington Redskins' offensive line was called "The Hogs."

The Bears could have been called "Ryan's Express."

Nicknames for entire groups of players began because those units were typically difference makers who remained anonymous. With all of the television Xs and Os and visual breakdowns it is easier than ever to be recognized as an outstanding guard or tackle. But the cachet of a flashy nickname is still worthy of bonus points in a society that always appreciates a brand name.

The best. No doubt about it.
—MIKE SINGLETARY ON BUDDY RYAN

Three of the greatest
linebackers in
Bears history: Mike
Singletary, Otis Wilson,
and Wilber Marshall.

as well. The players and the innovative mind behind the complexities made the Bears' 46 unique.

"Really, it's nuances that make it so effective," Walsh said.

Ryan did not have the look of a polished NFL coach. He was chunky and his vocabulary was more old-school than graduate school. He roared like a lion and many thought several doses of sensitivity classwork would have done him good. But Ryan knew his stuff, he was a great motivator, and even if he talked trash about his players sometimes he was a leader who made them want to play for him.

The Bears were never better than during the first two rounds of the playoffs on the road to the Super Bowl. Neither the Giants nor the Rams could move the ball. It was as if the line was always stacked heavily against them. The Bears simply devoured both top-notch teams, shutting them out.

Although the Bears did surrender some points to the Patriots, it wasn't as if the game was ever in jeopardy. New England collected only 113 yards in the game.

The night before the Super Bowl, "General" Ryan addressed his troops. Everyone believed that it was probably his last Bears game, that Ryan was on his way to becoming head coach of the Philadelphia Eagles. Ryan never said. But he did tell the players that regardless of what the team did in the game, "you're my heroes."

The Bears performed heroically on defense the next day and soon after Ryan left to take over the Eagles job. Brian Cabral, one of the backup linebackers, delivered a fitting laudatory valedictory with Ryan heading out the door.

"He raised all these guys," Cabral said. "He brought us to where we are. There were a lot of good athletes on this team, but Ryan made them great athletes."

And he definitely taught them to count to 46.

December 11, 1983

29 MISDIRECTION OFFENSE'S BEST FRIEND

Matt Suhey Throws a 74-Yard Touchdown Pass

It was no wonder it worked.

Matt Suhey didn't do flashy. Suhey was Mr. Reliable. He was the backfield complement to Walter Payton. He was the guy who spent most of his time blocking for Walter Payton. He was solid, dependable, and had some great moments rushing, piling up yards on the ground when called upon, but he was always the "other" back for the Bears.

Suhey grew up in Pennsylvania and it was virtually preordained that he would matriculate at Penn State, where he matured into a 5'11", 217-pound star. After being taken by the Bears in the second round of the 1980 NFL Draft, Suhey gradually worked himself into the lineup. He appeared in all 16 games as a rookie and became the starting fullback the next season.

He and Payton formed a special partnership. They did a lot of joking around. Few people besides Suhey knew just how powerful Payton's predilection for committing practical jokes ran. He was sometimes conspiring with Payton and sometimes the butt of his jokes. They complemented each other well on the field, respected one another, and became great friends off the field, staying close into retirement and right up until Payton's untimely death from liver disease in 1999.

Payton was a Hall of Fame player, but Suhey was an important piece of the Bears' puzzle. Payton left pro football as the leading rusher of all time. Suhey left football with the reputation of a hard-working, hard-nosed guy who got the most out of his talent.

Suhey was the king of fundamentals, a team guy with skill who could sublimate his ego when necessary and make the breakout play when Payton wasn't making one. And he earned a Super Bowl ring on one of the most flamboyant and dominating teams of all time.

After being more of a watcher than a participant during his rookie year, Suhey rushed for 521 yards in 1981. In 1983 he rushed for 681 yards and caught 49 passes. And during the 1985 regular season he rushed for 471 yards. These were all respectable totals for a guy who was never the first option for a handoff.

Matt Suhey proved he was more than just a blocking fullback in a game against the Vikings in 1983.

At one point during his career, Suhey annunciated his feelings about his sport, saying, "There are two rules in football. Rule No. 1 is it's a team game. Rule No. 2 is you don't change rule No. 1."

It was a philosophy he lived out during his time with the Bears. Football did not allow much room for making waves.

One thing that made Suhey's wild-and-crazy touchdown pass such a hit was that the opposition never saw it coming. No one pegged Suhey as a closet quarterback limbering up in the bullpen. The call by coach Mike Ditka was clever and daring and although it seemed possible, it was not drawn up on a napkin.

MATT SUHEY, BEARS QUARTERBACK?

Fullback Matt Suhey was a fine blocker for Hall of Fame running mate Walter Payton but wasn't known as a passing threat. That is what made his 74-yard touchdown pass to Payton so sweet in a 1983 game against the Minnesota Vikings. In a close game, quarterback Jim McMahon took the snap and pitched the ball to Suhey, who had lined up left and headed right. Suhey faked running an end-around; meanwhile, Payton vacated the backfield, took off downfield, and was open when Suhey stopped and threw deep. Payton gathered the surprise pass in for a touchdown and the Bears won 19–13.

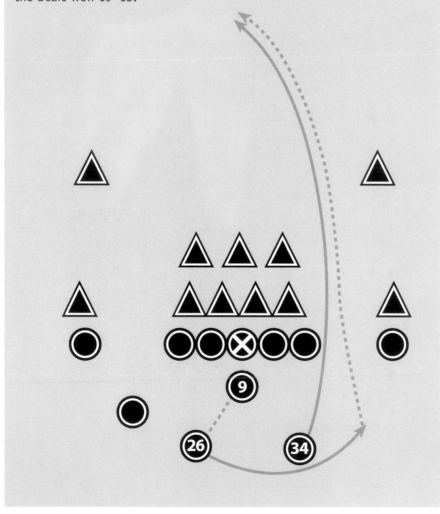

From the moment Ditka took over as Bears coach he preached one goal: championship. He was dedicated to making sure the Bears ended up back on top. The first step on the road to a title, he felt, was beating up on the teams in the NFC Central. No more cowering before the might of the Minnesota Vikings. No more losing to the Green Bay Packers. Ditka said it early and often that the Bears had to control their division to control their destiny.

The day he threw a pass for the ages, Suhey believes, was probably his most important as a Bear. It was a chance to show that Ditka's pep talks were taking hold. The tight game was played in Minneapolis and Ditka thought it was time to pull a slick play out of mothballs. The Bears practiced the play frequently and were just waiting for the right moment to spring it on another team.

Quarterback Jim McMahon took the snap. As he retreated into the pocket, McMahon lateraled the ball to Suhey rolling to the right side. Clearly, Suhey was going to tuck the ball into his gut and make a beeline downfield. Everybody knew that if the Bears employed a halfback option, the ball always went to Payton. Payton had a good track record of completing passes on that play, frequently to Suhey.

GAME DETAILS

Bears 19 • Vikings 13

Location: Metrodome, Minneapolis

Attendance: 62,074

Box Score:

To win the Super Bowl was a sensational feeling, hard to describe. But football has left me with such memories, memories I will treasure for the rest of my life.

—MATT SUHEY

Bears	10	6	0	3	**19**
Vikings	6	0	7	0	**13**

Scoring:

MIN Ricardo 30-yard field goal

MIN Ricardo 29-yard field goal

CHI Payton 74-yard pass from Suhey (Thomas PAT)

CHI Thomas 42-yard field goal

CHI Moorehead 2-yard pass from McMahon (PAT failed)

MIN Brown 1-yard run (Ricardo PAT)

CHI Thomas 22-yard field goal

But this was a variation, a counterintuitive maneuver where Ditka out-thought conventional wisdom. Instead of trying to dash around end, Suhey stopped behind the line of scrimmage. Payton had run a traditional pass route, but when the Vikings saw the pitch go to Suhey the defenders headed back toward the line of scrimmage to seal him off. Payton was wide open about 20 yards downfield. Suhey's pass might not have had the zing coaches are looking for on instructional videos, but it was straight and true. Payton caught the ball and rambled the rest of the way for a 74-yard touchdown pass.

The Bears defeated the Vikings 19–13 on the road. The accomplishment was telling. Suhey said it showed, "maybe we could be somebody." The next week the Bears defeated the Packers, the next season the Bears were in the playoffs, and the year after that they won the Super Bowl.

Talk about momentum flowing from one play.

The Bears' 1983 statistics showed Suhey with one completion in one attempt for a 100 percent completion percentage and a perfect 158.3 quarterback rating. Suhey threw only one more pass in his football career that spanned the 1980s. It was incomplete.

When he retired after the 1989 season, Suhey was reflective about what a tremendous experience he had with the Chicago Bears.

"I've had some fabulous relationships with the players and the coaches," he said. "They've been more than friends to me, they've been my family."

And if he had left well enough alone, Suhey would have been able to retire with a 1.000 completion percentage.

October 16, 1955

Rick Casares Proves He Belongs

Rookie's 81-Yard Run Gets Him the Ball

Rick Casares grew up in Tampa and was a star running back for the University of Florida Gators. He was just what the Bears were looking for in the 1954 draft: a big, strong fullback. He stood 6'2" and weighed 225 pounds, a hefty fullback in an era when fullbacks were also expected to turn on a dime when running the ball and possess the power to plunge ahead through the line of scrimmage for first downs and in goal-line situations.

As it so happened, Casares was drafted twice that year. He was the Bears' second-round selection in the NFL Draft and he was drafted by the U.S. Army. In that company, everyone was a number one draft choice. This wasn't exactly like being chosen by the NFL and the fledgling AFL in the 1960s. There was no choice in where Casares would report. The army had first dibs. Casares reacted with serious disappointment at first, resentful that this unanticipated career switch might derail his football opportunities for good.

While he was diverted from playing football for a while and his pro debut put on hold, by the time Casares appeared in a Bears uniform he was actually bigger and stronger than before, and at 24 a very mature rookie. When he reflected years later, he said the time spent in the army turned out to be a good investment for him physically and mentally.

Despite playing some football while in the service, Casares felt he would not know if his game instincts were still sharp until he suited up as a full-fledged Bears player. For one brief moment in his life, he lacked the confidence to back up his ability.

Coach George Halas was always a good judge of personnel, and he eased Casares into the lineup in spots, not merely handing over the starting job. During the first stretch of the season, Halas mostly called Casares's number in safe, short-yardage situations.

During the fourth game of the season against the Baltimore Colts, Casares was in the backfield with another rookie, Bobby Watkins. The play called by quarterback George Blanda was supposed to send the ball Watkins's way on a toss. However, Watkins had been slightly dinged up on a previous carry. Not wanting to come out of the game but needing to catch his breath,

Running back Rick Casares made the most of his unexpected opportunity, breaking off an 81-yard touchdown run against the Baltimore Colts in 1955.

CASARES'S SCAMPER

Fullback Rick Casares and halfback Bobby Watkins swapped places in the backfield, with Casares lining up on the left and Watkins on the right. When the ball was snapped, quarterback George Blanda pitched it to Casares (instead of Watkins), and the fullback slashed through a hole and burst 81 yards down the left sideline for the touchdown.

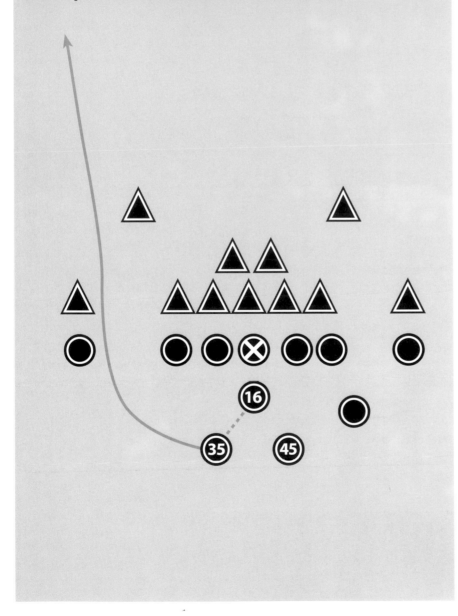

when the Bears broke from the huddle Watkins asked Casares to swap places with him. So they lined up on opposite sides in the backfield.

The backfield maneuver caught Blanda by surprise, but he did not have time to change the play. When the ball was snapped, Blanda followed through on the call, pitched the ball to Casares, and then watched with a certain level of astonishment, like all others at Wrigley Field, as Casares burst free on a wild gallop.

Casares ran left, then cut back as he reached open territory, angled right, dodged Colts linebacker Bill Pellington with the aid of a straight arm, and carried the ball into the end zone 81 yards later. It was an incredible play for the 40,184 fans and in Casares's mind a career maker. Tackle Stan Jones threw one block that got things rolling. But end Bill McColl threw the critical block—coincidentally on defensive back Don Shula, a man who had better football memories to be made in his future—that opened a hole large enough to float a sailboat through.

Casares was ecstatic and has called the play the most memorable of his pro career. The lasting image proved to him and Halas that Casares could play on the big stage.

The touchdown gave the Bears a 10–3 lead on their way to a 38–10 triumph. Casares scored a second

Game Details

Bears 38 • Colts 10

Location: Wrigley Field, Chicago

Attendance: 40,184

Box Score:

What a boy! Pain could not stop him, or slow him.

—GEORGE HALAS ON CASARES

Team					
Colts	3	0	0	7	**10**
Bears	3	14	14	7	**38**

Scoring:

BAL Rechichar 26-yard field goal

CHI Blanda 36-yard field goal

CHI Casares 81-yard run (Blanda PAT)

CHI Schroeder 51-yard pass from Blanda (Blanda PAT)

CHI Watkins 2-yard run (Blanda PAT)

CHI Casares 2-yard run (Blanda PAT)

BAL Ameche 2-yard run (Rechichar PAT)

CHI McColl 37-yard pass from Williams (Blanda PAT)

---

touchdown in the game, an icing-on-the-cake score on a two-yard power run. Casares's performance gave him the starting fullback job and that season he averaged 5.4 yards per carry. The next year Casares led the NFL in rushing with 1,126 yards and 12 rushing touchdowns.

And the Bears decided to add one play to their playbook, expanding the "toss option" to fullbacks as well as halfbacks.

Casares always had a good time playing football. He also enjoyed a reputation that he enjoyed partying. Halas was always on Casares's case to watch his weight and Casares's preferred method of trimming down to meet the boss's standards was to sweat weight off in the sauna. Center Mike Pyle suggested that sometimes

Casares drank so much the night before weigh-ins that he showed up dehydrated on purpose to come in under the limit.

It was Stan Jones, however, who recalled Casares's unique way to gain revenge on Halas for his restrictive policies. Casares brought a little dog to training camp in Indiana and he regularly walked it past Halas's room in the dormitory. By coincidence, the dog would suddenly have to "go" and each day there was a pile of crap outside Halas's door.

Funny how it always seemed to work out that way, Mr. Halas, but gee, who can control the bathroom habits of a dog?

That one play gave a push to my career.

—RICK CASARES

January 16, 1926

27 SHOWING FACE IS HALF THE BATTLE

Red Grange's Tour Goes Hollywood

It is often said that the 66-day, 19-game nationwide tour of Red Grange and the Chicago Bears made professional football. In the 1920s, football was seen as appropriate to play to defend the honor of an alma mater but felt it was somehow shady to be paid for doing so..

Grange helped change that attitude. The grand swing throughout the United States brought the sport to the masses who had never seen a live game and imprinted the quality of play in their minds. The tour was the beginning of a long-lasting growth spurt that provided a public relations bonanza and helped bring pro football out from under the shadow of college football.

As the Bears and Grange hit the road, the opener in Chicago was notable. A December 6, 1925, game at the Polo Grounds against the Giants in New York that attracted a pro football record 73,000 fans was a milestone. Grange ran back a 35-yard interception for a touchdown in that game. Giants owner Tim Mara said the phenomenal attendance and the publicity that accompanied his team's 19–7 loss to the Bears turned around his financially struggling franchise. The

Yankees' Babe Ruth attended the game and met privately with Grange to offer advice on dealing with celebrity and not picking up the check.

On they rolled, the Bears and Grange, from Chicago to St. Louis, Philadelphia, New York, Washington, D.C., Boston, Pittsburgh, Detroit, and Miami, with promoter C.C. Pyle cashing checks and distributing the profits. That took the circus up to Christmas and then a week's vacation. The break provided time for the players to rest and to heal the bruises and weariness accrued from colliding bodies in a schedule that was far more crowded than the typical once-a-week play.

A week of sunshine was all that the players received before resuming play on January 1 in Tampa, following up in Jacksonville, and then completing their journey through the East and South. Games in Los Angeles, San Diego, San Francisco, Portland, and Seattle lay ahead.

While the tour was an equal-opportunity show for fans in all those cities, the turnouts were not equal and a problem arose when headliner Grange got hurt and missed 2½

The 1925 barnstorming tour of the Bears and Red Grange (with helmet) put pro football on the map.

games. In Detroit, fans demanded refunds when they learned Grange would not play and attendance was about 4,000. Football fans had been hearing about Grange's exploits for Illinois for several years and they wanted to see him in the flesh. The Bears? Well, the clamor was not as great for a special chance to see them play in person. They were like backup singers for the front man.

The brainchild of C.C. Pyle and George Halas was a fabulous success. It mattered little that the Bears did not win every single game. Though it helped that Grange was on the winning side more often than not, that's not why people came. In an era before television, Grange was more mystery figure than flesh and blood. They wanted to see him in real life.

There had never been such evidence of public interest since our professional league began [in 1920]. I knew then and there that pro football was destined to be a big-time sport.

—GEORGE HALAS

Grange was not consistently great. After a full college season, draining travel, and playing professional games a couple times a week, he was not at full strength. But no one was going to say he was a bust. Grange offered fleeting, flashy hints of his talent.

Against the Columbus Tigers, Grange rushed for 140 yards and threw a 22-yard touchdown pass. Against the Donnelly Stars in St. Louis, he scored four touchdowns. Against the Frankford Yellow Jackets in Philadelphia, he scored two touchdowns. Against the Southern All-Stars in New Orleans, he rushed for 136 yards.

In Washington, Grange and Halas were introduced by Illinois Senator William Brown McKinley to President Calvin Coolidge and presented as "Mr. Grange and Mr. Halas with the Chicago Bears." Straight-faced, with absolute sincerity, the president uttered perhaps the pithiest sports comment ever to emanate from the White House: "Glad to meet you, young men. I always liked animal acts."

And, of course, Coolidge didn't even know he was being funny. Future presidents would be a little bit savvier about professional football.

When Pyle first approached him about the tour, Grange did not know the meaning of the word "barnstorming." In just over two months his vocabulary and his bank account were beneficiaries of it.

By the time the Grange-Bears tour reached California in mid-January of the new year, the sport and the main protagonists had reaped coast-to-coast publicity. Grange, it seemed, may have been self-effacing about his play and Midwesterners might have thought of him as a country boy made good. But Grange knew how to handle himself and how to have a good time. And it wasn't as if he was sending every penny back home to

JUST SHOW MY GOOD SIDE

Even before there was Hollywood interest in big-name athletes appearing in movies, stars of the playing field were invited to perform on stages around the country during their off-season. Baseball players were first. And it was not an unusual sight to catch an all-star ballplayer in full uniform on a vaudeville stage singing, dancing, or merely reciting a few lines during the winter months.

Chicago Cubs shortstop Joe Tinker, of the famed Tinker-to-Evers-to-Chance double play combination, performed in mini-melodramas designed to take advantage of his fame. Tinker and second baseman Johnny Evers had a home-run song called "Between You and Me" written under their names.

Babe Ruth was paid for a ghostwritten sports column and later his autobiography. Much later, linebacker Brian Bosworth, playing up an image of ferocity, performed in action movies.

Red Grange was the type of manly, glamorous figure Hollywood ate up, and he fit right in with his football exploits, his willingness to schmooze, and his lack of shyness in the public eye.

Wheaton, either. The folks were well enough on their own. He bought a raccoon coat and a Lincoln automobile.

Hollywood was not quite Hollywood when big-time professional football arrived in Los Angeles to play the Coliseum. The movies were still silent. But Grange and the Bears spoke for themselves on the field and residents apparently liked what they were saying because they turned out 75,000 strong, a record ticket count for a professional football game at the time.

In the 17–7 victory over the Los Angeles Tigers, Grange ran for two touchdowns. In some ways they were the biggest plays of the tour. The game was played on the biggest stage and the Bears were leading the National Football League into fresh territory where it could gain new fans. Offensive excitement would help the plot.

While he was in the neighborhood, Pyle kept the presses rolling for Grange, inking him to a movie deal. Grange appeared in a short called *One Minute to Play* and received half-decent reviews. This was not Grange's last flirtation with Hollywood. He later acted in a full-length movie called *The Racing Romeo*.

When the tour that had begun on Thanksgiving in Chicago ended on January 31 in Seattle, Grange and Halas shook hands and went their separate ways for a while.

True to his word, Pyle was a money-generating machine for Grange, lining up everything from Red Grange dolls to advertising endorsements. In 1926 Pyle even started his own professional football league to showcase Grange on a team in New York. But the league floundered and Grange rejoined the Bears for the rest of his playing career.

Beattie Feathers is credited with the NFL's first official 1,000-yard rushing season with 1,004 yards in 1934. But during his condensed barnstorming season, Grange was credited with 1,024 yards in the 17 games he played.

After he retired from football, Grange became an insurance salesman, then became a prominent member of the Bears' radio team, broadcasting games for years. It turned out that Grange could talk about football nearly as well as he could run with one.

Many popular athletes crossed over into Hollywood films, including Red Grange, the star of *One Minute to Play*.

Pyle came up with more ideas in one day than most men come up with in a lifetime.
—RED GRANGE

BOBBY DOUGLASS, THE GREAT RUNNING QUARTERBACK

Bears Great Scores Four Touchdowns

At the University of Kansas, quarterback Bobby Douglass had the chiseled build and size that would become the prototype for NFL quarterbacks in the coming years. He stood 6'4"and weighed 225 pounds.

Douglass's size meant that he was hard to bring down, even when full-speed-ahead linemen broke into the backfield. However, Douglass rarely waited around for hulking tackles to burst in upon him. By the time they got to where he had been standing, Douglass was on the go, scrambling around end to pick up big yardage. Douglass had the itch to run.

The man also had a strong arm but his passing game was not as honed as his running style. It had been nearly 20 years since Sid Luckman retired and the Bears were still on the prowl for more than a stopgap replacement. With a second-round draft pick in 1969, the Bears took a gamble on Douglass.

As most successful athletes do, Douglass had a head full of confidence and a belief that he could play at the professional level. Douglass had plenty of talent, but it was not often showcased in the passing game. In college, a quarterback whose legs were more reliable than his throwing arm wasn't that unusual. College offenses varied and many de-emphasized the pass in favor of the run depending on the current personnel.

It was a different story in the NFL. While it was always important to establish the run as part of a balanced offense, there was a growing reliance on the passing attack. The 1970s were the beginnings of offensive balance tilting in favor of passing. More passes began filling the sky than ever before.

As a rookie, Douglass saw a fair amount of action, participating in 11 games and throwing for 773 yards and five touchdowns. In the ensuing years, Douglass alternated between full-time starter and part-time player, never completing more than 46.6 percent of his passes in a season of major playing time.

What Douglass did was provide a dual-dimension threat at quarterback. In 1972

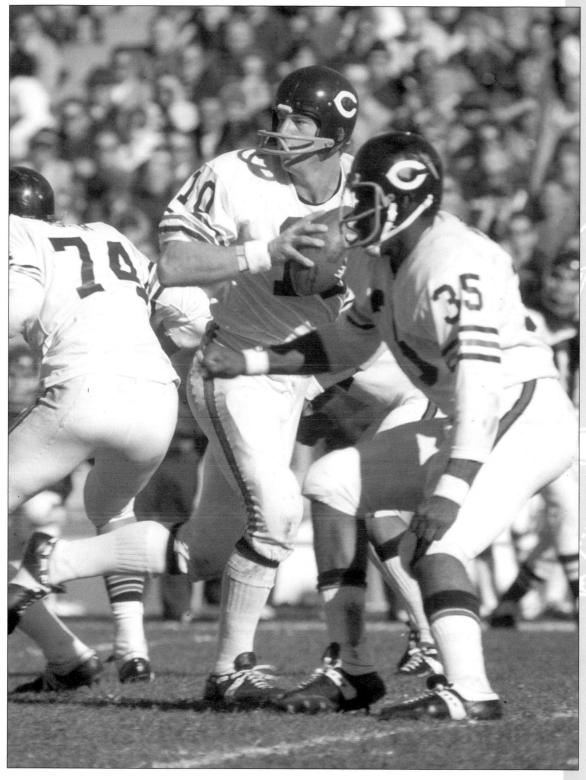

Bobby Douglass held the NFL record for most rushing yards by a quarterback for more than three decades.

Douglass set an NFL rushing record for a quarterback, collecting 968 yards. And that was before the expanded season took effect. The record lasted until 2006 when Michael Vick rushed for 1,039 yards in 16 games as a quarterback for the Atlanta Falcons.

Always a strong man with less-than-blazing speed, if Douglass had come along 20 years later it's very likely that some coach would have examined his attributes, harnessed his best talents, and turned him into a fullback. Nobody was going to stick around the NFL long completing just 45 percent of his passes. Douglass would probably have had a pro career, but he just might not have had as much fun blocking as lugging the football.

Appropriately, the best performance of Douglass's career mixed excellent passing and superb running on a November day in Green Bay. At one point trailing by 10 points, the Bears rebounded for a 31–17 victory with Douglass at the helm that showcased the El Dorado, Kansas, native at his best.

It was a day when Douglass's versatility paid off. Douglass finished the game with 100 yards rushing and

I've played as well this year.

—BOBBY DOUGLASS

four touchdowns on the ground, while completing 10 of 15 passes for 118 yards through the air, with most of the good stuff coming in the second half.

The Bears defense, led by Dick Butkus and Wally Chambers, shut down much of the Packers offense, but Green Bay had scored opportunistically on Chicago mistakes to lead 17–10 at the intermission. Coach Abe Gibron told the Bears in the locker room that they were playing well and predicted they would come back. Good pep talk.

Receiving the ball on the second-half kickoff, the Bears, directed by Douglass, put together a seven-play, 80-yard drive. On his finest day Douglass made his finest play during this stretch. Douglass faked a handoff to Jim Harrison, faked a pitch to Carl Garrett, then tucked the ball in and sped around the right side. As defenders closed in, Douglass angled left across the field

RUN FOR YOUR LIFE

With more than 100 NCAA Division I college football teams, not to mention Division I-AA, Division II, Division III, and NAIA teams, there are more offensive formations found than are in use in the NFL. And not every one of those schools can rely on a big thrower at quarterback. Coaches improvise. They deal with what they have. That's why it is still possible to see quarterbacks who depend on their legs as much as their arms in the college game.

At times, a coach strapped for a true signal caller will simply put his best athlete in at quarterback. That quarterback may not have the experience to make audibles or run sophisticated passing plays. So

he counts on his legs to bail him out. Although the NFL's offenses are built around drop-back quarterbacks, periodically someone comes along to upset the balance.

Bobby Douglass was a sterling example of what improvisation could do for a team. Vikings and Giants quarterback Fran Tarkenton knew his job was to throw first, but he was a genius at escaping pass rushers with his runs. Before he went to the dogs, Michael Vick of the Atlanta Falcons showed that it was possible to make the Pro Bowl by running as much as throwing. And in 2007 the University of Florida's Tim Tebow won the Heisman Trophy because he was an equal threat throwing and running.

GAME DETAILS

Bears 31 • Packers 17

Location: Lambeau Field, Green Bay

Attendance: 56,267

Box Score:

> **B**obby Douglass today played his greatest game as a Bear.
>
> —ABE GIBRON

Bears	7	3	14	7	**31**
Packers	7	10	0	0	**17**

Scoring:

CHI Douglass 1-yard run (Percival PAT)
GB Lane 5-yard pass from Hunter (Marcol PAT)
GB Hunter 1-yard run (Marcol PAT)
GB Marcol 25-yard field goal

CHI Percival 10-yard field goal
CHI Douglass 1-yard run (Percival PAT)
CHI Douglass 2-yard run (Percival PAT)
CHI Douglass 1-yard run (Percival PAT)

and finished off a 42-yard surprise play to give the Bears possession at the Green Bay 6-yard line.

Douglass moved the chains regularly after that, mixing passes and runs. His four touchdown rushes totaled just five yards, one a two-yard bootleg and the other three coming on a variety of one-yarders. Rarely has anyone run so little for so much productivity.

The spectacular all-around performance made Douglass the toast of the locker room and the toast of Chicago. For someone who had taken considerable criticism for not being Johnny Unitas, it was a delicious moment of vindication—maybe.

"I've heard the fans for years," Douglass said afterward. "Listen, I know how good a football player I am. I don't get any personal satisfaction out of telling people, 'I'll show you.' I didn't play that much of a better game today."

Douglass would not say that he played a better game than usual, hesitant to give any critic ammunition retroactively pertaining to other games that didn't turn out as well. If Douglass was reluctant to toot his own horn—after all, every player has to have a best game—Gibron gushed about his performance.

While the bulk of Douglass's career was spent with the Bears, he remained in the league through 1978 and had shorter stays with San Diego, New Orleans, and Green Bay.

Later, just before he turned 60, Douglass was diagnosed with squamous cell cancer. But a series of treatments beat back the illness and less than a year later he said he had regained full strength.

The day he scored four touchdowns to lead the Bears to a satisfying comeback victory over the Packers, Douglass's teammates gave him the game ball. Blocking backs seldom receive such rewards.

25 The Football Player America Wanted to See

Red Grange Makes His Pro Debut

The story of how Harold "Red" Grange, the "Wheaton Iceman," became the man who hoisted professional football on his shoulders—just like one of those blocks of ice he carried to build muscle and his bank account—is a flavorful one. It has gained currency over the years as the moment when the National Football League was transformed from an also-ran curiosity to mainstream sport in the eyes of the public.

Grange grew up in Wheaton, a suburb of Chicago, and at the height of the Roaring Twenties became a superstar athlete mentioned in the same breath as baseball's Babe Ruth, heavyweight champion Jack Dempsey, golfer Bobby Jones, and tennis star Big Bill Tilden. The difference initially was that Grange was a student at the University of Illinois, the only one among those revered household names who was not a professional in his sport.

In the 1920s college football players were seen as the purest of amateurs, competing in their sport only as an extracurricular school activity. When Grange completed his eligibility, it was assumed by most that he would parlay his fame into a job in the business world—the world of pro football was seen as a bit unsavory and certainly not a profession promising a lucrative livelihood.

Grange was a three-time All-American for Illinois, where his swiftness and shiftiness cemented his reputation as "The Galloping Ghost." He was much admired for what he could coax out of his 5'11", 175-pound frame, but one single game catapulted him into the highest pantheon of American sporting legends. It didn't hurt that Grange wore the flashy and easily identifiable No. 77 coming out of the backfield, a jersey number that would be assigned in later decades to anonymous linemen.

After scoring 75 touchdowns in high school, Grange was already on his way to greatness. The game that catapulted Grange's reputation into the stratosphere, raising him from anonymity to a name that transcended sport, occurred during his junior year at Illinois.

Grange single-handedly carried the Fighting Illini to a 39–14 victory over rival Michigan in front of 65,000 fans in Champaign. Michigan came into the contest with a 20-game unbeaten streak. Michigan came out of the game bruised in body and ego by Red Grange. Grange returned the opening kickoff 95 yards for a touchdown. Then in the next 12 minutes he ran for three more touchdowns. After a break, Grange scored a fifth touchdown and threw for a sixth. It was a wonder that the Wolverines didn't drop the sport right then.

The hosannas reverberated from coast to coast.

At a time when the concept of athletic celebrityhood was just dawning, C.C. Pyle, a savvy Champaign movie theater owner and promoter, recognized the wealth to be made from the Grange name. The moment Grange's Illini career ended, much to the chagrin of his Illinois coach Bob Zuppke, Grange signed a contract with Pyle.

There was definitely a body of opinion suggesting that Grange was soiling his hard-won reputation by turning pro to play with those ruffians whose only ideology was greenbacks. Grange seemed more bugged by the reaction than torn by any belief that he was selling his soul. Why shouldn't he make a buck playing his favorite game?

Pyle may have been history's first player agent. He bartered Grange's services to the Bears, selling the idea of a nationwide tour to take on all comers and to showcase Grange's talents. Bears owner George Halas bought in and Grange was guaranteed a minimum of $3,000 a game for a 17-game tour; Pyle assured his star that he would make much more.

Harold "Red" Grange was the first superstar in pro football history.

So although Grange was suiting up for the Bears, his paycheck came from Pyle. And while the Bears were a member of the NFL, this was an extracurricular tour where Chicago took on nonleague teams and league clubs across the country.

It is difficult to overestimate the magic of Grange's name at that time. It was party time all over the United States in the days before the Great Depression. Grange had established himself, and Americans who

C.C. Pyle and Red Grange arranged a barnstorming tour of the United States that changed sports history forever. *(Photo courtesy of AP Images)*

had never attended a football game were attracted by the opportunity to see a player they had heard about and felt might be the best player in the world.

The great "play" by Grange in his first appearance in a Bears uniform on Thanksgiving Day 1925 was simply showing up, being present in the flesh for a game against the crosstown Chicago Cardinals. Grange merely trotting onto the field had grand implications for the Bears, the league, and the sport. When the two Chicago teams met, crowds were often large, but with the extra added attraction of Grange, this game sold about 36,000 tickets. Since attendance fluctuated

IN POOR TASTE TO MAKE MONEY

For those who decry what big business college sports have become today—especially in NCAA basketball and big-time college football—it is interesting to look back at the outrage that descended upon Red Grange when he announced he was going to join the ranks of professional football players after starring for the University of Illinois.

In the mid-1920s, pro football was not regarded as a respectable profession. It was seen as a greedy offshoot of the sport made popular by collegians, populated by ruffians who made up for their lack of brainpower with their brawn.

Grange shattered the myth. He was a smart college man who didn't see anything morally corrupt in getting paid to exploit one of his talents. He loved playing football, so why not make it a career? He had

skill at the game and there were offers to make him instantly rich by using his talents to perform the same type of feats he had just performed for Illinois.

Given the lack of precedent, C.C. Pyle could have taken advantage of Grange when the promoter came calling with his wild plan to tour the country. But Pyle was honest and overnight Grange enhanced rather than diminished his reputation and expanded his bank account significantly.

Instead of being suckered by a bad deal, Grange actually became a barrier breaker. Pyle had the foresight to think big, Grange had the gumption to join him, and because they partnered with the Chicago Bears and carried out the grand tour, Grange is credited with being the man who elevated pro football's stature.

GAME DETAILS

Bears 0 • Cardinals 0

Location: Wrigley Field, Chicago

Attendance: 36,000

Box Score:

Cardinals	0	0	0	0	**0**
Bears	0	0	0	0	**0**

Grange was a true rarity—a perfectly conditioned athlete.

—GEORGE HALAS

wildly because of weather, it is difficult to determine how many fans would have turned out had Grange not appeared, but he was likely good for 5,000 to 10,000 paying customers.

The Bears were the better team that year, but the Cardinals produced a hard-fought game. One of the Cards' key strategies was to limit Grange's touches. In a game that played out 0–0, there were many possession changes, but the Cardinals' legendary and future Hall of Famer Paddy Driscoll smartly avoided punting to Grange whenever possible.

Driscoll, who eventually played five seasons with the Bears and was a confidante of Halas, almost single-handedly pulled off the upset with a drop kick that would have been the game-winning field goal. The kick bounced off the goal post. Driscoll's Grange-avoidance plan was not appreciated by spectators who paid to see Grange run wild and at times they booed Driscoll.

On plays the Cardinals could not control, the Bears gave Grange his opportunities on handoffs in the backfield. He gained 92 yards from scrimmage, a very respectable showing for a guy who had been a member of the team for only three days and admitted he did not even know all the signals. Playing both ways in the defensive backfield, Grange also intercepted a pass.

When a team hitches its wagon to a star there is pressure for that star to perform. The fact that the game ended in a tie and that Grange was held scoreless left disgruntled those who expected miracles from Grange every day on the gridiron.

What followed was a whirlwind tour that was headlined by Grange, made him rich virtually overnight, elevated the profile of the Chicago Bears, and helped stamp the NFL as a legitimate professional league.

Eventually Grange became a full-fledged member of the Bears roster, and for years ran, caught passes, and intercepted quarterbacks with deftness, grace, and toughness. When the Pro Football Hall of Fame was chartered and voted in its first class in 1963, Grange was one of the first members.

The customers left the park somewhat disappointed that I was unable to scamper for a touchdown, but satisfied they saw a good football game.

—RED GRANGE

24 Bears' Comeback Wows Monday Night Audience

Brian Urlacher Is a Showman on the Big Show

You don't want Brian Urlacher frowning at you, never mind running about 100 mph aimed straight at your chest.

The perfect physical specimen for a middle linebacker at 6'4" and 258 pounds, Urlacher has become one of the most distinctive and popular defensive players in the National Football League. He is admired not only because he is fearsome and hits like a truck, but also because he is fast enough to haul down running backs and wide receivers from behind.

Just when players thought they had escaped the clutches of the defense, here came Urlacher to pulverize them from the blind side.

What makes it so scary to face Urlacher on the field is that one minute he is nowhere in sight and the next minute he is in a player's face. Where had he come from so fast? How did he make it so quickly to the left sideline when after the snap he had first run toward the right sideline? He is an eyes-in-the-back-of-the-head player, one of those defensive monsters who seems capable of seeing where the play is headed even though there is no empirical evidence to point him in that direction. And he is one of those guys who hits so hard that opponents wished they had eyes in the back of their head so they could see him coming and take last-minute evasive action.

Urlacher had spent more time in the defensive backfield during his college days at New Mexico, but when he became the Bears number one draft pick in 2000, he was slated for middle linebacker. No team in the NFL had such a glorious history at the position. From Bill George to Dick Butkus to Mike Singletary, it was as if the Pro Football Hall of Fame in Canton, Ohio, had designated a special section among all of the greats just for Bears middle linebackers.

From the moment he joined the team Urlacher proved to be a worthy successor. That season he was in on 165 tackles, made

He was killing them, just running around and tackling anyone with the ball. It was probably one of the greatest games anyone has ever played.

—DEVIN HESTER ON BRIAN URLACHER'S DEFENSE

eight sacks, and was chosen the NFL's Defensive Rookie of the Year.

Play after play, season after season, Urlacher built his reputation. He made sacks by blowing in on quarterbacks. He forced fumbles by decking running backs. He intercepted passes by batting them in the air with one hand and plucking them out of the sky with the other. He ran side to side on the field, almost like a tracker in the woods hunting down prey to put the big hit on a guy who seemed about to slip away and run for pay dirt. Urlacher was selected for the Pro Bowl six times in his first seven seasons. He was in Honolulu so often that he could have almost qualified to register to vote in Hawaii.

Urlacher was consistently great. Youngsters nationwide scarfed up his No. 54 Bears jerseys and wore them to games. He made commercials. He was the personification of toughness. And then along came a game that solidified all facets of his Bears reputation. For a man who had played so many extraordinary games, Urlacher set a new standard during an improbable Chicago win over the Arizona Cardinals by virtually willing his teammates to make a comeback from what seemed like a hopeless situation.

At the time, six weeks into the NFL schedule in fall 2006, the Bears were

Brian Urlacher and the Bears defense snatched victory from the jaws of defeat against the Arizona Cardinals on October 16, 2006.

undefeated and running away with the NFC North Division. The Cardinals were still mired in a 40-year slump and were as big an underdog as if they had been playing real birds against real bears.

The *Monday Night Football* game, nationally televised from the desert against a backdrop of an orange sunset, figured to be a showcase for the best Bears team in years.

Only somebody tossed the script in a trash can. The 5–0 Bears were awful that night. The lowly Cardinals played with crispness and poise. The Bears, as they often had over the decades, had made something out of the early part of the schedule by playing superlative defense. Not this night. The defenders, with the exception of Urlacher, seemed to be bogged down in the sand by the road outside University of Phoenix Stadium. It seemed as if the Bears defenders were imposters, not All-Pros. Arizona had 20 points on the board at halftime and Bears defensive coordinator Ron Rivera went ballistic on his troops.

Well into the fourth quarter the Bears trailed the Cardinals by two touchdowns. Anyone who had to get up early the next morning had flicked off the TV, trying to salvage some extra sleep. Any yawning Bears fan who stuck with it deserved extra points for faith.

The idea of a Bears comeback seemed ludicrous, but those who believe in the anything-can-happen adage of sports hung with the game and watched a victory snatched from the jaws of defeat without any logical snatching going on. The Bears never were able to do much of anything on offense, either passing or running, and committed six turnovers. Of such ineptitude, comebacks are not made.

So the defense decided to win the game on its own. Defensive end Mark Anderson forced a fumble that defensive back Mike Brown ran in for a touchdown. Then Urlacher stripped the ball from Cardinals halfback Edgerrin James and Charles Tillman ran it back for a touchdown. Devin Hester's punt runback gave the Bears a 24–23 triumph.

IN THE MIDDLE OF IT ALL

Bill George may have invented the middle linebacker position as a Chicago Bear in the 1950s, but just because the team had one Hall of Fame selection at the spot didn't guarantee it would have an abundance of them. It just seemed to work out that way.

George was the first great Bears middle linebacker. He was followed by Dick Butkus, who some believe perfected the position. Butkus was big, fast, strong, and had a knack for getting his hands on the ball by making interceptions, forcing fumbles, or recovering fumbles. He hit like a freight train and covered more massive amounts of territory than modern radar systems.

Mike Singletary, known to be very religious during his sojourn with the Bears, was one of the focal points of the Bears' 46 defense during the 1980s. He must have been praying for forgiveness often after scaring the bejesus out of opposing running backs and sending all ball carriers silly enough to venture into his reach home groaning from aches and bruises.

And the Bears' lineage of great, admired, and feared middle linebackers continued with Brian Urlacher. Tradition and responsibility come with the role, but always there seems to be a Bears player up to the task.

GAME DETAILS

Bears 24 • Cardinals 23

Location: University of Phoenix Stadium, Phoenix

Attendance: 63,977

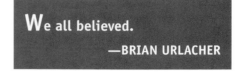

We all believed.

—BRIAN URLACHER

Box Score:

Bears	0	0	10	14	**24**
Cardinals	14	6	3	0	**23**

Scoring:

ARIZ Johnson 11-yard pass from Leinart (Rackers PAT)

ARIZ Boldin 26-yard pass from Leinart (Rackers PAT)

ARIZ Rackers 41-yard field goal

ARIZ Rackers 28-yard field goal

CHI Gould 23-yard field goal

ARIZ Rackers 29-yard field goal

CHI Brown 3-yard fumble return (Gould PAT)

CHI Tillman 40-yard fumble return (Gould PAT)

CHI Hester 83-yard punt return (Gould PAT)

Arizona coach Denny Green was so frustrated, so disappointed, and so mad that he could barely speak English in his postgame press conference and began looking around for fall guys to fire.

When the game ended, the original statistics credited Urlacher with 19 tackles. But once Bears coaches reviewed the game film they upped the total to 25 tackles. *Twenty-five tackles* in one game.

"They didn't block me," Urlacher said of the second half when he ran totally amok on the Cardinals.

Didn't try to or couldn't do it, the result was the same. Urlacher was the single most disruptive force in the Western Hemisphere that night unless there was a major earthquake in Missouri that everyone missed.

Bears teammates couldn't stop gushing about Urlacher's performance. The 25 tackles stunned even them. Urlacher also contributed two pass deflections, three quarterback hits, and the forced fumble.

"He showed why he's a superstar," Bears quarterback Rex Grossman said.

The game went from a major achievement for the Cardinals based on their first-half showing to being remembered with an insult—The Monday Night Meltdown. Green did fire offensive coordinator Keith Rowen the next day.

Bears players spent half the week praising Urlacher, trying to come up with one-upmanship laudatory descriptions of his play. One player joked that Urlacher's real father was Superman. And Hester, who has been likened to Superman himself on an occasion or two, called Urlacher The Incredible Hulk.

Even Urlacher seemed grudgingly impressed with himself.

"I've never had a game like that before," he said.

23 WILLIE GAULT TURNS IN SUPER GAME

Bears Dominate Super Bowl XX

Willie Gault has led a colorful life with success achieved on several fronts. Gault was a world champion track and field athlete, a Winter Olympian for the United States in the bobsled, a Hollywood guest actor on several television shows, and a fleet-footed wide receiver for the Super Bowl champion Chicago Bears.

Next thing you know, Gault will show up as a singer on *American Idol* or as a hoofer on *Dancing with the Stars*.

Many track stars with supersonic speed in Olympics-style 100-meter dash competitions have tried to cross over to the National Football League as wide receivers. For years, coaches' minds contained pictures of flankers and ends simply blowing past defenders, being wide open downfield for their quarterbacks to hit with simple passes. But for every high-profile success in that transition, such as the one made by world-record holder sprinter Bob Hayes with the Dallas Cowboys, there were probably five failures: men who could not adapt, run routes, or who had weak hands. And it turned out that as fast as they were, if they

were bumped at the line of scrimmage to interrupt their free-flowing run they could be thrown off stride and contained by a pretty fleet-footed defensive back.

Gault, whose playing dimensions were 6'0" and 181 pounds, possessed one attribute that some of the prominent disappointments lacked. He had played the game well at the University of Tennessee. Gault broke in with the Bears in 1983 and caught 40 passes for eight touchdowns as a rookie and also became a kickoff return threat. Gault knew how to cope with contact and he was one guy whom the defense was not going to catch from behind if he broke through the wedge.

The Bears were on the rise, building to a Super Bowl–caliber team when Gault joined. He was a piece of the puzzle, a weapon among the mix of weapons that supplemented the great Walter Payton's backfield moves. His speed was the added dimension for the offense. In a game where little things matter and margins are measured in inches, Gault was so much faster than other wide receivers that he gave

Wide receiver Willie Gault ran wild over the New England Patriots in Super Bowl XX.

the Bears a built-in advantage. He could gain separation from the safety or cornerback assigned to shadow him. Even if those guys were remarkably fast by athletic measurements, Gault was faster. And all he needed was to gain a step and sneak behind the coverage to become an inviting target for quarterback Jim McMahon.

Gault's special gifts made him dangerous and a distraction for opposing defensive coaches. Even if Gault never touched the ball, even if he was just the world's fastest decoy, he monopolized a good bit of planning. He simply could not be let loose or he would burn the defense; on the other hand, shifting double coverage to Gault left McMahon with options on the opposite side of the field or coming out of the backfield.

Thus Gault raised his status in the eyes of defensive coaches early in the 1985 season when a 99-yard kickoff return for a touchdown jump-started a Chicago victory over the Washington Redskins. While Washington built a small lead, Gault had been the near-goat on two kickoff plays. One was a botched reverse when he was giving the ball to linebacker Wilber Marshall. The other was losing the kick in the sun, but getting away with it because the ball rolled into the end zone for a touchback.

On the long return, Gault took the ball at the 1-yard line, watched his blockers form and clear a path, then darted through an opening in the middle of the field, cut to the left, and was gone. The Bears scored 31 points in the quarter to set a record.

Afterward, someone teasingly told Gault it took him 19 seconds to run the 100, a dawdle in comparison to his track times.

"I must be getting really slow," Gault joked.

Of course, with dodging tacklers, he probably ran 110 yards.

That was all prelude to the Super Bowl when the Bears matched up with the New England Patriots. The Bears dominated that game, winning 46–10, and Gault was at the root of many of the points. He caught four passes for 129 yards.

Early in the game, after the Patriots took a 3–0 lead, Gault made a 43-yard grab of a McMahon pass that set up a 28-yard field goal. It was hard to say which was the more important play: the 43-yarder, because it came at a time when the Bears were still vulnerable; or a Gault third-quarter play when he turned in a 60-yard reception setting up the touchdown that put the Patriots away.

Gault was not the man who put the Bears on the scoreboard that day, but he was the man who made the plays that enabled other Bears to get on the scoreboard with an all-around team-effort offense.

In his 11-year NFL career, Gault caught 333 passes. Gault also found himself edging into the Chicago newspapers' entertainment pages when he went onstage with the Chicago City Ballet. That was the show business in his heart. He was also the driving force in producing "The Super Bowl Shuffle," the bold music video that made the Bears the talk of the nation in a way their superb play could not. Eventually Gault moved into show business full-time, working as a regular on *The Predator*, appearing several times on *The West Wing*, and acting in many other TV shows.

Even in his forties, Gault retains much of the speed that helped make him famous. His muscles are still honed and he competes in master track and field events. One day he will probably be the fastest guy in a rocking chair.

I went into the game thinking I could score three touchdowns because of the plays in the game plan and the fact I have more speed than anyone on the field.

—WILLIE GAULT

GAME DETAILS

Bears 46 • Patriots 10

Location: Louisiana Superdome, New Orleans

Attendance: 73,818

That kickoff was the biggest play of the game.

—JIM MCMAHON

Box Score:

Bears	13	10	21	2	**46**
Patriots	3	0	0	7	**10**

Scoring:

NE Franklin 36-yard field goal
CHI Butler 28-yard field goal
CHI Butler 24-yard field goal
CHI Suhey 11-yard run (Butler PAT)
CHI McMahon 2-yard run (Butler PAT)

CHI Butler 24-yard field goal
CHI McMahon 1-yard run (Butler PAT)
CHI Phillips 28-yard interception return (Butler PAT)
CHI Perry 1-yard run (Butler PAT)
NE Fryar 8-yard pass from Grogan (Franklin PAT)
CHI Safety, Waechter tackled Grogan in end zone

Willie Gault's four catches for 129 yards jump-started the Bears offense in Super Bowl XX.

22 BEST OF ALL TIME

Walter Payton Breaks NFL Rushing Record

By attending Jackson State in Mississippi, Walter Payton forfeited the type of nationwide attention the best college football running backs receive from magazines and television reports. He did not escape the notice of professional scouts, however, and the Bears selected him as their number one draft pick in 1975.

The team believed it was drafting a star, but it likely had no idea Payton would turn into one of the greatest players in NFL history. Payton made his points from the backfield early in his career, took his yards where he found them, and made his yards where he could. His powerful, churning thighs helped him break tackles and his sturdy straight arm helped him fend off others.

Year by year, season by season, the 5'10", 200-pound halfback proved himself on the field and made his linemen proud to block for him. He also showed he was one of them when he enthusiastically led the blocking way when he didn't carry the ball. This ran counter to the image of many flashy running backs. Even the most down-to-earth among the top runners knew their primary job was to pile up yards for their team and they were

hesitant about risking their bodies on plays when they weren't lugging the football.

Not Payton. He was always in the middle of the action. The massive number of yards Payton accumulated year after year prompted many comparisons between his running prowess and that of other elite backs from Jim Brown and O.J. Simpson to Emmitt Smith. But his all-around play is what stuck in Bears coach Mike Ditka's memory and led him later to say that Payton was probably the best football player who ever lived. It was the ultimate compliment from the ultimate hard-nosed football man.

Payton's first big rushing year was 1976 when he collected 1,390 yards. The next season Payton rushed for a career-high 1,852 yards. In 1979 he racked up 1,610 yards. By the time the 1984 campaign began, Payton had seven 1,000-yard-plus rushing seasons to his credit.

For decades, before he walked away from the Cleveland Browns and football to start a movie career in *The Dirty Dozen* in 1966, fullback Jim Brown had been the gold standard for running backs. He was fast and powerful, had the best rushing average, and

Walter Payton broke Jim Brown's all-time rushing record against the New Orleans Saints on October 7, 1984.

his career total of 12,312 yards seemed out of reach for even the greatest of backs.

Pro football had changed. As Brown simultaneously developed his movie career and became known as a political activist, football provided more opportunities for running backs to shine longer. During the first four years of his career, Brown had just 12 games a season in which to compile his yardage total. The schedule later expanded to 14 games, then 16. That meant more carries and more chances for running backs to accumulate yards during individual seasons. Also, the 230-pound Brown left football after nine seasons (with his health intact). He might well have played a couple more years if premier players had been making millions of dollars during his era.

Brown's records withstood challenges from the best running backs for nearly 20 years. By the time the 1984 Bears season began, however, it was obvious that if Payton ran up to his usual standards and stayed healthy, he should easily set a new record early in the season.

The Bears carried a 3–2 record into their early-October matchup with the New Orleans Saints at Soldier Field. With heavy rains that drenched fans and kept the no-show count high, it was not a day for quarterbacks. It was a Walter Payton day.

In the third quarter, Bears quarterback Jim McMahon called Payton's number as he had so many times before. The ball was snapped and McMahon turned and flipped a pitchout to Payton on the left. Payton rumbled for six yards and established a new, all-time NFL career rushing record.

In his postgame remarks, Payton made special mention of certain running backs whose lives, never mind careers, had been cut short, singling out David Overstreet, Joe Delaney, and the Bears' own Brian Piccolo as players who didn't get the same chance he had to keep on running.

"This is a reflection of those guys," Payton said.

Although none of those players were ever considered a threat to become the league's all-time leading rusher, the spirit of Payton's comment was noted. He was essentially saying that things happen, things go awry, and not everyone gets a chance to live up to their potential or to live out long lives.

Weather aside, it was a great day all around for Payton and the Bears. The team won the game 20–7. Payton rushed for 154 yards, leaving him with a total of 12,400 at the end of the game. It was the 59th 100-yard game in his 10-year career. And the afternoon was topped off by a congratulatory phone call from

THE WHITE HOUSE ON LINE 1

After Walter Payton broke the NFL career rushing record of Jim Brown, the phone rang in Bears Land. It was President Ronald Reagan calling from Air Force One as he was approaching Louisville.

In part, Reagan said, "Congratulations on your marvelous day. Breaking Jim Brown's record is akin to Hank Aaron breaking Babe Ruth's home-run mark and Kareem Abdul-Jabbar breaking Wilt Chamberlain's point total. You've had a great career with the Bears in 10 years and 135 games and that is truly a most significant milestone that you reached today, and it would be for anyone. Good luck on your next 12,000 yards."

Payton thanked the president—and First Lady Nancy Reagan, who was also on the line—for calling. A reporter asked Payton if he was a Republican and he said, "I'm an American."

GAME DETAILS

Bears 20 • Saints 7

Location: Soldier Field, Chicago

Attendance: 53,752

Box Score:

Saints	0	7	0	0	**7**
Bears	6	7	0	7	**20**

Scoring:

CHI Thomas 48-yard field goal

CHI Thomas 46-yard field goal

NO Wilson 15-yard pass from Todd (Andersen PAT)

CHI Payton 1-yard run (Thomas PAT)

CHI McKinnon 16-yard pass from McMahon (Thomas PAT)

> **W**hen I finally got the record, I felt relieved.
>
> —WALTER PAYTON

President Ronald Reagan, the old sportscaster with Illinois ties who famously had played the role of ill-fated Notre Dame halfback George Gipp in the movies.

Almost always low-key in public, it was not until Payton celebrated breaking the record that he revealed the recent pursuit of it had placed unwanted pressure on his shoulders, maybe just a little bit like Hank Aaron's pursuit of Babe Ruth. All the attention, from the lead-up to the record-breaking moment, had gotten on Payton's nerves.

"For the last three weeks—and I've tried to conceal this—it's been hard on me, my family, and friends," Payton said.

The 1984 season was one of Payton's best. He rushed for 1,684 yards, scored 11 touchdowns, and also led the Bears in pass receiving with 45 catches. The team finished 10–6 in the regular season and won a playoff game. It was a prelude to the team's most satisfying performance during Payton's era. The Bears were on their way to a Super Bowl championship the next year.

When Payton retired after the 1987 season, his career total was 16,726 rushing yards, the new gold standard. It did not last as long as Brown's mark, though, with Emmitt Smith eventually doing something that few tacklers did to Payton during his career—catch him from behind.

> **T**o watch him just knock people over was very impressive.
>
> —BEARS LINEMAN KEITH VAN HORNE ON PAYTON'S RUNNING STYLE

October 15, 1939

21 A RECORD WITH LEGS

Fullback Bill Osmanski's 86-Yard Run

The Chicago Bears have always been a running team. Since the days of Bronko Nagurski and Red Grange, followed by the days of Rick Casares and Gale Sayers, and on to the great Walter Payton, the Bears have prospered more often on the ground than through the air.

So it is somewhat amazing that the Bears have never had a running back gain more than 90 yards on a play from scrimmage. There have been kick and fumble returns that have exceeded that number, but nearly 70 years after it occurred, Bill Osmanski's regular-season run of 86 yards in a 44–7 victory over the Chicago Cardinals remains the team record.

The Bears and the Cardinals were intense on-field rivals from the early days of the National Football League. Each game played within the city limits attracted a sizeable football following with supporters from both sides. Attendance was about 30,000 at Wrigley Field on this day when the Bears clobbered the Cardinals. For the most part, during the four decades the teams sought Chicagoans' allegiances, the Bears had the upper hand.

The Cardinals announced in 1960 that they were departing for St. Louis and the franchise later moved to Arizona. Any sense of rivalry was lost between the two clubs over time and now the games between Chicago and Arizona carry no special connection. But on Osmanski's big day, the game was more important, more immediate, and more like a Cubs–White Sox baseball game.

Osmanski's playing dimensions were listed at 5'11" and 197 pounds. In his autobiography, team owner George Halas said sportswriters commented that Osmanski was so strong "he could pick up a grand piano and run with it." Osmanski was born in 1915 and grew up in Providence, Rhode Island (where he reportedly ran two miles to school), before attending Holy Cross in Massachusetts. Osmanski was the Bears' number one draft pick that year and he also saw action at linebacker. A little bit later, Osmanski's younger brother Joe followed the same path to the Bears from Providence to Holy Cross to Chicago, joining the team as a fullback-linebacker in 1946.

The Bears of 1939 began the year well and were in second place, a half game behind the Detroit Lions in the Western Division standings, when they met the Cardinals for the first of two games that season. The Cardinals, however, were off to a poor start, winners of just one game.

Fullback Bill Osmanski, shown here against the Washington Redskins, broke free for an 86-yard touchdown run against the Chicago Cardinals in 1939—still the longest run from scrimmage in Bears history.

Chicago was about to embark on its winningest decade of football, despite the interruption of World War II, and the Bears were poised to inherit the "Monsters of the Midway" nickname from the University of Chicago. That school's once-proud college football program was being dropped, as administrators decided that education was more important to the identity of a university than any recreational pursuit. The balance between educational mission and big-time athletics was much easier to set right in 1939, but it still took commitment. Today, with the millions and millions of dollars at stake and the vast amount of free publicity attached to fielding a BCS-caliber football team, such breaks are not easy to come by.

"Monsters of the Midway" was catchy and it applied, so the rough, tough Bears became the monsters. Few people today probably recall the University of Chicago link.

True enough, the Bears were monsters on the day of the matchup with the Cardinals. Although there was nothing special at stake, the game is remembered as one of the wildest ever played by the Bears.

Although the Bears dominated on the scoreboard, the Cardinals had plenty of chances to take advantage of miscues. The game included eight interceptions and eight fumbles, with the ball truly being treated like a hot potato. No one could hang onto it long. The Cardinals simply made their big mistakes at the wrong time, keeping themselves out of the Bears' end zone.

During the chaos of possession changes in the first three quarters, Osmanski scored a touchdown. One of the newspapers covering the game joked that the Bears, "on orders from the purchasing department," were supposed to switch to passing for extra points instead of kicking them because of the cost of losing the balls to the fans. Given that it was 1939, the country had just come out of the Depression, and that Halas was the type of CEO to watch every penny spent, it might not have been a joke.

As the game was nearing the end of the fourth quarter, the score was 37–7. Osmanski took a handoff on his own 14-yard line and following the blocking of tackle Jack Torrance and guard Dick Bassi through the line, found a hole, and burst into the clear. He

WHEN A YARD WAS A YARD

The Bears are due for a 100-yard run from scrimmage. Bound to happen someday. It is intriguing that the Bears have not bested Bill Osmanski's 86-yard run for nearly 70 years. But the second-place run on the all-time list goes back to 1921, the third-longest run goes back to 1934, and the fourth-longest run goes back to 1955.

Ironically many of the longest Bears runs occurred during periods when the team's rushing leader didn't accumlulate many yards. Osmanski led the entire league with his 699 yards in 1939. Rick Casares totaled 672 yards in 1955, the same year he dashed 81 yards on a single rush.

The Bears went from 1934—when Beattie Feathers notched his milestone 1,004-yard season—to 1956—when Casares rushed for 1,126 yards—without a 1,000-yard runner. And only Gale Sayers, twice, topped the barrier between Casares and Walter Payton's 1976 season.

In all, despite their long history, the Bears have had only 10 different runners rush for 1,000 yards in a season. It would definitely boost the total if a runner broke Osmanski's single-run record.

GAME DETAILS

Bears 44 • Cardinals 7

Location: Wrigley Field, Chicago

Attendance: 29,592

Box Score:

> **I** probably used all of the words I learned on the Chicago streets.
>
> —GEORGE HALAS PROTESTING AN OFFICIAL'S NONCALL
> WHEN OSMANSKI WAS HELD AT THE END OF A GAME

Cardinals	0	7	0	0	**7**
Bears	17	7	0	20	**44**

Scoring:

CHI B Maniaci 12-yard fumble return (Maniaci PAT)

CHI B McDonald 10-yard pass from Masterson (Maniaci PAT)

CHI B Maniaci 21-yard field goal

CHI B Osmanski 3-yard run (Maniaci PAT)

CHI C Patrick 12-yard run (Patrick PAT)

CHI B Nolting 11-yard pass from Masterson (Stydahar PAT)

CHI B Nolting 35-yard interception return (PAT failed)

CHI B Osmanski 86-yard run (Stydahar PAT)

outran pursuing Cardinals Marshall Goldberg and Jack Robbins and sprinted the last 20 yards to the goal line untouched.

To that point, the 44–7 final score was the largest margin in the Bears-Cardinals series. However, in the last game of the season, the Bears delivered a slightly more overwhelming thumping 48–7. Osmanski led the league in rushing that season with 699 yards.

Osmanski played for the Bears from 1939 to 1943, then left the team for service in the navy during World War II. He returned to the Bears and played the 1946 and 1947 seasons before retiring. Osmanski scored the first of the 11 touchdowns the Bears totaled in their 73–0 rout of Washington in the 1940 championship

game. In all, Osmanski ran for 1,753 yards and 20 touchdowns for Chicago, with a rushing average of 4.8 yards a carry.

No carry, of course, was as extraordinary as Osmanski's rookie-year 86-yard run. The special run was just one yard longer than the team's old record of 85 yards set in 1921 by Pete Stinchcomb. The third-longest run from scrimmage in Bears history was Beattie Feathers's 82-yard gallop during his record-setting season of 1934.

It is remarkable that Osmanski's run has lasted so long atop the Bears' list and it is unlikely that whatever run exceeds it will still be a discussion topic almost 70 years after it is recorded.

> **H**e left them floundering behind and they gave up as he loped the last 20 yards of his 86-yard journey.
>
> —*CHICAGO TRIBUNE* SPORTSWRITER GEORGE STRICKLAND'S GAME ACCOUNT

October 16, 2006 and November 12, 2006

THE MOST EXPLOSIVE WEAPON IN FOOTBALL

Devin Hester Returns Kickoff, Missed FGA, and Punt for Touchdowns

20

On April 9, 2007, the featured guest at the Chicago Cubs' home opener was Chicago Bears kick returner Devin Hester. Hester threw out the ceremonial first pitch. If the Cubs were smarter, they would have signed Hester on the spot.

To pitch? Maybe. To hit? Possibly. To run? Definitely. Not only had Hester become insanely popular in Chicago for his spectacular kick returns, he was so good it seemed as if he could solve the problems of any or all of the other pro franchises in the city.

In a very short time Hester had become his own NFL highlight film. If a week passed without him scoring a touchdown on a flashy, creative, long-yardage runback, people wanted to know what was wrong. If he stays healthy and keeps up the pace, it won't be long before Hester claims 20 spots on any list of the 50 greatest plays in Bears history.

Fans and observers of Hester realize he is capable of taking one to the house from anywhere on the field, at any time, fielding any type of kick. It is really impossible to separate Hester's most phenomenal plays from one another since the Bears drafted him out of the University of Miami and turned him loose with a blessing and a smile at the start of the 2006 season. If equally discussed and analyzed, the *Devin Hester Great Plays* book alone would rival a James Michener novel in size.

During a Monday night game in the Arizona desert against the Cardinals, the Bears looked dead in the fourth quarter. They had trailed 20–0 at the half and 23–10 after three quarters. Televisions were being turned off all over America. Too bad for those yawning football fans. Hester would have woken them up faster than a gulp of Red Bull.

The Cardinals tried to pin the Bears deep in their own territory with a punt that traveled to the 17-yard line. Hester gathered it in, got his legs churning, and decided that although the blocking scheme was set up for him to run right there was more room in the middle. So he adjusted on the fly and darted through a big hole

Devin Hester scores the winning touchdown in a thrilling comeback victory over the Arizona Cardinals on *Monday Night Football.*
(Photo courtesy of AP Images)

Weeks after beating the Cardinals, Devin Hester ran back a missed field goal 108 yards for a touchdown against the New York Giants.

in the center of the field, going 83 yards for the game-winning touchdown.

"Basically," Hester said later, "everybody blocked. It was the right time and I give all the credit to my teammates."

When the Bears' Nathan Vasher returned a missed field goal 108 yards for a touchdown in 2005, it set a record for the NFL's longest-ever runback. It seemed possible it would never be duplicated, or at least not for a few decades.

Of course, that was the year before everyone in the league had heard of Devin Hester. Maybe if the play had not worked the year before, Bears special teams coach Dave Toub would have been skittish about positioning a return man so deep in the end zone and even thinking of trying to run back a potential missed boot.

A month after the Cardinals game, Hester turned around a potential scoring play against the New York Giants. The Giants' Jay Feely lined up to try a field goal in the fourth quarter. It was a reach from 52 yards, but New York felt it was worth the gamble. If the kick fell short, the Bears would take over on their own 34-yard line. But if Feely connected, it would account for a valuable three points.

Toub actually dropped Hester back from the line because he thought the Giants might fake the field goal and try to get off a punt that would fall dead inside the 5-yard line. But Feely went for the field goal and the boot fell short. Hester caught it eight yards deep in the end zone and made the quick assessment that it was worth trying to run it out rather than simply taking a knee.

The Bears players on the field weren't sure Hester was doing the right thing when he revved up the engines. At first, linebacker Brian Urlacher yelled at him not to go. Lineman John Tait wondered what Hester was doing and where he was going. Hester saw the possibilities before they did. Hester was off on an odds-defying 108-yard romp to put himself into the record book next to Vasher. Hester and Vasher could only laugh together about the coincidence and double achievement.

"He said it's a great chance to make it to the Hall of Fame," Hester said. "I said if I get my hands on it [the missed field goal], I'll be given the green light."

Hester was forcing his way into the NFL record book from the start of his career. Nobody had ever scored more runback touchdowns faster. Bears fans can only hope he continues to put the "special" in "special teams."

DIDN'T YOU USED TO BE...?

In some ways it was amazing that there still was a Cardinals franchise in the NFL for the Bears to play in 2006.

Once upon a time, the Cardinals were the Bears' greatest rivals. Just like the Cubs on the north side and the White Sox on the south side in baseball, football fans had the north side Bears and the south side Cardinals to support.

Ultimately the Cardinals realized Chicago wasn't big enough for two teams and moved to St. Louis and eventually on to Phoenix. Nothing remains of the rivalry itself between the players. All Bears fans and players will flatly state that their top rival is the Green Bay Packers. It takes an old-time fan to remember the good old days.

However, during their days in Chicago the Cardinals had some tremendously popular and talented personalities, including Ernie Nevers, Jimmy Conzelman, Charlie Trippi, Marshall Goldberg, and Ollie Matson. Jim Thorpe also suited up for the Cardinals.

GAME DETAILS

Bears 38 • Giants 20

Location: Giants Stadium, East Rutherford, New Jersey

Attendance: 78,641

Box Score:

Bears	3	7	14	14	**38**
Giants	7	6	7	0	**20**

Scoring:

NY Jacobs 1-yard run (Feely PAT)
CHI Gould 49-yard field goal
NY Feely 46-yard field goal
NY Feely 40-yard field goal
CHI Bradley 29-yard pass from Grossman (Gould PAT)

CHI Muhammad 10-yard pass from Grossman (Gould PAT)
CHI Clark 2-yard pass from Grossman (Gould PAT)
NY Jacobs 8-yard run (Feely PAT)
CHI Hester 108-yard missed field goal return (Gould PAT)
CHI Jones 2-yard run (Gould PAT)

> **W**hen I went out on the field all my teammates said, "We need a big play."
> —DEVIN HESTER AFTER AN 83-YARD PUNT RETURN FOR A TOUCHDOWN

GAME DETAILS

Bears 24 • Cardinals 23

Location: University of Phoenix Stadium, Phoenix

Attendance: 63,977

Box Score:

Bears	0	0	10	14	**24**
Cardinals	14	6	3	0	**23**

Scoring:

ARIZ Johnson 11-yard pass from Leinart (Rackers PAT)
ARIZ Boldin 26-yard pass from Leinart (Rackers PAT)
ARIZ Rackers 41-yard field goal
ARIZ Rackers 28-yard field goal

CHI Gould 23-yard field goal
ARIZ Rackers 29-yard field goal
CHI Brown 3-yard fumble return (Gould PAT)
CHI Tillman 40-yard fumble return (Gould PAT)
CHI Hester 83-yard punt return (Gould PAT)

> **H**e's gone. He is gone.
> —BEARS LINEMAN RUBEN BROWN ON DEVIN HESTER'S 108-YARD RETURN OF A MISSED FIELD GOAL

November 25, 1934

19 RUSHING PAST 1,000

Beattie Feathers Breaks the Barrier

He is the answer to a trivia question, but one not easily answered by anyone who is not a professional football historian.

Even among those who know his last name and claim to fame as the first National Football League runner to exceed 1,000 yards in a season, few would recall that his given first name was William. Beattie Feathers is the name fans know and for one season the Chicago Bears halfback was the greatest running back of all time.

In a season shortened by injury, Feathers rushed for 1,004 yards in just 11 games for the Bears. The total number of yards advanced does not seem to be in any dispute. However, a couple other numbers attached to Feathers's name remain murky.

In his remarkable, cut-short season, Feathers carried just 101 times and averaged 9.9 yards per rush. Or he carried 117 times. Or he carried 119 times. Regardless of the accuracy of attempts, the stats were extraordinary.

Born in 1909, Feathers was of Native American heritage and grew up in Bristol, Virginia. At the University of Tennessee, Feathers lettered in football, basketball, and track and was an All-American in football. He was the Most Valuable Player

in the Southeastern Conference as a senior, rushing for 1,052 yards with an average gain of 9.8 yards per attempt. He later was elected to the College Football Hall of Fame.

The Bears squad that Feathers joined was already a powerful one. The 7–1–6 team in 1932 won the championship game played indoors, also known as the "Tom Thumb Game." The 10–2–1 club of 1933 won the first conference-against-conference NFL title. And in 1934, Feathers's rookie season, the Bears blitzed all of their foes, outscoring them 286–86 and finishing the regular season 13–0.

Chicago was loaded with talent. But with Red Grange's knees failing him to the point he could no longer cut with the shiftiness of his past, the addition of Feathers was just what George Halas's offense needed. Feathers was known for hitting the line slowly after a handoff, but accelerating sharply as he hit the line of scrimmage. He was helped immeasurably in piling up massive yardage by following the blocking of fullback Bronko Nagurski.

"It takes two things above all others to make a 1,000-yarder," Feathers said years after recording the achievement. "A back must be fortunate enough to avoid injuries,

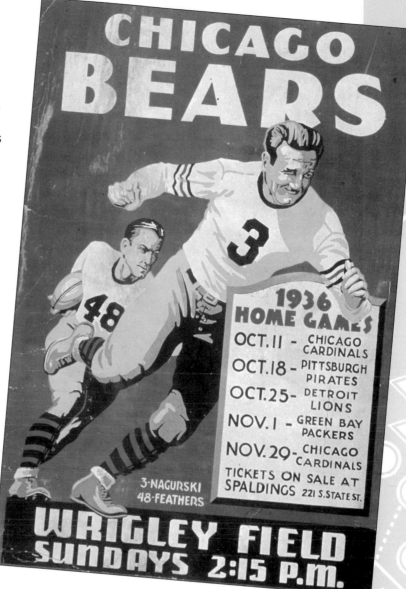

Though teammate Bronko Nagurski was a bigger star, Beattie Feathers was the first player to break the 1,000-yard rushing barrier.

and he must be fortunate enough to have good blocking."

Actually, Feathers was only completely healthy during the Bears' march to a 10–0 start. Then in the team's 11th game against the crosstown rival Chicago Cardinals, Feathers was hit hard. He suffered a separated shoulder and was sidelined for the final two regular-season games, both against the Detroit Lions. Even worse, Feathers's injury did not heal in time for him to compete in the Bears championship game against the New York Giants later that December, a game Chicago lost in an upset 30–13.

With three attempts for 42 yards, Feathers stayed healthy just long enough in the Cardinals game to crack the 1,000-yard mark, the milestone barely eked out by four yards.

Feathers was an old rookie. He was 25 during his first season in Chicago, the result of dropping out of school a few times as a youth before football focused his mind sufficiently to obtain the type of grades he needed to enroll at Tennessee. He said that physical maturity helped him during his debut year with the Bears. He wasn't wide-eyed, away from home for the first time and soaking up the bright lights of the big city. Feathers was married and had been around a couple of blocks a couple of times. He made his running sound easy.

"Whichever way Nagurski knocked them, I cut into that hole," Feathers said.

There was no particular attention focused on a running back being the first to reach 1,000 yards on

UNDEFEATED TILL THE END

The Bears went 13–0 during the 1934 regular season, but couldn't finish the undefeated season, falling to the New York Giants 30–13 in the title game.

This was the famous Sneakers Game. The Bears were outsmarted by the Giants: on an icy field where Chicago's cleats wouldn't hold, the Giants substituted sneakers for better traction and blew away the Bears in the second half.

The idea came from Giants captain Ray Flaherty, who would later coach the Redskins teams in their rivalry against the Bears. New York coach Steve Owen doubted the idea would work, but consented to the footwear change when all-around team aide Abe Cohen said he could obtain the shoes from Manhattan College.

At halftime the Bears led 10–3, but in the second half the Giants powered away. Bears tacklers went slipping and sliding while Giants runners maintained their footing.

"We were helpless," Bronko Nagurski said of the Bears. "We had to mince about."

The Giants topped the Bears for the 1934 championship in the infamous "Sneakers Game."

GAME DETAILS

Bears 17 • Cardinals 6

Location: Wrigley Field

Attendance: 13,800

Box Score:

Cardinals	0	0	0	6	**6**
Bears	10	0	0	7	**17**

Scoring:

CHI B Hewitt 13-yard lateral from Ronzani after pass from Molesworth (Manders PAT)

CHI B Manders 30-yard field goal

CHI B Nagurski short run (Manders PAT)

CHI C Hortsman 2-yard run (PAT failed)

> **I** had the greatest blocker who ever lived—Bronko Nagurski.
>
> —BEATTIE FEATHERS

the ground, not with the same intensity as someone becoming the first to scale Mount Everest, for example. Feathers was feted more and occasionally celebrated for the accomplishment in years to come.

Feathers was so far ahead of his time, it took 13 years for a player to break his record. The Philadelphia Eagles' Steve Van Buren was the second National Football League runner to crack 1,000 yards, and when he did in 1947 he finished with 1,008 yards, just a few more than Feathers.

As time passed and the NFL settled into a 12-game regular-season schedule, the 1,000-yard mark became the status symbol for running backs. It was the milestone number that all good runners aspired to reach. That remained true through expansion to 14 games and to a lesser extent during the current 16-game schedule. The 1,000 number is nice and round. Even if runners carry the ball much more frequently and are afforded more games per season to reach it, 1,000 yards still carries a certain cachet.

As it turned out, Feathers was pretty much a one-season wonder. The Cardinals game was the last time he competed at full strength for the Bears in 1934, and when he returned to the lineup in 1935 Feathers was comparatively ineffective. He rushed just 56 times for 281 yards, a good average of 5.0, but the sparkle was gone.

Feathers lasted with the Bears through the 1937 season, and he drifted around the league to Brooklyn and finally to Green Bay before retiring after the 1940 season. Feathers entered college coaching, spending 24 years as an assistant coach at Wake Forest and also coaching Appalachian State and North Carolina State.

Feathers was a supernova as a pro player. The most he ever rushed for in a season after his Bears rookie campaign was 350 yards. The magic of 1934 was gone the moment Feathers's shoulder was knocked out of alignment.

> **I** was healthy all the way.
>
> —BEATTIE FEATHERS

November 13, 2005

18 A BREATHLESS 108 YARDS

Nathan Vasher Takes It to the House

These are the moments fans live for—to be electrified by a spectacular player doing the thing he does best. These are the moments explosive players live for—shocking the opposition with a play that lives forever in memory.

And if the play sets a National Football League record, all the better.

You can't squeeze many more yards out of a single play without being under the grandstands in a tunnel than Nathan Vasher did when he returned a missed field-goal attempt 108 yards for a Bears touchdown against the San Francisco 49ers.

Vasher, a fourth-round draft pick out of the University of Texas in 2004, quickly established himself as a solid cornerback with terrific hands during his rookie year. He was a ballhawk, the type of player who on defense is a constant threat and annoyance to quarterbacks. If Vasher did not merely tip intended passes, he caught them. During Vasher's rookie season, he intercepted five balls—and he started only seven of 16 regular season games.

At 5'10" and 183 pounds, Vasher is no giant. He is a player with great instincts, awesome speed, excellent leaping ability, and someone who always knows where the ball is when it is zipping through the air. He scored high in intangibles.

This was evident dating back to high school. Vasher played cornerback and wide receiver in Texarkana, Texas, and as a senior was selected first-team all-state at both positions. That's a true distinction in any league, but in Texas the football competition is fiercer than just about anywhere else.

It didn't take long for the Bears to realize they had a very valuable draft pick on their hands. In just his second season, Vasher was a full-time starter in the defensive backfield and still took on the chore of occasional runbacks.

Some days the winds that swirl inside Soldier Field, located adjacent to Lake Michigan, are gale force in nature and are hazardous to any small craft. Those days can also be nightmares for punters, kickers, quarterbacks, and wide receivers.

It's the weirdest play I've ever seen.
—BRIAN URLACHER

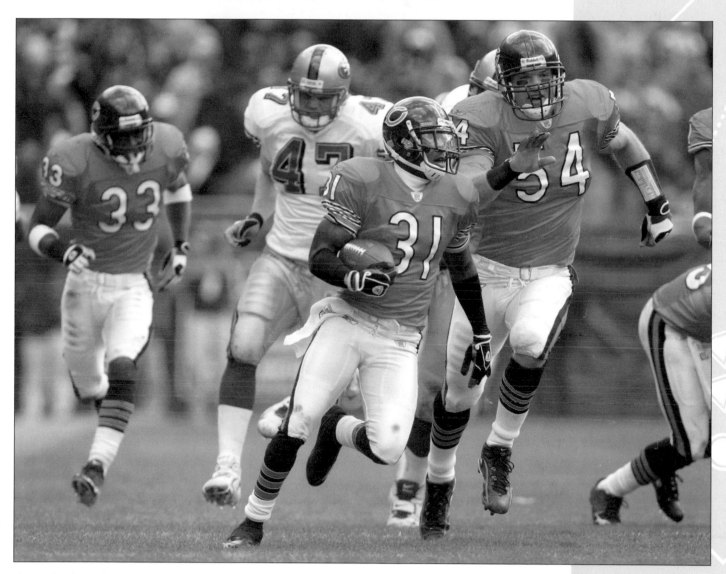

Cornerback Nathan Vasher runs a missed field goal back 108 yards for a touchdown against the 49ers on November 13, 2005. *(Photo courtesy of AP Images)*

The high-velocity winds on this day clocked steadily at 26 mph, drove players crazy, and played a key role in Vasher's monumental runback.

That didn't stop the Bears or 49ers from attempting field goals when game strategy called for it. Lovie Smith looked at Robbie Gould and said, "Do it." The 49ers looked at Joe Nedney and said, "Do it." Both kickers would need to earn their six-figure salaries under challenging conditions.

Nedney kicked a 30-yard field goal in the second quarter. Major achievement. Meanwhile, Gould missed a 39-yard field-goal attempt that seemed to be blown so far off course it might have landed in Oz. The second time the Bears tried a field goal, the wind was so strong—gusting up to an announced 47 mph—the snap was affected and Gould didn't even get the kick off.

Pieces of trash and paper whirled across the field in the wind throughout the game. No fun at all for kickers. This explains why the Bears had a man hanging around the end zone when the 49ers decided to brave the odds and try a long field goal at the end of the second quarter.

San Francisco was ahead 3–0 and the last few seconds of the first half were ticking away when the 49ers lined up for a what-the-heck 52-yard field-goal attempt by Nedney. There were three seconds on the clock when the ball was snapped. Vasher was in the game essentially as a potential kick blocker, but the Bears did not bring the full rush and at the last moment he dropped back.

Nedney's kick was short of the goal posts, stationed on the end line 110 yards from the opposite endzone. The ball wobbled in the air, Vasher tracked it down, hugged it to his body, and given that he had nothing to lose with no time left on the clock, ran it out of the end zone.

Before Vasher accelerated to full speed, he stumbled and nearly fell flat on his face. Surveying the array of 21 players spread out before him, Vasher saw a wall of Bears interference forming to his right. He cut right,

THAT'S A LONG WAY

Nathan Vasher's 108-yard return with a missed field-goal attempt is a play most fans have never seen before. At the time it was the undisputed record.

Any time fans see a play that travels longer than the actual 100-yard boundaries of the field they should consider themselves fortunate because they have witnessed an incredible rarity.

The NFL record for the longest kick-off return is 108 yards, established by Ellis Hobbs of the New England Patriots against the New York Jets on September 9, 2007.

The longest punt return in NFL history is 103 yards, returned by Robert Bailey of the Los Angeles Rams against the New Orleans Saints on October 23, 1994.

Some other very long Bears runs: Gale Sayers's 103-yard kickoff return against Pittsburgh on September 17, 1967; Don Bingham's 100-yard kickoff return against the Los Angeles Rams on November 18, 1956; and Johnny Bailey's 95-yard punt return against Kansas City on December 29, 1990.

GAME DETAILS

Bears 17 • 49ers 9

Location: Soldier Field, Chicago

Attendance: 57,747

Box Score:

49ers	0	3	3	3	**9**
Bears	0	7	0	10	**17**

Scoring:

SF Nedney 30-yard field goal

CHI Vasher 108-yard missed field-goal return (Gould PAT)

SF Nedney 34-yard field goal

CHI Peterson 7-yard run (Gould PAT)

SF Nedney 29-yard field goal

CHI Gould 37-yard field goal

> **W**e practice that play in special teams and it looks like a waste of time.
>
> —BEARS QUARTERBACK KYLE ORTON

watched as linebackers Brian Urlacher and Lance Briggs made big blocks, and he broke into the open.

He was unmolested during the long trip downfield, but the sound wave from 57,747 shocked and happy Bears fans' chants chased him into the distant end zone.

One reason the play worked so well, Vasher said, was the composition of the 49ers' lineup for the kick. Because it was a field-goal attempt rather than a punt, San Francisco's unit was heavy with lineman rather than speedier cornerbacks and receivers.

"There's no defensive backs or wide receivers," Vasher said. "I was out there with the big boys."

Translated, that meant nobody had the quickness to catch him.

The surprise touchdown gave Chicago a 7–3 halftime lead and was the game's turning point, while the distance of the return established a new record. Vasher's play would have stood out in any game, but it was more dramatic because the weather conditions made it so difficult for anybody to catch anything. There were only nine completed passes in the game and the Bears' main returner Bobby Wade fumbled three punts.

Vasher had a pretty good bead on the ball he caught and it was the biggest play in the 17–9 Bears victory. Nedney scored all of San Francisco's points on three good field goals. But the one he missed is the one that haunted the 49ers.

17

GOULD FLIES PAST SEATTLE

Kicker Beats Seahawks on Overtime Field Goal

The Bears finished the 2006 regular season 13–3. They dominated the NFC North Division, seemingly clinching a playoff spot the moment they laced up their cleats. Back at the beginning of October, the Bears crushed the Seattle Seahawks 37–6.

Except for a late-season loss to the Green Bay Packers, the Bears had looked superb all season, like the sure-thing NFC representative for the Super Bowl. But after an earned bye, the Bears' first playoff game against Seattle turned into a much tougher tussle than they expected.

Some Seahawks players who missed the regular season game had recovered from injuries and were back. Some Bears were injured. Game plans changed. What occurred on the field was no walk in Grant Park for the Bears this time. If the Bears took Seattle lightly, it was not obvious. Both teams played hard, played well, and scored often in the first half. Nobody wanted to go home for the season. There was a lot more at stake than there had been in the first encounter. Both teams hungered for a Super Bowl appearance.

The Bears worked hard to build a 21–14 lead at halftime, but the Seahawks readjusted and moved ahead 24–21 in the third quarter. As time grew precious, the Bears marched into Seattle territory in the fourth period and turned over responsibility to kicker Robbie Gould. Gould kicked a 41-yard field goal to tie the game at 24–24 and send it into overtime.

Gould had been the personnel find of the year in 2005. He had a good reputation coming out of Penn State, but the 6'0", 183-pound place-kicker was waived by the Baltimore Ravens. The Bears picked up Gould as a free agent and pitted him head-to-head in training camp against veteran Paul Edinger. Edinger was established and had done some good things for the Bears. Yet Gould won the competition and became Chicago's full-time place-kicker in 2005, sending Edinger to the waiver wire.

That season Gould hit 21 of 27 field-goal attempts, or 77.8 percent of his tries, and made 19 out of 20 extra points for a total of 82 points. He acquitted himself well and gained experience.

During the 2006 season, as the Bears became a dominant team, Gould grew with his teammates. He had more opportunities to kick and kicked better, whether in the normal course of a game or under pressure. In his 16 regular season games, Gould made 88.9 percent of his field goals and hit all 47 of his extra points. Gould's total of 143 points was one shy of the team record, and by the time the playoffs began he had been selected to the Pro Bowl.

And at the time Gould was called upon in the struggle against Seattle, he was on a hot streak. A few weeks earlier, a Gould kick in overtime defeated the Tampa Bay Buccaneers, and in the Bears' recent defeat of the Detroit Lions, Gould kicked three field goals in the fourth quarter to win it. The Bears had come to rely on Gould as money in the bank every time he flexed his toe muscles.

Gould—whose last name is pronounced "Gold"—calmly hit the tying field goal solidly to propel the Seattle playoff game into OT. Bears coach Lovie Smith did not have the slightest hesitation in calling upon Gould again in overtime, this time to try to bury the Seahawks.

The temperature was about 32 degrees and the wind was swirling in Soldier Field. When the snap came to holder Brad Maynard, the Bears' punter, he placed the ball on the turf, Gould took a couple of steps, swung his leg, and smacked the ball through the uprights.

Robbie Gould sent the Bears to the NFC Championship Game with this game-winning field goal against the Seahawks in 2007.

The 49-yard field goal was good and the Bears had a dramatic 27–24 victory that sent them to the next round of the playoffs. More than 62,000 fans in Soldier Field went bananas. Gould hugged Maynard, but for the most part showed less emotion than a winner on *American Idol*.

Reporters swarmed around Gould after the game, insisting that with the magnitude of the situation, with the game and the season riding on him, he must have been nervous.

Robbie Gould has proven to be a reliable, accurate kicker since being signed as a free agent by the Bears in 2005.

"Big Foot" is an NFL Kicker, not a Monster

In the early days of pro football, place-kicking was almost nonexistent. Kickoffs, extra points, and field goals were booted by using the drop kick, not by relying on holders or kicking tees. The ball was rounder in shape and bounces were truer.

Over time, as the passing game morphed into a serious weapon and became a more sophisticated part of the offense, the ball was streamlined for better throwing accuracy. For several decades kickers were not really specialists. They were all-around football players, members of the offensive or defensive units who kicked when the occasion arose in the flow of the game. This was a necessity when roster limits were 33 players. Some memorable kickers who were full-time position players include Lou Groza and Lou Michaels.

Eventually, roster sizes expanded and kicking specialists emerged. They were straight-ahead kickers who stood behind the ball, took one step, and booted. In the 1960s the first soccer-style kickers appeared in brothers Pete and Charlie Gogolak, who approached the ball from the side.

Initially hooted at as showboating, soccer-style football kicking took over because it offered superior accuracy and now no kicker uses the old style. Field-goal kickers became so good at hitting long tries that the league moved the goal posts back 10 yards from the goal line to the back of the end zone in 1974.

Illustrating the improvement in accuracy, while Bears kicker Roger Leclerc made all of his extra points in 1965, he hit just 11 of 26 field-goal attempts. In 2006, when Gould made all of his extra points, he also hit 32 of 36 field goals.

GAME DETAILS

Bears 27 • Seahawks 24

Location: Soldier Field, Chicago

Attendance: 62,184

Box Score:

> This game right here, it'll be an instant classic.
>
> —BEARS DEFENSIVE END ALEX BROWN

Seahawks	0	14	10	0	0	**24**
Bears	7	14	0	3	3	**27**

Scoring:

CHI Jones 9-yard run (Gould PAT)
SEA Burleson 16-yard pass from Hasselbeck (Brown PAT)
CHI Berrian 68-yard pass from Grossman (Gould PAT)
SEA Alexander 4-yard run (Brown PAT)
CHI Jones 7-yard run (Gould PAT)
SEA Brown 40-yard field goal
SEA Alexander 13-yard run (Brown PAT)
CHI Gould 41-yard field goal
CHI Gould 49-yard field goal

"No, I really don't get nervous," Gould said. "Once you start getting nervous, you end up missing kicks."

One of the job requirements of kickers is that they have ice water in their veins. Gould wasn't about to go hot-blooded on the Bears just because he did what he was hired to do.

Those with the most emotion committed to one side or the other always prefer blowouts so they don't have to worry about the outcome. Those who just love football root for close, suspense-filled games with many highlight plays. Those fans were the winners. Even the players understood they had participated in an extraordinary game.

Certainly, when he passes beyond the days of making heart-stopping plays, Gould will appreciate this one the most.

Kickers must believe they are going to make every kick or they start second-guessing themselves, start tinkering with their form, start missing, and find themselves out of a job. They are on the field for only a few seconds at a time, but frequently those are the most important seconds of the game. Kickers do not share practice routines with linemen or running backs, but they are counted on to come through when everything is on the line.

When quarterbacks were limbering up before the game throwing to wide receivers, when other players were stretching, Gould was measuring the wind velocity and direction at the base of the Soldier Field bowl. That's how he prepared for his kick three hours later.

Kickers earn their teammates' faith by performing. Many large men sweat and grunt to hold off other teams or to put the ball in position for a kicker to trot onto the field and make a winning score. They have to believe that he will make it and he has to make it to retain their belief. When Gould made the 49-yard kick that kept the Bears alive and kicking for another playoff game, someone asked Chicago defensive tackle Tank Johnson what he thought of Gould.

"He's gold," Johnson said.

16 TWO MIRACLES IN TWO WEEKS

Mike Brown Steals the Show

Not much was expected from the 2001 Chicago Bears. Preseason prognosticators eyed the team's 5–11 record of 2000 in the second year under coach Dick Jauron and figured 2001 would feature more of the same. The Bears had shown little evidence of a major turnaround, and no one put any particular faith in the good things shown in the preseason.

When the Bears bored America to tears in their opener, a 17–6 loss to the defending Super Bowl champion Baltimore Ravens, many Bears fans prepared themselves for a long season of mediocrity.

However, riding a defense keyed by Brian Urlacher at middle linebacker and solid players in all 11 slots, the Bears followed up their opening defeat by ripping off four straight victories without allowing more than 13 points in any game. Chicago's blood pressure and excitement levels rose simultaneously.

It has never taken much to jump-start a Bears bandwagon in Chicago, and the thousands of fans itching for a ride could have filled a dozen CTA trains. The next week, in a matchup against the San Francisco

49ers at Soldier Field, it appeared the joyride would be momentarily derailed as the clock ticked down with the Bears trailing.

The Bears fell behind early 14–0 and stayed behind, trailing by as many as 19 points. With the game heading into its final four minutes and Chicago still on the short end of a 31–16 score, spectators began making their way to the exits to beat the always-gnarly postgame traffic.

Wrong move. In rapid succession, receiver David Terrell caught touchdown passes of 13 yards and four yards from quarterback Shane Matthews, an extra point was kicked, and running back Anthony Thomas dove into the end zone to tie the score with a two-point conversion and send the game into overtime. The speed of the comeback was dizzying.

Those who stayed around to watch were delirious. And then things got better. The 49ers had possession in OT and quarterback Jeff Garcia scanned the horizon for his favorite receiver, the ever-dangerous Terrell Owens. Garcia whipped a pass to Owens, the ball hit his hands, and bounced directly to Mike Brown, the Bears'

Mike Brown snatched the ball off the hands of the 49ers' Terrell Owens and returned it 33 yards for the game-winning score in the Bears' 37–31 overtime victory. (*Photo courtesy of AP Images*)

5'10", 207-pound safety. Brown revved up the afterburners and rushed into the end zone with a 33-yard return that gave Chicago an unlikely 37–31 victory. The play came just 16 seconds into overtime, the quickest OT finish in league history. Talk about stealing a victory.

Brown, who dismissed the always talkative Owens as "probably the most arrogant player in the NFL," happily pinned the San Francisco loss on the receiver: "Terrell Owens was running a slant and he just dropped the ball. The ball went into the air and fell into my hands."

Some backstory played into Brown's comments. In a game played the year before, Owens caught a humiliating 20 passes against the Bears and Brown remembered San Francisco's reaction in the easy win.

"San Francisco didn't respect us at all," he said. "You could just tell it by what they were saying in the papers and in interviews. We had the belief and the will to win the game."

It was difficult to measure who was more stunned by the happenings, the joyous Bears or the discouraged 49ers.

Owens, who did have six catches on this day, was still shaking his head after the game.

"We shouldn't have let them back in the game," Owens said. "This is one that got away from us."

It was a huge victory for a Bears team trying to establish itself. The comeback was the largest margin Chicago had overcome since 1987, and by putting a fifth straight win on the board the team's confidence escalated. And the triumph in the face of defeat also scored bonus points with the fans. The tradition of pregame tailgating in Soldier Field parking lots had slumped in recent years right along with the team's on-field performance. But now it was back in full force. Cars lined up to get into the parking areas hours before kickoff. Fans wanted to revel in being on the scene, grilling their brats, and toasting the team for as long as they could on a home Sunday.

When legal betting on the Super Bowl is offered in Las Vegas, the combinations of what those wagering can choose to put their money on is boggling. There are about 300 betting choices beyond just picking a point spread for a winner and loser. But it's a guarantee that no one in Las Vegas had the foresight to offer a betting proposition on the Bears–Cleveland Browns game the next week and whether or not Mike Brown would again intercept a pass for a touchdown in overtime to win the game. Those odds could only have been measured in numbers dealing with mileage between planets.

Just like the 49ers game, the Bears were playing at Soldier Field. Once again, the Bears fell behind in the game. It was another hopeless case. The Bears trailed 21–7 at the end of the third quarter. Once again, the faithless among the faithful started abandoning the stadium in the fourth quarter as the diminishment of the game clock seemed to outpace the probability of the Bears scoring.

Wrong again. If the departed fans were listening to the finish on their car radios they likely bashed their heads against the steering wheel in frustration because of what they were missing. It was a twice-offered lesson—don't walk out on these Bears before the final gun.

If anything, the Bears' comeback against the Browns was even more unbelievable than their stunner against the Niners. The Bears invested an entire four minutes in obtaining a tie. This time the Bears scored

A Tie is Like Kissing Your Sister

The Bears benefited from the NFL's sudden-death overtime rules where the first team that puts any kind of points on the scoreboard wins the game.

Overtime rules are dramatically different in high school and college football. Although both use different plans to carry out overtime, each team is guaranteed at least one possession, so even if a team falls behind by a touchdown and extra point, it can still rally to tie and keep the game going. In the NFL, once a team scores the game is over—not even extra points are attempted.

Ties were once a much larger part of the game in the NFL. During the Bears' 1963 regular season leading up to the championship, the team experienced two ties. In 1932, the year the Bears won the "Tom Thumb Game" playing the championship event indoors, they posted the strangest record in team history. The Bears finished 7–1–6. That's six ties.

GAME DETAILS

Bears 27 • Browns 21

Location: Soldier Field, Chicago

Attendance: 66,944

We can't keep doing this. We're giving people heart attacks.

—MIKE BROWN

Box Score:

Browns	7	0	14	0	0	**21**
Bears	0	7	0	14	6	**27**

Scoring:

CLE Brown 25-yard fumble return (Dawson PAT)

CHI Thomas 3-yard run (Edinger PAT)

CLE Sellers 3-yard pass from Couch (Dawson PAT)

CLE Johnson 55-yard pass from Couch (Dawson PAT)

CHI Booker 9-yard pass from Matthews (Edinger PAT)

CHI Allen 34-yard pass from Matthews (Edinger PAT)

CHI Brown 16-yard interception return

GAME DETAILS

Bears 34 • 49ers 31

Location: Soldier Field, Chicago

Attendance: 63,265

To lose a game like that, this is a shock.

—JEFF GARCIA

Box Score:

49ers	14	0	14	3	0	**31**
Bears	0	9	7	15	6	**34**

Scoring:

SF Peterson 26-yard fumble return (Cortez PAT)

SF Swift 1-yard pass from Garcia (Cortez PAT)

CHI Safety, punt snap out of end zone

CHI Shelton 3-yard pass from Matthews (Edinger PAT)

SF Hearst 60-yard pass from Garcia (Cortez PAT)

SF Bronson 97-yard interception return (Cortez PAT)

CHI Thomas 19-yard run (Edinger PAT)

SF Cortez 40-yard field goal

CHI Terrell 13-yard pass from Matthews (Edinger PAT)

CHI Terrell 4-yard pass from Matthews (Thomas run)

CHI Brown 33-yard interception return

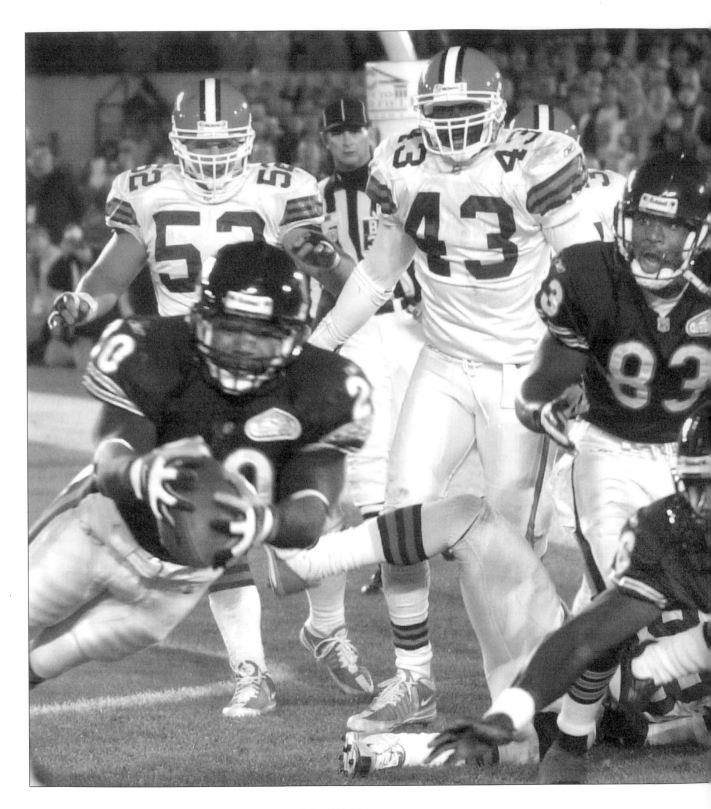

two touchdowns in the final 28 seconds of the fourth quarter to force overtime.

The Bears trailed 21–7 when they took possession of the ball on their own 20-yard line with 1:52 to play. Matthews, subbing for the injured Jim Miller, was at the controls again. He completed pass after pass, culminating with a nine-yarder to Marty Booker for a touchdown with 28 seconds left.

Okay. Nice drive. Showing no quit was cool. Still, game over, right? Nope. Paul Edinger booted an onside kick recovered by Bobbie Howard at the Cleveland 47. Tiny ray of hope. The Bears had just about half a field to cover in less than half a minute.

Two short passes to running back James Allen only brought the Bears to the 34-yard line with time for one last play. Nothing but a Hail Mary into the end zone had a chance to pay off. The clock ticked down to :00 by the time Matthews threw into a crowd. The ball was tipped by the Browns' Percy Ellsworth in the free-for-all; Allen was nearby and dove as the pigskin began fluttering to the ground and he caught it for the touchdown to tie the game.

"Shane threw the ball where he was supposed to," Jauron said, "but you've got to have your stars lined up and somebody looking out for you to have it bounce the way it did."

In overtime, the Browns had a chance to regroup and retaliate. Quarterback Tim Couch faded back, looking for room to make a completion. He threw. A big hand belonging to Bears defensive end Bryan Robinson shot up in the air and deflected the pass.

Where did it land? Improbably into the arms of Mike Brown. This time Brown returned the interception 16 yards for the game-winning touchdown. It was an astounding finish and thoroughly unreal given that almost the exact same circumstances prevailed the week before.

Booker didn't have to worry too much about it all happening again. A once-in-a-lifetime finish had already become a twice-in-a-lifetime finish. The Bears apparently used up their miracle quota for quite some time.

James Allen's Hail Mary catch set up another game-winning, overtime score by teammate Mike Brown.
(Photo courtesy of AP Images)

December 8, 1940

The Greatest NFL Massacre of All Time

Bears 73–0!

Given that the Bears demolished the Washington Redskins 73–0 in the 1940 NFL Championship Game, it is difficult to highlight one play that made a difference. The result, the greatest blowout in the history of the National Football League, brings to mind many stereotypical jokes.

The turning point was when the Bears showed up.

The turning point was when the teams came out of the locker room.

The turning point was the kickoff.

In this case, all three were true, not just Bob Hope–type jokes.

The winning margin was doubly surprising because the Bears and Redskins were fierce rivals in the 1940s and the rivalry was not nearly as one-sided as the score of this game indicated.

Perhaps the true turning point was something that occurred well before the game began. During the regular season, only a few weeks beforehand, the Redskins defeated the Bears 7–3. Not content merely to absorb the hardfought victory, Washington owner George Preston Marshall gloated and taunted the Bears. Marshall described the

Bears as "a team that folds under pressure in the second half against a good team." A win is a win is a win, but it wasn't as if the Skins' 7–3 victory was a rout.

George Halas and Marshall had worked together on various NFL committees and forged programs they felt were for the betterment of the league, but their useful business relationship frayed as the intensity of the rivalry increased. After Marshall's inflammatory statement and others like it appeared in Washington, D.C., newspapers, Halas posted the clips on the bulletin board in the Bears' locker room. Publicly Halas resented the remarks and said he wouldn't be surprised if the Bears won big; privately he told his 33 players they comprised the best football team he had ever seen.

Halas's approach worked. The Bears were angry going into the 1940 Championship Game. They believed they were the best team in the world, just as Halas said, and the earlier loss to Washington wounded their pride. Then to have the result rubbed in by the opposing organization infuriated them. The title match was truly a revenge game for Chicago.

We beat a good football team.
—SID LUCKMAN

The contest was played at Griffith Stadium in D.C., on a sunny 39-degree afternoon before 36,034 Redskin fans. The Bears won the coin toss (another possible turning point) and elected to receive the kickoff. The Bears started the series on their own 25-yard line and promptly charged down the field. On second down, Bill Osmanski took a handoff from Sid Luckman, dashed around left end, and took the ball 68 yards to the house. A Jack Manders extra point made it 7–0.

That may well have been the play of the game right there, the big-play touchdown giving the Bears the lead they never relinquished in a shutout victory. It was a sign of superiority, but the Redskins did not give up immediately.

Washington, led by the incredible Sammy Baugh, the best all-around player in the game, hung around for a little while longer. The Redskins brought the kickoff back 51 yards and began their own drive at the Bears' 39-yard line. On the fifth play, Baugh spotted receiver Charley Malone wide open at the 5-yard line. He fired a pass only to see Malone drop the pass (Malone said later he lost it in the sun). A 32-yard field-goal attempt missed. That was the closest the Redskins came to scoring all day, and if Malone had been able to lug the ball into the end zone, the score might have been tied 7–7.

After the game a subdued Baugh was asked if things might have been different if Malone had hung onto the pass and knotted the game at that moment.

The Redskins' Jimmy Johnston is swarmed by Bears defenders during Chicago's 73–0 blowout victory in the 1940 NFL Championship Game. *(Photo courtesy of AP Images)*

"If Charley had caught the ball, the final score would have been 73–7," Baugh glumly replied.

After that double Redskins miscue of a dropped pass and missed field goal, it was open season on Washington. The Bears came right back and upped the score to 14–0 on a one-yard Sid Luckman quarterback sneak. The next series ended with a Baugh punt

The scoreboard at Griffith Stadium in Washington, D.C., illustrates the Bears' dominance over the Redskins in 1940. *(Photo courtesy of AP Images)*

A FLUKE

There is no doubt that the stunning 73–0 result was an anomaly. Given how closely matched the teams were, there was every likelihood the Redskins would have won that day.

Many years later, Washington quarterback Sammy Baugh said he had heard rumors that some members of the Redskins had not played with their full passion and heart, implying they had conspired to throw the game, but the suggestion was quickly dismissed.

As good as the Redskins were, the Bears were the best team of the era. The team won another championship, easing past the Giants in 1941, and was favored to make it three in a row in 1942. The Bears finished the regular season 11–0.

Much has been made of the dearth of undefeated NFL champions. The Miami Dolphins finished 17–0 in 1972 and the zero at the end of their record was unique. In 2008 the New England Patriots entered the Super Bowl with an 18–0 record, expecting to join the Dolphins in the undefeated ranks. But they lost to the Giants in Super Bowl XLII.

The same disappointment befell the Bears of 1942. The opponent on that cold December day was the Washington Redskins, featuring many of the same players who faced the Bears in 1940. This time, with the backdrop of the worst beating in league history casting a shadow, the Redskins upended the Bears 14–6. No three-peat.

GAME DETAILS

Bears 73 • Redskins 0

Location: Griffith Stadium, Washington, D.C.

Attendance: 36,034

The memory of a lifetime. It was like a miracle.

—SID LUCKMAN

Box Score:

Bears	21	7	26	19	**73**
Redskins	0	0	0	0	**0**

Scoring:

CHI Osmanski 68-yard run (Manders PAT)

CHI Luckman 1-yard run (Snyder PAT)

CHI Maniaci 42-yard run (Martinovich PAT)

CHI Kavanaugh 30-yard pass from Luckman (Snyder PAT)

CHI Pool 15-yard interception return (Plasman PAT)

CHI Nolting 7-yard run (PAT failed)

CHI McAfee 35-yard interception return (Snyder PAT)

CHI Turner 24-yard interception return (PAT blocked)

CHI Clark 44-yard run (PAT failed)

CHI Famiglietti 2-yard run (Maniaci pass from Sherman)

CHI Clark 1-yard run (PAT failed)

being partially blocked. The Bears obtained excellent field position at the Washington 42, and on the first play of the possession, running back Joe Maniaci tucked the ball under his arm and rambled 42 yards for another score. It was 21–0 and the Redskins were dead with a long, long afternoon ahead of them.

The Bears were in no mood to let up after being verbally assaulted by the Redskins' owner. And whatever they did turned to gold all game long.

Possession after possession, the Bears scored. They scored through the air and they scored on the ground. They scored with the first string and they scored with the subs. For one day, the Bears did everything right and the Redskins did everything wrong.

The most remarkable part of the entire blowout was that the Redskins weren't exactly pushovers. Washington was led by a Hall of Fame player like Baugh who was an All-Pro quarterback, defensive back, and punter. The Bears did not beat the last-place team by 73 points. The Bears did not beat a team decimated by injuries

by 73 points. The Bears did not even have home field advantage in the game. However the stars were aligned that day; the brightest constellation was Ursa Major, also known as The Great Bear.

As the game wore on and the Bears racked up touchdowns about as fast as statisticians could count—11 in all—officials noted that they were running out of footballs. In those days, there was no net behind the goal posts to catch extra points booted and the balls were not returned by spectators. The refs asked Halas to run or pass for extra points if the Bears were going to be so inhospitable as to keep scoring touchdowns.

The Bears did score more touchdowns and the final two extra-point efforts came on passes.

When he was 82, someone asked George Halas what his best memory of a lifetime in pro football was. He said, "The 73–to–nothing."

There has never been another day like it in pro football history.

 14 Mr. Defense Takes the Offensive

Dick Butkus Score Wins Game

More than 30 years after his retirement, Dick Butkus retains the image as one of the toughest men in the history of professional football.

When a player was tackled by Butkus, he knew it. When Butkus plowed a player in the ribs, the pain was felt for days. Butkus was an All-Pro middle linebacker who was a Mack truck in human form. During his playing days for the Bears between 1965 and 1973, Butkus measured in at 6'3" and 245 pounds, yet he seemed larger, more along the lines of a skyscraper on feet.

If pro football is legalized mayhem, then Butkus was the consummate hitman. Butkus was a two-time All-American at the University of Illinois, a first-round pick of the Bears in the 1965 draft, and a star from the moment he set foot on a pro football field. During his career as a linebacker he intercepted 22 passes and recovered 27 fumbles. He probably caused half of them by merely roaring at the ball carrier and scaring him half to death. NFL runners of the period would probably have been happier to come upon a grizzly bear in the woods than they were bumping into Butkus in the middle of the field. Butkus was selected for participation in eight straight Pro Bowls.

Butkus was supremely skilled, fast, and strong, and he enhanced his aura of dominance by also talking a big game. He was thorough in his methodology of intimidation, making sure to let opponents know he was a heat-seeking missile who would find them and catch them, allowing that he didn't much care just how hard he hit a runner in a no-mercy sport. *The San Diego Union-Tribune* once ran a headline reading, "Never Met Man He Didn't Hate." The first comment from Butkus, speaking on the telephone to the writer, read, "I don't personally like anybody."

Butkus did not want anyone thinking they could take advantage of him on the field just because he was their friend off the field. He couldn't be a selective enforcer or opponents would tend to think he was all bark and no bite. Butkus sank his teeth in.

All of which made it more unusual, more surprising, and more satisfying for Butkus when he won a game for the Bears by doing something that didn't involve delivering a forearm shiver or plowing into

Legendary for his play on defense, linebacker Dick Butkus won a game for the Bears in 1971 with his play on offense.

THE DICK BUTKUS JITTERBUG

Chicago Bears middle linebacker Dick Butkus's assignment when he got into the game was usually very simple: he was supposed to clobber the ball carrier or sack the quarterback. Sometimes, Butkus was used on special teams, and against the Washington Redskins he was in at blocking back for an extra-point attempt in a 15–15 game. Quarterback Bobby Douglass, kicker Mac Percival's holder, couldn't handle the snap. The ball squirted loose and Douglass scooped it up. Meanwhile, as Douglass rolled left, Butkus ran for the end zone, where he was open to catch a 30-yard pass for the game-winning extra point.

> **I** never scored on a screwier play.
>
> —DICK BUTKUS

a quarterback: Butkus's big play actually took place on offense.

The Bears met the Washington Redskins before 55,049 witnesses during the team's first season at Soldier Field. This was the era when Chicago relied on Bobby Douglass, perhaps the greatest running quarterback of all time, as its field general. Douglass, never perceived as a master of the two-minute drill, was whipping the ball downfield play after play in an attempt to bring his team back. Mac Percival had kicked a 42-yard field goal to trim Washington's margin from 15–3 to 15–6, then added a nine-yard field goal to bring the Bears within a score. Just put up a touchdown for the tie and the game could be won on a chip shot extra point.

The Bears got the ball on their own 40-yard line and this time Douglass was up to the assignment of moving the chains fast. His first pass found end Jim Seymour cutting across the middle for a gain of 20 yards and a first down at the Washington 40.

On the next play, running back Cyril Pinder, who played sparingly in two seasons with the Bears, broke loose and ran 40 yards into the end zone.

That made for a tie game, 15–15, just the circumstances the Bears had hoped to arrange. Let Mac kick the extra point and the Bears would escape with a close one.

Game Details

Bears 16 • Redskins 15

Location: Soldier Field, Chicago

Attendance: 55,049

I think the last time I caught a pass for a point was in high school.

—DICK BUTKUS

Box Score:

Redskins	6	6	3	0	**15**	
Bears	0	3	3	10	**16**	

Scoring:

WAS Knight 30-yard field goal

WAS Knight 12-yard field goal

CHI Percival 15-yard field goal

WAS Knight 37-yard field goal

WAS Knight 9-yard field goal

WAS Knight 27-yard field goal

CHI Percival 42-yard field goal

CHI Percival 9-yard field goal

CHI Pinder 40-yard run (Butkus pass from Douglass)

What seemed likely to be a win quickly became more complicated. In those days, while the American Football League had adopted the two-point conversion before the merger a year earlier, the NFL still disdained that option. Although an NFL team would be rewarded for running or passing the ball into the end zone, it would receive just a single point. But no one was thinking about that rule. The kick for one point was good enough.

Butkus was inserted into the game to perform as a blocking back. The sure-thing play came unglued immediately. The snap to Douglass as the holder for Percival went awry. Douglass got control of the ball and began scrambling as the Redskins' rush closed in. As Douglass desperately searched for a solution to his predicament, Butkus drifted into the end zone.

"When the play was broken, I knew I was an eligible receiver, so I started for the end zone," Butkus said.

Butkus stood in the end zone and jumped up and down, waving his arms as if it was a schoolyard game. Finally, Douglass, under pressure, saw him and heaved the ball. It was a 30-yard extra-point pass and Butkus had to dive to grab it and twist to stay in bounds. He held on to the ball, and the Bears held on to win 16–15.

The Bears celebrated the unlikely play and Butkus greeted sportswriters after the game with a big smile on his face. In the same way pitchers seem to relish getting a base hit because nobody expects it of them, Butkus took special pleasure in his offensive contribution.

No one, however, suggested that Butkus should be shifted to wide receiver full-time to make his living catching balls instead of catching ball carriers.

13 TWO SNEAKS ALL THEY NEED

Bill Wade Leads Bears to 1963 Title

Conventional wisdom said the Giants had too much offensive firepower for the Bears' stingy defense in the 1963 NFL title game. Prognosticators figured that Y.A. Tittle would find an open Del Shofner for touchdown passes more often than the Bears would find ways to stop him.

Few would have guessed that the star quarterback of the day would be Bill Wade, not New York's Tittle, who had thrown a record 36 touchdown passes during the regular season and was in the midst of a Hall of Fame career.

The Bears advanced to the NFL Championship Game for the first time since 1956 and they were looking for their first title since 1946. That was a very long drought for George Halas and Chicago fans. This was a veteran Bears team with many savvy players who put in their time going back to the mid-1950s. Linebackers Bill George and Joe Fortunato, lineman Stan

Jones, fullback Rick Casares, and defensive back Richie Petitbon were hard-nosed guys hungry to put championship rings on their fingers. They were supplemented by a young Mike Ditka and Wade, who had spent most of his career with the Los Angeles Rams. Meanwhile, they were aware that Vince Lombardi was building something special, that he had a possible dynasty in the making in Green Bay, so this was the time to grab for it all. As many key performers approached athletic middle age, they had to wonder if there would ever be a second chance to get back to the top of the mountain.

The temperature at Wrigley Field was 11 degrees as kickoff approached. Many of the 45,801 fans hunkered down in blankets. The players were too keyed up to worry about the cold.

The Bears were stopped on their first possession and punted to the Giants. Tittle

> **I** would have to say the defense did its job.
>
> — JOE FORTUNATO ON INTERCEPTING FIVE NEW YORK PASSES

Doug Atkins stops the Giants' Joe Morrison during the 1963 NFL Championship Game, and Bill Wade's two quarterback sneaks provided all the offense the Bears would need.

went to work, guiding New York down the field on a mix of runs and passes. On the seventh play of the drive, Tittle whipped a pass to Frank Gifford in the end zone for a touchdown. The extra point made it 7–0. This is what the experts envisioned.

But the pattern changed. The heavy Bears pass rush forced Tittle to hurry his throws and the Chicago secondary and linebackers were waiting for him, poised to seize upon any mistake. Near the end of the first quarter, Bears linebacker Larry Morris picked off a pass and returned it 61 yards. That gave Chicago a first-and-goal on the 5-yard line. After a Ronnie Bull rush, Wade kept the ball and plunged two yards into the end zone for the tying touchdown. The extra point was good to make it 7–7.

There was nothing fancy about Wade's play. It was one of football's fundamental plays: the quarterback puts his head down and pushes forward behind a wall of blockers. Simple. It was like a layup in basketball.

Wade, who attended Vanderbilt and lives in Nashville, Tennessee, said recently that was a typical call for the Bears in those circumstances.

"I called the quarterback sneaks when we were two or three yards away from the goal line," Wade said. "Usually, the 1-yard line. Mike Pyle [center] and Ted Karras [right guard] were excellent blockers. They opened up a big hole."

Wade said that shortly before the title game, he had watched another quarterback fumble a handoff to a halfback near the goal line and "that cost them the game. So I thought there was no need. I didn't want to have that happen." Keeping the ball worked out fine and minimized any mixups.

The Giants came back in the second quarter and drove to the Bears' 6-yard line. On fourth down, Don Chandler booted a 13-yard field goal for a 10–7 New York lead. The score stayed that way, frozen on the scoreboard the way spectators froze in their seats, until near the end of the third quarter.

A Tittle screen pass was picked off by defensive end Ed O'Bradovich, who ran it back to the Giants' 14-yard line. A Wade pass to Joe Marconi, a Ronnie Bull run, and a 12-yard pass to Ditka set the Bears up on the 1-yard line. The Giants stopped the first try, but Wade's next quarterback sneak paid off. The one-yard touchdown gave Chicago a 14–10 lead.

Two quarterback sneaks, two touchdowns.

That was the end of the scoring. Chicago's defense, as it turned out, could trump New York's offense. It was an awful day for the hotly chased Tittle. The Bears intercepted five passes. The Giants' quarterback injured his left knee against the Bears' pash rush in the first quarter, then was hit a second time by Morris and was forced to leave the game. Tittle returned for the second half, but the injury affected his accuracy. New York attempted 30 passes, but gained just 140 yards through the air.

TAKE THAT, PACK

The 1963 Bears were heavy on veterans who had played on good teams but had yet to win a world championship. The closest many of the long-time players had come was losing 47–7 to the New York Giants in the 1956 title game.

The unexpected rise of the Green Bay Packers under Vince Lombardi caught the Bears off balance. Suddenly the rivals to the north, featuring Paul Hornung, Jim Taylor, Bart Starr, Willie Davis, Herb Adderley, and others moved into a position of dominance. From a 1–10 record only a few seasons before, Lombardi lifted the Packers into a championship team, winning the league crown in 1961 and 1962.

It was the Packers' time and it seemed as if the Bears' championship window had closed. But in 1963 the Bears interrupted the Packers' dynasty—barely. The Bears finished 11–1–2 during the regular season and the Packers finished 11–2–1.

Under the playoff system in place at the time— winner of the Western Division meeting the winner of the Eastern Division—that meant the Bears advanced to play the New York Giants and the Packers went home.

Game Details

Bears 14 • Giants 10

Location: Wrigley Field, Chicago

Attendance: 45,801

Box Score:

Giants	7	3	0	0	**10**
Bears	7	0	7	0	**14**

Scoring:
NY Gifford 14-yard pass from Tittle (Chandler PAT)
CHI Wade 2-yard run (Jencks PAT)

NY Chandler 13-yard field goal
CHI Wade 1-yard run (Jencks PAT)

> **R**ight up the middle. That was the quickest way to get to the goal line.
> —BILL WADE

To illustrate how a conservative offense was aided by a spectacular defense using an unusual five-man front, the Bears gave the game ball to defensive coordinator George Allen.

On a day when Wade only completed 10 of 28 passes for 129 yards through the air, the littlest things he did—namely hanging onto the ball and pushing a few feet across the goal line—were the most important. Wade's safety-first attitude was in precise tune with Halas.

Years later Patrick McCaskey, a member of the Bears' board of directors, spoke of attending games with Halas, his grandfather, after the older man retired from coaching. The simple quarterback sneak, McCaskey said, was his grandfather's favorite offensive call.

"He always said the quarterback sneak was the greatest play in football," McCaskey said. "When he was retired from coaching he would stand up all of the time and yell for the coach to call it."

Wade's two successful executions of the quarterback keeper ranked right at the top of Halas's favorite plays and favorite memories, McCaskey said.

Wade was pleased and surprised to hear that.

"I didn't know I was in that category," Wade said.

Wade, always considered one of the friendliest and most upbeat among players from the championship team, stayed with the Bears through the 1966 season, then retired with 124 touchdown passes and a 54.3 percent completion percentage. Later in life he endured some hardships. A son in his late 20s was killed and as he aged into his 70s, Wade lost his sight.

By the time the 1963 Bears gathered for a 25th reunion in 1988, Wade had endured three knee operations. But that didn't seem to bother him much.

"So what?" Wade said. "I wish I could play today."

The memories of that championship season were that sweet. And who would have imagined that two of the most important plays would have covered a grand total of three yards.

12

AN NFL RUSHING RECORD FOR PAYTON

275 Yards in a Single Game

For most of his 13-season career with the Chicago Bears, Walter Payton was virtually unstoppable coming out of the backfield. But on one day Payton truly was unstoppable on just about every carry. Call it inevitability. Call it alignment of the stars. Whatever the case, the perfect storm descended on the Minnesota Vikings' heads.

By the time Payton stopped running in a hard-fought 10–7 victory over the Vikings at Soldier Field, he had accumulated 275 yards, a new single-game NFL rushing record. Payton barely eclipsed the old mark of 273 yards, set by O.J. Simpson about a year earlier. And his performance set a new Bears record, overwhelming the old one-game record of 205 yards set by Gale Sayers in 1968, a mark Payton had previously tied.

It took 40 rushing attempts for Payton to establish the record on a very busy day out of the Bears' backfield when no other offensive weapon was working. It was a gritty between-the-tackles encounter and the Bears needed every one of Payton's hard-fought yards to win the game. Play calling was affected by a strong wind, with defenders on both sides geared up to stop the run. But nothing Minnesota tried stopped Payton.

Payton gained renown as a superb runner at Jackson State, the Division I-AA school with a proud heritage but not a team that saw action on television or was recognized much by the casual fan. The Bears noticed Payton's ability, however, and made him their number one draft pick in 1975. During Payton's lengthy career with the Bears—from the earliest years when he was often the only offensive option like he was against Minnesota, to the end when he was the crown jewel on a Super Bowl champion—he was a stalwart. Payton was selected to play in nine Pro Bowls, held 16

> **I** just wanted to get that game over with.
> —WALTER PAYTON

Walter Payton set an NFL record with 275 yards rushing in the Bears' 10–7 victory over the Vikings on November 20, 1977. *(Photo courtesy of WireImages)*

league records and 27 Bears records when he retired (including most yards rushing ever with 16,726), and was voted into the Pro Football Hall of Fame.

Teammates and coaches considered Payton the complete football player. Besides his uncanny instincts to find holes when rushing, he had good hands and caught 492 passes during his career. What gained Payton even more admiration was his willingness to risk his body making hard-hitting blocks for teammates. Payton's overall skills led coach Mike Ditka to call him the best football player he had ever seen. Not the best ground gainer. The best football player, period.

In 1977 under head coach Jack Pardee, the Bears were on their way back from a terrible stretch of losing seasons. Still, there were days when all they had going for them was Payton. In the days leading up to the Vikings game, Payton was more like a sick bear cub than a punishing runner. He had a fever, felt nauseous, and his availability was in question. But on game day Payton decided he might be strong enough to give it a go.

Once the adrenaline started flowing Payton apparently forgot he was sick, and once his legs started eating up chunks of yardage, the Bears forgot they had any other plays to call. Quarterback Bob Avellini threw just seven times in the game. Coaches grew increasingly skittish about relying on the passing game as the day went on because of high winds. Several passes hung in the air and some were as wobbly as dying waterfowl twisting in the breeze after being shot out of the sky.

For a guy who carried the offensive load while under the weather, Payton was remarkably fresh at the end of his day. He had no idea how many times he toted the ball.

"Forty?" he said when informed. "It felt like about 20."

Who can explain the things elite athletes do when even they are surprised by the results?

Another offshoot of the big day was Payton setting a new team single-season record of 1,404 yards rushing with four games still remaining.

The play that pushed a great day into the realm of record-threatening day was a 58-yard run in the fourth quarter, on Payton's 38th carry of the game. That was also a huge play in the context of the contest. The Bears had a first-and-goal on the Minnesota 9-yard line. Fullback Robin Earl ran for one yard. Payton moved the ball another three yards and then Avellini lost a yard.

GOOD COMPANY

The NFL is heavily populated with good running backs. At any given time there are also a half dozen or so true superstar running backs. Yet for all of those who pass through NFL rosters and even achieve excellence for a time, only a few retain the health and ability to run for more than 1,000 yards season after season.

Two things that set Walter Payton apart were his longevity and durability. And for an NFL running back to achieve long-term greatness, move up on the lifetime statistical lists, and become a candidate for the Hall of Fame, those traits are nearly as important as speed and elusiveness.

Many contend that Cleveland Browns fullback Jim Brown, who played during the 1950s and 1960s, was the greatest running back and perhaps the greatest football player of all time. The two halfbacks that Payton is most frequently compared to in accomplishments and ability are Barry Sanders, who played his entire career with the Detroit Lions and also retired young, and Emmitt Smith, who mainly performed for the Dallas Cowboys. Smith surpassed Payton as the all-time league yards leader in 2002.

GAME DETAILS

Bears 10 • Vikings 7

Location: Soldier Field, Chicago

Attendance: 49,563

Box Score:

Vikings	0	0	7	0	**7**
Bears	0	10	0	0	**10**

Scoring:

CHI Payton 1-yard run (Thomas PAT)

CHI Thomas 37-yard field goal

MIN Blair 10-yard blocked punt return (Cox PAT)

> **W**hat I remember best about that game was seeing the back of Walter's jersey.
>
> —TED ALBRECHT

Avellini jogged off the field, assuming the Bears' next move was to try a chip shot field goal. But Pardee sent him back onto the field with instructions to give the ball to Payton on a sweep.

Payton broke the record on a fourth-down, four-yard sweep around right end. The play brought the Bears to the Minnesota 2-yard line and despite the failure to score, on the exchange of possession it pinned the Vikings so deep in their own territory with just 2:12 to go, they couldn't come back.

Pardee later said he called the handoff to Payton rather than attempting a field goal because he figured the runner might get the touchdown from the 6-yard line, and if he did not, the Vikings couldn't possibly advance 98 yards in time to win. Pardee said he didn't even know Payton was close to setting a record until after the game. Payton got the record, was stopped at the two, and the Vikings stalled against the wind, sealing the Bears' victory.

Payton was rather matter-of-fact about setting the record, reacting much the way Sayers did after his six-touchdown game. He issued comments pretty much saying he was only doing his job. Twenty years later, when Payton recounted the game, his memory was clouded by how lousy he truly felt that day. Having the flu was always going to be intertwined with his top rushing showing.

"I had the flu," Payton said. "I was throwing up. I didn't care about 275 yards."

But Bears tackle Ted Albrecht, taking pride in the accomplishment as only a helping-hand lineman can, had a wonderful observation on the way the game unfolded. Time and again Albrecht threw his block and got to watch Payton run away. Albrecht recognized the impact of the performance immediately, proclaiming it a "historical day."

Regardless of where one was watching—from the line of scrimmage, the Bears' sideline, or the Soldier Field stands—watching the back of Payton's jersey running over the horizon was indeed the view of the game.

January 26, 1986

FRIDGE'S SUPER BOWL PLUNGE

The Bears Are Super Champs

One thing that William Perry, also known as "The Refrigerator," was not going to endorse was body-shaping, muscle-toning equipment.

Cupcakes, maybe.

Hot dogs, you bet.

Pizza with everything on it, makes sense.

A happy-go-lucky, star-of-the-moment, the Bears' number one draft pick was an All-American defensive tackle out of Clemson who tipped the scales at...at...at something around 300 pounds.

Whereas now every team in the National Football League easily has a dozen offensive or defensive linemen on the roster who exceed 300 pounds, more than 20 years ago the rotund player was still uncommon. And of those, most are somewhat anonymous outside of their own households or their own playing city.

What set the 6'2" Perry apart from the start was his geniality, his outgoing nature, and his ability to make a joke and take a joke. He was easy to identify and easy to fall in love with. He seemed like a great big teddy bear that needed a hug. On a team that was serious about its business, especially on the defensive side of the ball with no-nonsense coordinator Buddy Ryan setting the destruction-mode tone, Perry stuck out.

Ryan was presiding over a potentially record-setting defense, a defense that felt it had to do more than take care of 50 percent of the team's business for it to succeed. There was frivolity among the personalities that were as strong as their biceps, but Ryan's harsh comments, prodding remarks, and sarcasm left little room for whimsical humor. And there was little doubt that Ryan considered Perry more of a clown than a serious contender for a regular spot on his defensive line.

The fact that Ryan seemed opposed to Perry played a role in the rookie eventually finding his way into the offensive playbook. Head coach Mike Ditka and Ryan did not exactly interact like blood brothers. There seemed to be resentment between them most of the time and it ended up boiling over before the end of the season. Ditka decided that if Ryan wasn't going to use Perry on defense, he might, on occasion, borrow him for the offense.

William Perry's touchdown plunge is perhaps the most memorable moment from the Bears' 46–10 demolition of the New England Patriots in Super Bowl XX.

Six weeks into the season the Bears played against the defending Super Bowl champion San Francisco 49ers. The year before the 49ers ended the Bears' season with a 23–0 thrashing in the playoffs. It was a humbling game for a team with high hopes. During that game San Francisco coach Bill Walsh inserted guard Guy McIntyre into his backfield as a fullback. The Bears resented it, thinking Walsh was making fun of them and trying to humiliate them.

When the regular season matchup in San Francisco rolled around the following October, the Bears were the superior team on their way to a 26–10 victory. On the final series of the game, Ditka brought The Fridge in to play fullback and the big man carried the ball twice, gaining four yards. A 300-pounder in the backfield carrying the ball. What will they think of next? Go, Fridge, go.

Bears players went along with the lightheartedness that engulfed Perry and his weight. Center Jay Hilgenberg, the man who snapped the ball to the quarterback and knew what was coming, explained his blocking strategy with The Fridge getting ready to rumble behind him.

"I mostly tried to get out of his way," Hilgenberg said of Perry. "I didn't want him falling on me."

It was not a special play put in just for Perry. Normally, the play called "34 dive straight" was run for regular Bears fullback Matt Suhey. Ditka just subbed out personnel to make his point clear to Walsh, and he had his team practice it quietly in the week leading up to the game.

"If they can do it, we can do it better," said tackle Keith Van Horne pointedly about the 49ers' move the year before.

The play also added to the growing legend of The Fridge. Even back in training camp, Perry's No. 72 had loomed large in sportswriters' thoughts. Comedic headline after headline followed his every move, from "He's Mean, He's Fat, He's Cool" to "Bears want Perry to Pull his Weight." In polite description, it seemed as if the word "hefty" was Perry's middle name, though "The Fridge" was definitely more colorful.

Although Perry's weight was generally rounded off at 300 pounds, there was constant speculation that he weighed perhaps as much as 340 pounds. At one point back when he was still at Clemson, it was acknowledged he had reached 360 pounds. One story went that Perry downed $22 worth of McDonald's hamburgers and fries at a sitting—and that was at 1980s prices.

Perry was so good-natured that he played along with reporters in the game of how much he weighed and how much he ate. He was a quote machine with a grin, a jolly fat man with surprising athleticism. Perry could dunk a basketball, bench press 420 pounds, and squat with 600 pounds of free weights. He lapped up the attention and the sports media loved dishing it out because Perry was such a fun guy.

Indeed, Madison Avenue jumped on the bandwagon early and Perry became an endorser of various foodstuffs, including hamburgers.

As the Bears steamrolled through their schedule, dominating other teams in most games, with a plethora of stars who had their own very high-profile personalities, the Perry fan club only grew. The rookie known for his girth, his grin, and the gap between his two front teeth also had a starring role in "The Super Bowl Shuffle" recording.

Perry was already a distinctive football celebrity by the time the Bears reached Super Bowl XX. They proceeded to clobber the New England Patriots 46–10 and to many people the best-remembered moment came when Ditka, seemingly playing along with the frivolity of Perry's image, once again inserted him into the lineup as a running back, this time near the goal line.

The first time occurred in the first quarter with the ball on New England's 5-yard line, when the coach called a play that was an offshoot of Perry's first appearance

ADDING INSULT TO INJURY

Fans got a chuckle when Bears coach Mike Ditka inserted 315-pound defensive tackle William "The Refrigerator" Perry into the game at fullback during Chicago's Super Bowl XX demolition of the New England Patriots. When the Bears reached the 1-yard line, Ditka called on Perry to run the ball on a plunge at the goal line. Quarterback Jim McMahon took the snap from center Jay Hilgenberg and handed off to Perry, who nestled the ball against his ample belly, lowered his head, and followed right tackle Keith Van Horne into the end zone for a touchdown.

GAME DETAILS

Bears 46 • Patriots 10

Location: Louisiana Superdome, New Orleans

Attendance: 73,818

Box Score:

Bears	13	10	21	2	**46**
Patriots	3	0	0	7	**10**

Scoring:

NE Franklin 36-yard field goal

CHI Butler 28-yard field goal

CHI Butler 24-yard field goal

CHI Suhey 11-yard run (Butler PAT)

CHI McMahon 2-yard run (Butler PAT)

CHI Butler 24-yard field goal

CHI McMahon 1-yard run (Butler PAT)

CHI Phillips 28-yard interception return (Butler PAT)

CHI Perry 1-yard run (Butler PAT)

NE Fryar 8-yard pass from Grogan (Franklin PAT)

CHI Safety, Waechter tackled Grogan in end zone

> **I** want you to score, big guy.
>
> —MIKE DITKA TO WILLIAM PERRY
> BEFORE THE FRIDGE'S TOUCHDOWN

of the season against San Francisco. Instead of just running up the middle, Perry actually played the role of a roll-out quarterback, running to his right with his arm cocked, searching the end zone to throw a pass. Perry was tackled before he could throw to tight end Emery Moorehead.

In the third quarter, Perry played the part of blocking back, opening a big hole in the line that led to a touchdown. And finally, in the third quarter Perry took a handoff from quarterback Jim McMahon and plunged over left guard to score a touchdown. That pushed the Bears' lead to 44–3.

It was a howl of a moment, the capstone to a wacky season. Bears fans yucked it up as Perry grinned his trademark grin. It wasn't until later that Ditka realized that amidst all of the pinball-machine-like tallying of points, the only guy who didn't score was the guy who absolutely, positively should have: the great Walter Payton, in his only Super Bowl, was shut out. Payton admitted that he felt slighted and as time passed and people reflected, many felt badly that Payton did not get a touchdown. It came to be seen that Perry's one-yard run for six points rightfully belonged to Payton.

At the time nobody made a big deal about that. Perry's score was just part of the hilarity of the moment, the frosting on the cake of a tremendous season.

The Fridge played for the Bears through the 1993 season, but he often battled weight problems, was written about as much for his diets as his tackles, and eventually had disagreements about his weight with Ditka.

Despite the passage of more than two decades, and perhaps some lingering disappointment over the absence of a Payton Super Bowl touchdown, the mere mention of Perry's name to a Bears fan brings a smile to the face. And ironically enough, in 2008, Perry's smile itself changed. He underwent major dental surgery to fix his decaying teeth and in the process eliminated the gap between his two front teeth.

10 ARROGANCE IN THE AIR

Recording "The Super Bowl Shuffle"

It would be difficult to find any event in Chicago Bears history that was more arrogant than recording "The Super Bowl Shuffle" before the Bears won the Super Bowl, even if the action took place off the field, was done in fun, and turned a large share of the proceeds over to a charity food drive.

Making a record about how great you are before you have won the title takes a group of supersized egos to think up the project and execute it. Certainly, the 1985 Bears had the brass to do such a thing. Rarely has a team walked on the pro football stage that had as much swagger as the Mike Ditka–coached Bears of the mid-1980s.

When a team can back up its feeling of invulnerability by performing the same way, it's not opinion, it's fact, Jack.

The Bears had color and flavor and personality and they won just about all of the time. What more could any fan ask for? They were flattered by high exposure nationally on games of the week, and they were beloved locally by a populace that always revered the Bears, even when the team was far less successful.

The team as a whole had personality, from the cigar-chomping Ditka and his say-anything defensive partner Buddy Ryan, from "Sweetness" Walter Payton to "Samurai" Mike Singletary, from cocky Jim McMahon to the amazing exploits of William "The Refrigerator" Perry, the world's most athletic appliance.

Therefore, it wasn't a huge surprise when show business–oriented receiver Willie Gault dreamed up the idea of a team song.

On an off day, several prominent members of the Bears gathered in a recording studio. There was not room enough for several dozen solo crooners without recording an hour-long song, but 24 guys did participate in the making of the video by singing and "playing" drums, guitars, or other instruments. Some said the Bears made beautiful music on the field the way they meshed. The team tested the theory off the field with "The Super Bowl Shuffle."

Still, not every player thought it was such a grand idea to sing about success before all the wins were in the bank. Unlikely as it seemed given his stature on the team and his outspoken and fun-loving nature, Steve McMichael refused to be involved in the recording. He worried about the song

I think it was a really gutsy thing that we did. It was revolutionary. Historic. We gave about $250,000 to charity.

—WILLIE GAULT

The '85 Bears were immortalized in "The Super Bowl Shuffle," a song that would crack the Billboard charts, earn a Grammy nomination, and become a cultural phenomenon. *(Photo courtesy of WireImages)*

jinxing the Bears before they completed their season's resume. Since athletes are often superstitious, it seemed to be a reasonable argument.

The majority of the Bears did not worry the way McMichael did. For many of them, the "Super Bowl Shuffle" extravaganza was just a way for boys to bond and have fun. It was more of a lark than anything else. There wasn't much of a history of novelty sports songs becoming appreciated in the music

world. Maybe it would make a few bucks and charities would benefit.

As popular as the team was, none of the players envisioned that the song would take off as a hit the moment it was released on December 23, 1985, and later be nominated for a Grammy. That was stunning to all of them.

There had long been a crossover factor between athletes and other entertainers. They had mingled as long ago as the 1920s, but never had a group of sports team members come so close to also being classified as rock stars. Heck, quarterback McMahon even made the cover of *Rolling Stone*.

Gault took care of the original organizing, but with a truck full of egos along for the ride, there was no shortage of helpful suggestions in the recording of the tune.

Lyrics to "The Super Bowl Shuffle" were credited to Richard E. Meyer and Melvin Owens—though it has been said some Bears such as Richard Dent and William Perry helped with the writing—and the music was attributed to Bobby Daniels and Lloyd Barry.

The song was undeniably catchy, and fans of the team and players knew the words sung by each individual truly rang true. It may have been surprising to see certain players singing, but what they said about themselves in their stanzas was believable. It was also genuinely funny and the spirit of the song was taken just that way: that it was all about fun. Listening and viewing the video seemed somewhat surreal and almost as if it had jumped off the drawing board at *Saturday Night Live*.

The players who sang solo parts were Payton, Gault, Singletary, McMahon, Otis Wilson, Steve Fuller, Mike Richardson, Dent, Gary Fencik, and Perry. What an unlikely group. The typical first reaction to hearing the song by fans was that they laughed so hard tears ran down their cheeks.

In part, the chorus went like this:

We are the Bears Shufflin' Crew
Shufflin' on down, doin' it for you.
We're so bad, we know we're good.
Blowin' your mind like we knew we would.

And, given his sky-high Q rating, there was no doubt that The Fridge was one of the star attractions:

You're lookin' at the Fridge,
I'm the rookie.
I may be large, but I'm no dumb cookie.

Neither, as it turned out, were the Bears dumb cookies. As rappers, the Bears did not have a star among them, but together the whole sounded better

ONE FINE TUNE

In its own way, "The Super Bowl Shuffle" may be the best sports song of all time, though it is difficult to argue with "Take Me Out to the Ballgame."

"Take Me Out to the Ballgame" has been around longer and gets more play when fans sing it during seventh-inning stretches at baseball games all summer long.

The Harlem Globetrotters' use of "Sweet Georgia Brown" for their warmups deserves special mention, but it is not strictly a sports song.

"The Super Bowl Shuffle" lyrics suffer in the public's mind because they are dated, geared to the one specific season in Bears history, and because they refer to players for one team. They are narrowly focused on individual Bears, not broadly aimed at a wide football audience.

Ironically, even among Bears fans another song gets more attention. The official Bears theme song, "Bear Down, Chicago Bears," written in 1941 by Jerry Downs using the alias Al Hoffman, is played at every home game at Soldier Field and the words are splashed on a message board so fans can sing along.

It ends with these words: "You're the pride and joy of Illinois, Chicago Bears, bear down."

than the individual parts, the same way the team performed on the field. The song became a sensation and the Bears were a nationwide phenomenon, except among fans of teams that still harbored hopes of knocking Chicago off its pedestal in the postseason.

If "The Super Bowl Shuffle" was any kind of distraction on the field, as most coaches would fear it would be, evidence to support the claim was negligible. The team finished the regular season with a 15–1 record, then blitzed through the playoffs with equal-opportunity destruction of the New York Giants, Los Angeles Rams, and New England Patriots.

Surely, whether it was right or wrong to record the song during the season, "The Super Bowl Shuffle" must go down in history as the best sports team song of all time.

One measure of the temporary insanity the hit song provoked was that by the end of the next season there was a humorous parody of the humorous parody. By then the Super Bowl champions were ex-Super Bowl champions, knocked out of the playoffs. The Shuffle parody was called "Super EmBEARassed" and was penned by brothers Al and Howard Fleishman.

Jim McMahon and Walter Payton joke while recording their parts for "The Super Bowl Shuffle." *(Photo courtesy of WireImages)*

November 14, 1943

AIR LUCKMAN

Sid Luckman's Seven Touchdown Passes

When Sid Luckman was a kid growing up as the son of a trucker in Brooklyn, he developed his arm strength playing street football, while also dodging cars in his busy neighborhood. When it was time to attend college, he didn't stray very far, enrolling in Columbia University at a time when the Ivy League was still a top football conference.

New York is where the Bears' George Halas found Luckman, pursued him, wooed him, and signed him. Rarely has there been a better meshing of coach and quarterback. Approaching six decades after his retirement, Luckman remains the premier quarterback in Bears history. He was the leader of the glorious 1940s accomplishments when the Bears first became the Monsters of the Midway and remained the top team in the NFL while World War II raged.

Sometimes the greatest of athletes have the best drawn out of them by the greatest of rivals. In boxing that was true of Muhammad Ali and Joe Frazier. In tennis it was true of Chris Evert and Martina Navratilova. And in basketball it was true of Bill Russell and Wilt Chamberlain. Sid Luckman joined the Bears in 1939, two years after Sammy Baugh joined the Washington Redskins. For a decade they were indisputably the

best quarterbacks in football, foils for one another in championship contests as their Bears and Redskins fought for the ultimate prize.

Under Luckman, the Bears won league crowns in 1940, 1941, 1943, and 1946. They finished second in the Western Division in 1939, 1944, 1947, 1948, 1949, and second in the National Division in 1950.

Although Luckman was primarily a tailback in a single-wing formation in college, Halas felt the young man could be the linchpin of the Bears' shift to the T-formation and lead them as a passer. Halas made a trade with the Pittsburgh Steelers to obtain the top pick in the draft, then plucked Luckman. There was some adjustment time for Luckman behind center, but Halas was eventually proven correct.

What Luckman possessed, Halas saw, were leadership qualities more than a rifle arm. Surrounded by star teammates, several bound for the Hall of Fame, Luckman had the powerful personality to win them over, the smarts to direct an offense, and just enough firepower in his arm to make the big plays when passing was called for.

As Luckman wrapped up his college days at Columbia, he gave little thought to playing professional football. He was

Though not known for the strength of his arm, quarterback Sid Luckman tossed seven touchdown passes against the New York Giants in 1943.

Sid Luckman Celebrates Sid Luckman Day

A New York native and a graduate of Columbia University, Sid Luckman, the Bears' All-Pro quarterback, was honored with a special day recognizing his achievements when Chicago came to town to meet the Giants in November 1943. Showing just what type of damage he could do when the passing game was on, Luckman threw for seven touchdowns, still an NFL record. On this play, end Hampton Pool, who already had one touchdown catch in the game, lined up on the right side. At the snap, Pool angled slightly to the left across the middle of the field and into the end zone. Luckman threw deep, but a little high, forcing Pool to make a jumping grab for the 25-yard touchdown.

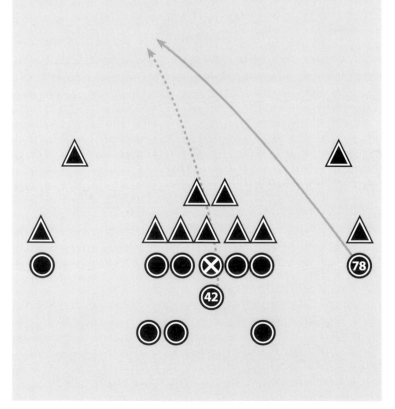

married and shared a New York apartment with his wife, Estelle. They planned to start a family soon and Luckman, whose dark curly hair helped make him Hollywood handsome, planned to put his degree to work for him.

Halas, who was not famous for his charm, convinced Luckman to hear his offer and made enough of a case for Luckman to try pro ball. Luckman's family had been deeply impacted by the Depression and when Halas agreed to pay him $10,000, Luckman thought it made sense to keep playing rather than move into the business world immediately.

By 1943, Luckman was established as the field general of the Bears and as a well-established league star. The Bears were losing players one by one to the service and even talked Bronko Nagurski out of retirement to fill in.

Late that fall the Bears were scheduled to play the New York Giants at the Polo Grounds. Luckman had a sore right shoulder and didn't know if he was healthy enough to play. In order to suit up, Luckman took a novacaine shot to numb the shoulder.

It was a homecoming situation for Luckman and was billed as a tribute game for the city native. It certainly turned out to be. He was presented with a $1,000 war bond and his mother, brothers, and sisters were in attendance for the occasion. The rivalry between two of the league's top teams, combined with the fanfare surrounding Luckman's return to New York, contributed to the turnout of 56,681 fans. Many were there for spectacle, but they were rewarded with history.

Luckman came out firing at the renowned Giants defense. Before the end of the first quarter, Luckman completed touchdown passes to Jim Benton and Connie Berry. The Giants fought back within one score before Luckman

GAME DETAILS

Bears 56 • Giants 7

Location: Polo Grounds, New York

Attendance: 56,681

I just threw the ball and there was always a Bear around to catch it.

—SID LUCKMAN

Box Score:

Bears	14	14	14	14	**56**
Giants	0	7	0	0	**7**

Scoring:

CHI Benton 4-yard pass from Luckman (Snyder PAT)

CHI Berry 31-yard pass from Luckman (Snyder PAT)

NY Kinscherf 1-yard run (Cuff PAT)

CHI Pool 27-yard pass from Luckman (Snyder PAT)

CHI Clark 4-yard run (Snyder PAT)

CHI Clark 62-yard pass from Luckman (Snyder PAT)

CHI Benton 15-yard pass from Luckman (Snyder PAT)

CHI Wilson 3-yard pass from Luckman (Snyder PAT)

CHI Pool 40-yard pass from Luckman (Snyder PAT)

completed his third touchdown throw of the day to Hampton Pool.

The fourth Luckman touchdown pass went to Harry Clark and the fifth time around Luckman found Benton again. By then the Bears led 42–7. The Giants were vanquished with more than a quarter to play. Co-coaches Hunk Anderson and Luke Johnsos (filing in for Halas who was doing another tour in the navy) wanted to take Luckman out of the game and put in backup Bob Snyder to show mercy on the Giants and to prevent injury.

However, Johnsos was sitting in the press box and was informed by a sportswriter that the league record for touchdown passes in a game—held by Baugh—was six. Teammates lobbied Anderson to leave Luckman in. They shouted that it was his day and urged the coach, "Let him go for it!"

So the Bears stuck with Luckman. Luckman tied the single-game mark with a three-yard touchdown pass over the middle to George Wilson, the fiery player who later had success coaching the Detroit Lions. Finally,

midway through the fourth quarter, Luckman swung a pass to Pool that was slightly off target, but Pool made a spectacular grab and fought his way into the end zone for the 40-yard completion. The seventh touchdown throw was the most memorable and spectacular play of the game.

The final score was 56–7 in favor of the Bears as Luckman became the first man to throw seven touchdown passes in a single game. Snyder never got his chance to fill in for Luckman behind center, but he kicked a record eight extra points that day.

Luckman completed 23 of 30 attempts for 433 yards, also a record at the time. That season Luckman finished with 28 touchdown passes, a record for a single year and the best of his career.

The Bears finished out the season—Luckman's greatest—by winning the NFL championship and sending Nagurski back into retirement with a smile on his face. Eight days after the Bears defeated the Redskins for the title, Luckman was in the U.S. Merchant Marines.

November 24, 1963

HOLDING TIGHT TO FIRST PLACE

Mike Ditka's Big Catch Saves the Bears

Forty-five years ago, when Mike Ditka growled as much as he spoke in complete sentences and caught passes as effortlessly as he growled, Chicago Bear teammates might have had difficulty envisioning their All-Pro tight end as a pitchman for his own brand of wine.

The operator of Mike Ditka's, a famous steakhouse in downtown Chicago, is a mini-conglomerate as a senior citizen, but when he was taking his position along the line of scrimmage in the early 1960s he was one of the most respected and feared players in football.

Always a great athlete, Ditka possessed the all-around skills of strength, savvy, and speed to reinvent the tight end spot amidst the Xs and Os on the chalkboard. For decades the tight end was almost a misnamed position in football lexicon. In most formations, he acted more like a third offensive tackle than a dual-threat blocker/receiver. Any passes thrown in the direction of the tight end seemed to be heaved out of desperation or by accident, not as part of the planned offensive game plan.

When the Bears made the 6'3", 230-pound Ditka their number one draft choice in 1961, the wheels in George Halas's creative football mind were spinning. He saw a guy tough enough to block the big boys on the line and also agile enough to be integrated into the attack.

Ditka had been an All-American bruiser at the University of Pittsburgh after growing up in the eastern Pennsylvania community of Aliquippa, but he thought at the time and said many years later that if another team had drafted him he probably would have ended up as a linebacker. There were no antecedents for big pass-catching tight ends. Halas came up with the idea and Ditka was the instrument of implementation.

The modification of the tight end's role was an immediate sensation. During his rookie year of 1961, Ditka caught 56 passes. That was a huge number for a tight end. Stunningly, he averaged 19.2 yards per catch, a statistic proving that he could run downfield as well as any speedy wide receiver. And he scored 12 touchdowns.

Mike Ditka's return to Pittsburgh in 1963 brought out the best in the Bears' fiery tight end.
(Photo courtesy of WireImages)

We'll settle for the tie.

—GEORGE HALAS

Ditka came along when the Bears were trying to dent the budding dynasty of the Green Bay Packers. In 1963, with the mix of veterans and youthful players, the Bears had their best chance to win their division since 1956. To stay ahead of the Packers, the pressure was on to win just about every game and by late November the Bears were in first place with a one-game lead.

The game against the Pittsburgh Steelers on November 24 at Forbes Field was Ditka's first time back in his home area as a player since his student days at Pitt, located only a couple blocks away. The homecoming, with many friends and relatives in the stands, was a special day for him. As had become his trademark, Ditka played with hunger and ferocity that day, hooking up with quarterback Bill Wade for seven passes and 146 yards. Even in today's game, that would be a fine day for any receiver, but it was unheard of for a tight end at the

time. The performance symbolized how well Ditka and Halas had adapted the tight end role.

It seemed as if Ditka had burned up most of his energy in the late going when the pesky Steelers, poised for an upset, kept fending off the Bears' best offensive charges. It has been said Ditka played himself to exhaustion in trying to reach the end zone that day, but while he did not score, his biggest play of the game positioned the Bears to notch the tying points in a 17–17 game.

Pittsburgh's double-duty defensive end/kicker Lou Michaels had missed two field goals, but an 11-yard kick provided the Steelers with a 17–14 lead.

For the Bears, for once a tie was as good as a win. With about five minutes remaining in the fourth quarter, the Bears trailed by that three-point margin and were stuck deep in their own territory. Really stuck. It was third-and-33 to go for a first down. The

AS TOUGH AS ME

Mike Ditka spent his NFL coaching career looking for players who were as passionate, hardworking, and rugged as he was on the field. If ever there was a player who would be better suited to become identified with cigar smoking, it would be hard to name him.

When he was a younger man in Pennsylvania, Ditka also played some baseball. It figured that he was a catcher. How would you like to be the base runner steaming for home and see Iron Mike blocking the plate? It wouldn't be difficult to imagine Ditka playing hockey, either, especially in the days before helmets

and visors. If Mike Ditka checked you into the boards, you would stay checked.

Longtime sports broadcaster Beano Cook once said of Ditka, "In an earlier life Ditka was probably Achilles—a great, great fighter—and he came back as Mike Ditka."

For a guy who chewed nails for breakfast, lunch, and dinner, it is ironic that Ditka is a purveyor of fine food in his two Chicago-area restaurants. Of course, he specializes in meat like any good football player would.

GAME DETAILS

Bears 17 • Steelers 17

Location: Forbes Field, Pittsburgh

Attendance: 36,465

Box Score:

Bears	7	7	0	3	**17**
Steelers	0	14	0	3	**17**

Scoring:

CHI Galimore 1-yard run (Jencks PAT)
PIT Hoak 6-yard run (Michaels PAT)
CHI Bull 1-yard run (Jencks PAT)

PIT Curry 31-yard pass from Brown (Michaels PAT)
PIT Michaels 11-yard field goal
CHI Leclerc 18-yard field goal

> **M**ike just ran out of gas with that superhuman effort.
>
> —GEORGE HALAS

situation seemed fairly hopeless, with the odds stacked as high as a pile of IHOP pancakes against the Bears even obtaining a first down, never mind scoring a touchdown.

On the snap, Ditka slashed across the middle of the field. Wade fired and the tight end gathered in the ball and hugged it to his chest as six Steelers defenders converged for a tackle that would doom the Bears. Ditka was surrounded, but he was determined to go down fighting. One by one, Steelers tacklers hit him or missed him, but Ditka fought past them all, breaking into the clear and lugging the ball for a 63-yard gain before he was brought down. Who gets a first down when they need 33 yards?

The Bears had new life. Riding the momentum swing, Wade threw into the end zone twice. The first pass was out of reach. The second pass was dropped by end Bo Farrington. The Bears could not ram the ball in

for a touchdown against a stung Steelers defense, so they played for the tie.

Kicker Roger Leclerc stepped up and booted a field goal from the 18-yard line. Ditka's heroic run after the catch set up the tying points that kept the Bears ahead of the Packers by a half-game in the standings.

It was one of those sigh-of-relief results, where the better team knows it was lucky to escape.

"Our future is still in our hands," Halas said.

The Bears finished 11–1–2 in the regular season, which was good enough to edge the Packers and propel them into the NFL title game against the New York Giants. The "disappointing" tie was a season-saver and the most important play in that game was Ditka's phenomenal catch and run.

"They didn't bring him down," Halas said.

It was a pretty spiffy catch and run for a guy who was only a tight end.

September 19, 1985

7 THE BEARS FOLLOW THEIR LEADER

Jim McMahon Shows His Heart

To the public, Jim McMahon often seemed like a flake, like a good-time boy who rated having fun as the most important thing on his personal agenda. And while McMahon did much to enhance the image and little to debunk it, he knew himself well enough to understand what was truly important as a measuring stick with the Bears.

So did his teammates. The playful McMahon was not the whole man, just one aspect of his personality. Players understood that beneath the veneer of playfulness was a tough layer of grit. McMahon was a leader and a winner and he inspired his teammates to play harder and to do whatever it took to win. Those who were quick to judge McMahon for being a silly guy never understood all of what was taking place inside him. He was made up of equal parts guts and heart.

A superstar quarterback in college at Brigham Young, McMahon's intangible traits were more important in the pros. Some viewed the demonstrative McMahon as a player with a bad attitude, but the reality is that his attitude was more focused on winning than most others.

Frequently injured, McMahon's mental toughness was more critical to his success than whether or not he was able to walk during the week leading up to a game. Football clings to the adage that if you can't practice, you can't play. It is often difficult to convince coaches otherwise.

It just so happened that in the early part of the 1985 season, McMahon could barely walk. He could barely straighten up because of a back injury and an infected right leg. All week leading up to the Vikings game, McMahon took treatment instead of snaps.

He willed himself to readiness, but on the day of the nationally televised matchup, coach Mike Ditka started backup Steve Fuller against the Vikings. Ditka told McMahon that he wanted him to use the week for recuperation to prepare himself for the rest of the season. McMahon did not like the idea of resting. Even upon digesting Ditka's speech, McMahon urged the coach to call on him if needed.

He is known to have miracles happen.

—DENNIS MCKINNON ON JIM MCMAHON

Jim McMahon came off the bench to lead the Bears to victory over the Vikings in 1985, one of the signature wins in the punky QB's playing career.

McMahon was too hurt to play, it was announced. McMahon was in uniform but his injury precluded him throwing passes. End of story. McMahon was a bit miffed because despite not practicing he thought he was capable of playing and darn it, the quarterback job was his.

Put me in Coach, McMahon said to Ditka before the game. No, said the coach. Leave me alone and let me coach. As the day wore on and the result seemed in jeopardy, McMahon grew more insistent.

Put me in Coach, McMahon said to Ditka in the first quarter. No, said the coach. Don't bother me.

Put me in Coach, McMahon said to Ditka at halftime. No, said the coach. Get away from me.

Repeatedly, McMahon pleaded with Ditka to put him in the game, and over and over Ditka refused. It was like a child in the backseat of the car repeating over and over, "Are we there yet?" McMahon was driving Ditka nuts on the sideline.

Behind quarterback Tommy Kramer, Minnesota worked itself into a 17–9 lead in the third quarter. Finally, annoyed and sick of McMahon's pleadings and with the game in danger of slipping away, Ditka inserted McMahon into the lineup. The Bears had the ball on their own 30-yard line. On the first play, McMahon faded back while ducking an all-out Minnesota blitz and connected on a 70-yard touchdown pass to receiver Willie Gault.

One McMahon play, one pass, one touchdown.

The Bears defense quickly got the ball back. Linebacker Wilber Marshall intercepted a Kramer toss and set Chicago up on the Minnesota 25. McMahon trotted back onto the field, this time without any argument from Ditka. On first down, McMahon faded back again, and dodging Viking pressure, spotted streaking receiver Dennis McKinnon on a crossing pattern. McMahon pinpointed the pass between defenders and into McKinnon's grasp for a 25-yard touchdown.

Two McMahon plays, two passes, two touchdowns.

On the next series it took him five plays to complete a 43-yard touchdown pass to McKinnon. Ditka shook his head in disbelief. Three touchdown passes for McMahon in just over six and a half minutes. In all he completed eight passes in 15 attempts for 236 yards in less than a half of play, producing a 33–24 Chicago victory.

HERO STUFF

To fans, Jim McMahon was Mr. Cool with his shades and wisecracking demeanor, the guy who would moon a passing helicopter in New Orleans prior to Super Bowl XX.

To his teammates, McMahon was an inspired leader. He was like a captain in the field with his men during a firefight. He may have been an officer, but they knew they could count on him as one of their own. One of the great athletic clichés is the story of the game where the quarterback, slugger, or outside shooter limps off the bench to lead his team to victory.

Dismissed as too predictable now because it has been seen so often, there have been true-life examples of players consigned to the sideline who do force themselves into game action and do inspire their teammates. Willis Reed did it with the New York Knicks. Larry Bird did it with the Boston Celtics. And Jim McMahon did it for the Bears.

Performances such as the unlikely one McMahon turned in against the Vikings build a foundation of respect and belief. After the Vikings game, McMahon's teammates had to be thinking, *When the chips are down, that guy is going to bail us out.*

Jim McMahon was the unquestioned leader of the '85 Bears.

Game Details

Bears 33 • Vikings 24

Location: Metrodome, Minneapolis

Attendance: 61,242

Box Score:

Bears	3	3	24	3	**33**
Vikings	3	7	7	7	**24**

Scoring:

CHI Butler 24-yard field goal

MIN Stenerud 25-yard field goal

CHI Butler 19-yard field goal

MIN Carter 14-yard pass from Kramer (Stenerud PAT)

CHI Butler 34-yard field goal

MIN Jones 9-yard pass from Kramer (Stenerud PAT)

CHI Gault 70-yard pass from McMahon (Butler PAT)

CHI McKinnon 25-yard pass from McMahon (Butler PAT)

CHI McKinnon 43-yard pass from McMahon (Butler PAT)

MIN Carter 57-yard pass from Kramer (Stenerud PAT)

CHI Butler 31-yard field goal

> **T**he first play I almost fell on my face. I felt like a fool and thought, *What a start...*
>
> —JIM MCMAHON

When the Bears were playing sluggishly and the offense was stagnant, McKinnon said he prayed Ditka would put McMahon into the game.

Maybe it was adrenaline. Maybe it was simple fortitude. But for one hour McMahon's injuries seemed fine to thousands of witnesses.

"I must have been blessed tonight," McMahon said after the game. "I can't remember when I threw three touchdowns like that."

Probably because he never had before. Probably because only a few other quarterbacks in NFL history might have approached the accomplishment for its speed and drama.

"I don't know how you write scripts for the kind of game you saw out there," Ditka said.

Running back Walter Payton, clearly a more avid aficionado of black-and-white football movies run on late-night television, understood better how those scripts come out.

"It was like one of those Notre Dame old-time movies," Payton said.

McMahon admitted lobbying Ditka harder than if he was buttonholing a congressman for support on legislation dear to his heart. The sight of the Bears offense moving well, then bogging down short of the goal line, motivated him to argue he could do better. McMahon probably also wanted to show Steve Fuller that he really was the team's quarterback.

The Bears were jubilant after the victory and players realized how special McMahon's showing was. The Vikings were a little more tepid in their praise, with Kramer saying, "I thought he did a heck of a job."

The astounding performance in the face of adversity and risk to his physical well-being further solidified in his teammates' minds that McMahon was the leader who could take them to the Super Bowl. And he did that season. The Bears completed the regular season 15–1, mashed the Rams and Giants in the playoffs, and then steamrolled the Patriots in Super Bowl XX.

February 4, 2007

BEARS BLAZE TO SUPER BOWL LEAD

Touchdown Machine Devin Hester Runs Back Kickoff

By the end of his rookie year, Devin Hester was such an electrifying, explosive, fleet-footed presence as the Bears' kick return specialist he had fans wondering if from infancy he had jumped out of his crib and darted in and out of the arms of parents or siblings who tried to catch him.

In the nine decades of Bears history, the only comparable elusive weapon the team had ever fielded was Gale Sayers. And as spectacular as Sayers was, after a short while of watching the newcomer, even he admitted that Hester was doing things on the gridiron Sayers himself never did.

Hester was chosen in the second round of the 2006 draft out of the University of Miami. At 5'11" and 186 pounds, he was compact dynamite with the ability to shift gears like a Ferrari. Although Bears general manager Jerry Angelo felt Hester had promise, there was no way to foresee that Hester would so swiftly emerge as a once-in-a-generation returner who shook up the entire league.

It was apparent quickly that Hester had a special gift that could not be quantified by stopwatches or other straightforward measurements. Hester had the uncanny sense of being able to read the developing situation in front of him and to react with incredible quickness to take advantage of oncoming defenders being overshifted, off-balance, or failing to plug a lane.

It was Sayers who said that while he only needed a foot of daylight to run to freedom, Hester needed only six inches.

Hester's actual position was thought to be defensive back, but in piling up a league record six returns for touchdowns as a rookie it became obvious he was most valuable and dangerous with the ball in his hands. Any time he was given to rev up a run, whether it was fielding a kickoff, a punt return, or famously, a missed field goal, Hester made opponents pay. Open space made him salivate. Slashing through tiny openings served up only a minor challenge.

Naturally sportswriters wanted to know how Hester performed his magic tricks. Hester, who always gave credit to the other 10 men on the return team for their blocking, once compared the unit to playing the card game spades.

Devin Hester returned the opening kickoff of Super Bowl XLI for a touchdown; it would prove to be the only highlight of the day for the Bears.

"You finally find a partner, y'all just click and y'all willing to bet anything," he said.

Hester set such a high-confidence tone about the likelihood of scoring on the usually long-shot plays that his blockers competed to lead him upfield. They joked that he should follow them left or follow them right. Right this way, Mr. Hester. Pick me, Mr. Hester. Follow me, Mr. Hester. That presupposed that Hester acted more out of premeditation than instant judgment.

Israel Idonije, who also has made a reputation on special teams with the Bears, leads the squad's wedge on kickoff returns. Yet he acknowledges Hester's special abilities.

"It's all Devin," Idonije said. "All Devin needs is a piece [of space]. I call him 'the autobahn' because he has no speed limit."

Even when he didn't score, Hester's savvy and speed repeatedly provided the Bears with excellent field position, shortening the field for touchdown drives. It was a tremendous advantage to be able to start offensive drives from the 40 rather than the 20. As the Bears marched to a 13–3 season and easy conquering of the NFC North Division, Hester became one of the centerpieces of foes' scouting and game-planning. Chicago fans embraced him deliriously. Opposing coaches smacked their foreheads in frustration. To them, watching Hester film was like watching Godzilla rampage through cities, only at a higher rate of speed.

The 2006 Bears earned a first-round bye in the playoffs, then bested Seattle and New Orleans to reach the Super Bowl at Dolphin Stadium in Miami against the Indianapolis Colts. The Colts entered the showdown game ranked 30th in the league in punt coverage and 31st on kickoffs. The sound in the distance was Hester smacking his lips. Much pregame speculation focused on whether or not the Colts would even be willing to kick the ball to him. Do anything but, seemed the theory. Kick the ball out of bounds. Kick the ball to the other side of the field. Kick the ball to another Bear. But football coaches play the percentages. Just how often could Hester run back the kickoff all the way for a touchdown? The odds were against it. Whereas if they kept giving the Bears the ball closer to their own end zone, they would definitely be tempting fate.

SPECIAL SKILLS

A kick returner is the only football player who can make a name for himself by succeeding once every few weeks. Coaches look for consistency in their quarterbacks' throwing and play calling. Coaches want running backs who can make yardage on every down. Coaches look for blockers and tacklers who come to play on every snap.

But the man who can return punts, kickoffs, or any other sort of ball kicked to the wrong place at the wrong time is like a nuclear weapon, a sudden explosion that reshapes the landscape.

Historically, NFL return men only periodically run kicks back for touchdowns. Each time a return man lines up, the odds are against him. There are 11 people running down the field chasing him, trying to put him face down on the turf. For him to break free from all of them, his blockers must block, he must see the field well, he must anticipate, and would-be tacklers must guess wrong.

What made Devin Hester so remarkable for the Bears during his first two seasons was the frequency of his eruptions. He broke loose for touchdowns of 80, 90, and even 100 yards time after time.

GAME DETAILS

Bears 17 • Colts 29

Location: Dolphin Stadium, Miami

Attendance: 74,512

Box Score:

> This is what I had been envisioning all week, and actually for the past two weeks.
>
> —DEVIN HESTER

Colts	6	10	6	7	**29**
Bears	14	0	3	0	**17**

Scoring:

CHI Hester 92-yard kickoff return (Gould PAT)

IND Wayne 53-yard pass from Manning (PAT aborted)

CHI Muhammad 4-yard pass from Grossman (Gould PAT)

IND Vinatieri 29-yard field goal

IND Vinatieri 20-yard field goal

CHI Gould 44-yard field goal

IND Hayden 56-yard interception return (Vinatieri PAT)

Before the Super Bowl, both Hester and special teams coach Dave Toub said the Colts might be skittish about kicking the ball out of bounds on kickoffs because that would allow the Bears to start a series on the 40-yard line.

"We'll take the 40 anytime," Toub said.

It was a dream come true for the Bears when they made it to the Super Bowl for the first time since 1986. It symbolized that the rebuilding of the franchise had worked. And the game began auspiciously with the Bears ready to receive.

The kickoff floated inside the 10-yard line and the Bears got what they wanted. The ball came to Hester. Hester promptly did what he was famous for—grabbing the pigskin and turning on the afterburners.

As the Colts' coverage team pounded toward him, Hester sidestepped tacklers, bobbed and weaved, cut to the sideline, and broke into the open in full flight. Hester dashed 92 yards with the kickoff, the first time in the history of the Super Bowl that the opening kickoff was returned for a touchdown.

The game was only seconds old and Bears fans were jumping up and down, for the moment feeling invincible. Their team was going to do it. Super Bowl champs! Hester had shown the way.

Unfortunately, the rest of the game did not unfold with such clarity. Indianapolis was stunned, but under the steady hand of quarterback Peyton Manning, the Colts regrouped. The blip passed and the Colts surpassed the Bears on the scoreboard to win the title 29–17. Hester's shining moment was the best moment of the game for the Bears, but they couldn't sustain the high for the remaining 59:40 on the game clock.

"We had a chance to come out with the kickoff return on the first play of the game," Hester said.

Alas, there is no rule that reads a great play must clinch a great triumph.

November 4, 1923

5 98 Yards to Daylight

Papa Bear Outraces Thorpe for Touchdown

Few photographs endure of young George Halas, the Decatur Staleys/ Chicago Bears football player. And perhaps few were taken. It wasn't as if National Football League fields were teeming with photographers in the early days. Halas is best remembered as an older man stalking the sideline wearing an overcoat and fedora, the coach of the Monsters of the Midway. Or secondarily seen in pictures as a front office magnate wearing suits in his role as president of the Bears or carrying out committee work or assignments on behalf of the NFL.

It is true that Halas is best known for his role in founding the NFL and the Bears and his decades as the then-winningest coach in league history. But the man could also play the game he promoted. Halas was a very good athlete who grew up in Chicago and played football for the University of Illinois.

He was also an excellent baseball player and although his time spent as a right fielder

with the New York Yankees was brief enough to classify as "a cup of coffee," he was good enough to make the big leagues.

Halas's true love was football, of course, and after he was benched for hitting less than his weight in favor of the young slugger Babe Ruth, Halas devoted the rest of his life to the gridiron.

Halas did not go to work at the Decatur starch company that founded the Staleys in order to obtain a factory job. He joined because he was given the power to start, organize, coach, and play for a professional football team. More than anything else in this arrangement, Halas wanted to keep playing football. He was excited to be able to continue his football days beyond college, but not even Halas could have imagined he would spend the last 63 years of his life connected with one team.

Because of his affiliation with the starch company, Halas was present at the creation of the NFL, and because he was the face of the team he inherited its organization when

> **I** ran faster and faster, but I sensed he was gaining.
> —GEORGE HALAS OF JIM THORPE'S HOT PURSUIT

Before he became "Papa Bear," George Halas used his legs to propel the Bears past Jim Thorpe and the Oorang Indians in 1923. *(Photo courtesy of AP Images)*

the business could no longer support the effort. But throughout it all—the meetings in Ohio to form a league and the hard times suffered financially in Decatur—Halas played for the Staleys and the Bears.

Often overlooked—perhaps because of his otherwise sterling resume—is that Halas was the perpetrator of one of the greatest and most memorable plays in Bears history. As a player Halas was 6'0" and weighed 182 pounds. He was primarily a two-way end (though sometimes a running back) when statistics were not strictly kept or effectively preserved. But well-documented was the greatest play of Halas's on-field career.

The Bears were facing the Oorang Indians—one of the many franchises that came and went during the early days of the NFL—on a damp and chilly afternoon at Wrigley Field.

It had long been established that Jim Thorpe, Olympic gold medal-winner and fabulous all-around runner, thrower, and kicker for the Carlisle Indian Industrial School and then the pros, was the greatest athlete in the world. Indeed, as a public relations maneuver, the founders of the NFL appointed Thorpe as the league's first president to capitalize on his fame.

This was hardly a desk job for Thorpe, who continued playing and became player/coach near the end of his career for the Indians. The Bears were in the midst of a 9–2–1 season and were the superior team on that yucky November day.

But Thorpe was an athlete of great pride and if he occasionally lacked purpose it did not take much to stir him up. Thorpe had a legendary temper that he often called upon to avenge any slight. In that sense he was like basketball legend Michael Jordan, employing seemingly mild external factors as a jump-start to his motivation.

On this particular day, Thorpe received a handoff and just as he started to run, the slippery, wet ball sprung free of his usually sure hands. The ball bounced around loose on the turf, settling on the Bears' 2-yard line. Halas scooped up the fumble, tucked it away, and turned in the other direction. It appeared that he had clear sailing down the field.

Halas's legs began churning as he aimed for the end zone 98 yards away. An infuriated Thorpe, angered

THE OTHER GUY IN THE PLAY

George Halas, known as "Papa Bear," helped put Jim Thorpe into the driver's seat of the NFL when the league began, but Thorpe did not gravitate to desk jobs. He was a big name and nearly a century after his athletic prime his name still resonates with sports fans. Even if they do not know the particulars of his sporting career, many casual fans know simply that he was a tremendous athlete. Thorpe won Olympic gold medals and played professional football and Major League Baseball. Accomplishing any one of those things is the embodiment of the American athletic dream.

It is no wonder that Thorpe was considered by most to be the greatest athlete of the first half of the 20th century. Thorpe was also remembered for his casual acceptance of the compliment from the King of Sweden in 1912 that he was the world's greatest athlete. "Thanks, King," Thorpe responded in a short but sweet retort.

Thorpe stood 6'1" and weighed 190 pounds in his prime football days before the NFL's existence. Many of those occurred in the 1915–1919 era when he was paid $250 a game to play for the Canton Bulldogs.

GAME DETAILS

Bears 26 • Indians 0

Location: Wrigley Field, Chicago

Attendance: 1,000

Box Score:

> **I** could hear the squishing of his shoes in the mud.
>
> —GEORGE HALAS

Indians	0	0	0	0	**0**
Bears	13	13	0	0	**26**

Scoring:
CHI Knop 5-yard run (Sternaman PAT)
CHI Lanum 5-yard run (PAT failed)
CHI Sternaman 16-yard run (Sternaman PAT)
CHI Halas 98-yard fumble return (PAT failed)

that he made the mistake that lost the ball, saw Halas running, and embarked on the chase determined to prevent a touchdown that rightfully belonged to him.

Thorpe, who had the reputation as a fierce runner who could level tacklers with a straight arm on offense, was just as renowned for his hard hits on defense. Over the years, in retelling the story many times with self-effacing commentary and chuckles, Halas said he was scared to death Thorpe was going to catch him and dismember him with a vengeance.

"I heard an angry roar," Halas wrote years later. "It was Thorpe coming after me."

There was no time to take the ill-advised chance of looking back, but Halas would dearly have loved temporary possession of a rearview mirror.

"When I could almost feel his breath, I dug in a cleat and did a sharp zig," Halas continued. "Thorpe's

momentum carried him on and gave me a few feet of running room. He narrowed the gap. I zagged. Again he lost a stride. He turned and came on. I zigged. I zagged. Zig. Zag. Just short of the goal, Thorpe threw himself at me and down I went, into a pool of water."

The last-gasp tackle came too late. Halas was already in the end zone. The 98-yard run for a touchdown with a recovered fumble was an NFL record and it lasted 49 years until the 1972 season.

Halas's life in football lasted even longer. Halas played for the Bears from 1920 to 1928, but coached the team with a few breaks into the 1960s, collecting 324 victories, and he ran the front office until his death in 1983. By then, Halas could only walk 98 yards with a cane, but he never forgot the most colorful on-field play of his career.

December 15, 1946

SID LUCKMAN'S BOOTLEG FOOLS GIANTS

Bears Gain Another Title

America was starting over, and so were the Bears.

At the end of World War II, the Monsters of the Midway were coming together again. Star players returned to the team from fighting the Germans and Japanese. George Halas returned to coaching the Bears after his second sideline leave of absence to serve as a commander in the navy.

The Bears had been the league's powerhouse when World War II began. But as so many teams did, they lost players one by one to different branches of the service. When the team regrouped to start the 1946 season it was not clear if the old group still had its magic. Halas said he didn't know what to expect when the team gathered for preseason training camp at St. Joseph's College in Indiana. He was doubtful about the game fitness of players who had been in the military for three or four years and away from the sport, saying it was "questionable whether they could regain their football legs."

The other teams faced the same circumstances, however, and since the Bears began with more talent than those teams, the Bears were in position to recover better than most.

Under the clever hand of quarterback Sid Luckman and the guiding hand of Halas, the Bears came together again, recording a solid 8–2–1 season. That mark was good enough to win the West and earn the right to play the New York Giants in another NFL title game.

Luckman, along with Sammy Baugh, was one of the best two quarterbacks of the decade. Luckman joined the Bears in 1939 after playing at Columbia University. Halas recognized that Luckman was the perfect quarterback for his offense and pushed hard to convince him to be a Bear. Pro football did not promise either riches or job security at the time so it was not easy to convince the college star to choose the Bears over other stable careers in business. Halas had to do some convincing to obtain Luckman's autograph on a contract. Over time, the two men became very close.

During World War II, Luckman had been lucky compared to many other NFL players. Luckman was not a multiple-year

Sid Luckman's bootleg run against the New York Giants keyed the Bears' 24–14 victory in the 1946 NFL Championship Game. *(Photo courtesy of WireImages)*

SID LUCKMAN TRICKS THE GIANTS

Sid Luckman was the greatest passing quarterback in Chicago Bears history, but in the 1946 championship game against the Giants, it was his legs that made the difference. Luckman lined up at his usual place behind center. He backpedaled a few yards, but then shocked the entire Polo Grounds crowd by executing a play called "Bingo, Keep It 97." Faking the handoff to halfback George McAfee in the backfield and then hiding the ball on his right hip the best he could, Luckman darted around right end to score a crucial touchdown.

> **T**he easiest [touchdown] of my life.
>
> —SID LUCKMAN

military man battling on foreign soil. He missed less than half of the 1944 season. So the Bears had their sharp leader at the key quarterback position and he was not as rusty as many others.

In an ideal football relationship, the head coach and the quarterback are like extensions of one another, always on the same page, thinking alike, agreeing on approaches. Since not even football players live in a perfect world, it does not always work out that way, but in Luckman, Halas had an alter ego on the field.

During the 1946 regular season, Luckman led the NFL in passing yards with 1,826 and also threw 17 touchdown passes. When it came time for the championship game, a peace-time nation once again showed its hunger for normalcy by turning out a record 58,346 fans at the Polo Grounds. The day was marred because some Giants players were accused of being involved in a bribery scheme that could have fixed the game, and after some quick investigation one New York player was held out of the game.

The Bears got off to a good start in the contest, building a 14–0 lead in the first quarter behind Luckman's touchdown pass to Ken Kavanaugh, and then an interception return. The Giants tied the score at 14–14 in the third quarter and it stayed that way into the fourth.

Luckman was the ultimate pocket quarterback. He had a terrific arm and knew how to use it. Rolling out was a major departure for Luckman. In fact, he ran the ball just 25 times during the 1946 regular season. He was not inclined to run, and Halas didn't want to risk injury

GAME DETAILS

Bears 24 • Giants 14

Location: Polo Grounds, New York

Attendance: 58,346

Box Score:

Bears	14	0	0	10	**24**
Giants	7	0	7	0	**14**

Scoring:

CHI Kavanaugh 21-yard pass from Luckman (Maznicki PAT)
CHI Magnani 34-yard interception return (Maznicki PAT)
NY Liebel 38-yard pass from Filchock (Strong PAT)

NY Filipowicz 5-yard pass from Filchock (Strong PAT)
CHI Luckman 19-yard run (Maznicki PAT)
CHI Maznicki 26-yard field goal

> **S**id put the ball on his hip, drifted around right end and made a touchdown. Nobody touched him.
>
> —GEORGE HALAS

to his main man, so rarely called his number for a rush.

Which is why the Bears' game-winning play was such a shocker, a strategy of such audacity that Halas was left chortling. The Bears started their key drive on their own 34 yard line after a poor Giants punt. With Luckman passing to George McAfee and mixing in running plays, plus the benefit of a Giants penalty, the Bears advanced to the New York 19 about three minutes into the fourth quarter.

The Bears called timeout. Luckman strolled to the sideline, looked at Halas and said, "Now?" He knew the moment was ripe for the overlooked play in the offense's repertoire. Halas answered, "Now." With a tie score and time running out in the championship game, it was the perfect moment to attempt a trick play that might baffle the opposition. It was a bold call, deviating from the norm when things were running smoothly, but it proved to be the right one.

As Bears fans edged forward in anticipation, Luckman stunned the crowd with a bootleg run around right end, dashing free and clear for 19 yards and the winning touchdown. The play was called "Bingo Keep It, 97," devised by Halas to be used inside the 20-yard line only. The strategy called for the left side of the line to pull left, then turn right past the line of scrimmage, as the right side of the line held its ground blocking. All this while Luckman ran to the right after a fake handoff to McAfee and while trying to disguise the ball beside his body. The last Giants defender between Luckman and the end zone was faked out at the 10-yard line.

Patrick McCaskey, a member of the Bears' board of directors, reminisced later that Luckman's touchdown run is just about his favorite play in Bears history because it was designed by Halas himself.

"It was a favorite of my grandfather's," McCaskey said. "It won the 1946 championship game."

Luckman said the Bears practiced the play all year, but hadn't found the appropriate occasion to use it.

The touchdown was the play that broke the Giants' backs. The Bears added a field goal for the 24–14 margin of victory. Luckman's bootleg, the highlight play, had all of the Bears smiling.

December 17, 1933

Razzle-Dazzle Makes the Difference

Bears Win First Official NFL Title

When people said Bill Hewitt was hardheaded, they meant it in two ways. First, they assumed his head must be as solid as a metal bucket. Second, they believed the stubbornness contained in his noggin exceeded the bounds of common sense.

That was because the Chicago Bears' star end was the last man standing in the National Football League who refused to wear a helmet during games. Hewitt was bugged by the leather headgear the way some people are irked by the itchiness of a wool sweater. He just didn't like it and he said the helmet hindered his play.

Hewitt, a 5'9", 190-pound receiver, was so fast off the line of scrimmage that he was nicknamed "The Offside Kid." He was a living optical illusion, his reactions so good it only looked like he was breaking offside on every play. Hewitt was elected to the Pro Football Hall of Fame in 1971.

The play of Hewitt's career with the Bears that provided the most excitement and won a championship for Chicago occurred in the 1933 title game against the New York Giants.

This was the first NFL game staged between the winners of Eastern and Western conferences and marked the beginning of a decades-long championship rivalry with the New Yorkers. In later years some began referring to the event as "the original Super Sunday." The 1933 game may have been one of the best big games ever played with the lead changing hands six times during the game. The contest had more suspense than an Agatha Christie novel.

The Bears showed up for the game before 30,000 fans at Wrigley Field with a record of 10–2–1. The Giants' mark was 11–3. Several famous players fated to enter the Hall of Fame lined up this day. Bronko Nagurski and Red Grange were members of the Bears' backfield and Roy Lyman blocked for them. Harry Newman, Mel Hein, and Ken Strong were among the Giants' stars. And after concluding his leave of absence from the bench during the Ralph Jones years, George Halas had come back to coaching.

The pro game was opening up, employing more sophisticated offenses, and in the year since Nagurski had completed his controversial jump pass to beat Portsmouth,

Bill Hewitt laterals the ball to teammate Bill Karr for the winning score in the 1933 NFL Championship Game.

the play had been perfected by the Bears. It was an era of trick plays, of thinking outside the box. The Giants attempted one hidden ball play designed for the center to mask the ball and drift away from the action. Unnoticed, Hein casually began walking downfield and gained 30 yards before the Bears defense wised up and tackled him.

It sounded like Marx Brothers foolishness, but it worked.

The action seesawed back and forth on the wintry afternoon and whenever the Giants defense proved too formidable and shut down the Bears' progress outside the end zone, Halas called on his premier field-goal kicker. The toe of Jack Manders kept

Bill Hewitt and Bill Karr Create Razzle-Dazzle

In the 1933 NFL Championship Game, the Bears trailed the New York Giants and had the ball on the Giants' 33-yard line. Bronko Nagurski took a handoff, then scanned receivers running downfield. Left end Bill Hewitt, the last player to compete in the NFL without wearing a helmet, outran the coverage on the left side. Nagurski delivered the ball, but Giants defenders swarmed around Hewitt, seemingly trapping him. Bill Karr, who had started the play on the far right side of the field but slashed across the middle, came up behind Hewitt. Hewitt pitched the ball back to Karr, who sped the rest of the way into the end zone.

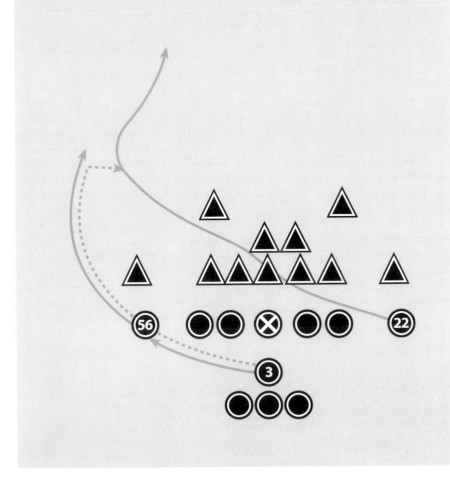

the Bears in the hunt all day as he booted three field goals. Still, the Giants held a 21–16 lead with five minutes to go when the Bears got a break.

A weak Strong punt gave the Bears the ball on the New York 47-yard line. The Bears advanced to the 33. It was then that Chicago reverted to what appeared to be its now-favorite play.

The snap went to Nagurski, and just as he had the year before, he faked a run into the line before dropping back a few yards with the intent to pass. Nagurski threw a jump pass to Hewitt, who gathered the ball in and stampeded toward the Giants' goal line. Defenders began closing in on him, but rather than simply protect the ball and go down after a significant gain, Hewitt had other plans.

Coming up from behind was Bears right end Bill Karr, a less-fabled rookie receiver out of West Virginia who already had an eight-yard touchdown catch in the game. Before the game, a Chicago tailor announced he would provide a new suit to the first Bear to score. Karr was about to gain greater fame, if not additional clothing for his wardrobe.

As Hewitt was swarmed by Giants tacklers, he lateraled the ball to Karr. Gene Ronzani, another backfield Bear who liked contact, had also followed the play downfield. Ronzani had the perfect blocking

GAME DETAILS

Bears 23 • Giants 21

Location: Wrigley Field, Chicago

Attendance: 30,000

It was the greatest game I have ever seen.

—RED GRANGE

Box Score:

Giants	0	7	7	7	**21**
Bears	3	3	10	7	**23**

Scoring:

CHI Manders 16-yard field goal

CHI Manders 40-yard field goal

NY Badgro 29-yard pass from Newman (Strong PAT)

CHI Manders 28-yard field goal

NY Krause 1-yard run (Strong PAT)

CHI Karr 8-yard pass from Nagurski (Manders PAT)

NY Strong 8-yard pass from Newman (Strong PAT)

CHI Karr 33-yard lateral from Hewitt after 14-yard pass from Nagurski (Manders PAT)

angle to knock the remaining two Giants between Karr and the end zone into one another. The terrific block saved Karr.

"I guess I must have thrown a pretty good block," Ronzani said years later, "because those two fellows there, I knocked them right on their cans. I can still remember it, maybe because one of the things I liked to do best was put people on their fannies."

That spectacular play—Nagurski to Hewitt to Karr—gave the Bears the lead and represented the game-winning touchdown. The ball handlers got most of the credit. But Ronzani's hit was just as important. If the play occurred in a more modern era of football, it would have been replayed a thousand times on highlight shows and John Madden would have added Ronzani to the All-Madden team.

The Giants turned in a last-gasp drive to try to change the lead one more time, but from his defensive backfield spot, Red Grange made a game-saving tackle and the Bears claimed the 1933 championship.

Karr spent six years with the Bears, catching 48 passes. He was always a big-play receiver, scoring 18 touchdowns among those limited number of receptions and averaging 21.5 yards per catch for his career. But he never made a bigger play than grabbing hold of the lateral from Hewitt that won the Bears a championship.

Bronk and the two Bills got the credit, but the guy we all patted on the back was Ronzani.

—BEARS QUARTERBACK CARL BRUMBAUGH

December 12, 1965

2 GALE SAYERS SCORES SIX TOUCHDOWNS

85-Yard Punt Return Caps Day

There was magic in Gale Sayers's legs that day when everyone around him, from blockers to tacklers—especially tacklers—could barely maintain balance on the slippery, wet, muddy grass at Wrigley Field.

It was a day when the "Kansas Comet," so nicknamed because of his speed and elusiveness while carrying the ball as a two-time All-American at the University of Kansas, would write history with his National Football League-tying six-touchdown day. On a dreary afternoon, Sayers completely discouraged the San Francisco 49ers and energized the 46,278 Chicago Bears fans who shrugged off the nasty weather.

The bleak gray sky alternated between unleashing drizzle and downpour as Sayers, on his way to a rookie-record 22 touchdowns that autumn, and his Bears poured it on the 49ers. By the fourth quarter, Sayers had recorded touchdowns on runs of 21, 7, 50, and one yards and added a fifth score on an 80-yard screen pass. While everyone around him flailed, Sayers seemed to glide effortlessly across the muddy surface.

When asked to explain his performance, all Sayers could say was that everyone else seemed to slip and he didn't. Observers could see that, but Sayers could not add any insight without sounding boastful and admitting he was simply otherworldly that day. After all, it would have been a variation of saying he could walk on water while others drowned.

Sayers was 6'0" and weighed 198 pounds. He and linebacker Dick Butkus, both future Hall of Fame selections, were drafted in the first round by the Bears earlier in 1965 in one of the most valuable drafts ever conducted by any team. By the time the Bears faced the 49ers in this late-season game, Sayers had made his professional mark. He had scored four touchdowns in a game to lift Chicago over the Minnesota Vikings. That eye-catching effort persuaded San Francisco to install a defense aimed at containing Sayers and shutting down the Bears' running game.

All the time spent on pregame preparations went for nothing, however. The Bears led 47–20 when Sayers dropped back

> **Y**ou could go through a full game and never get to touch that man.
>
> —MATT HAZELTINE

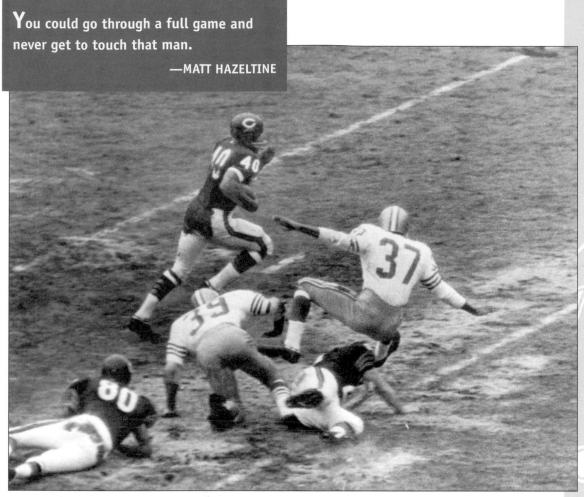

Gale Sayers scores one of his record-setting six touchdowns against the San Francisco 49ers on December 12, 1965. *(Photo courtesy of WireImages)*

to field a punt in the fourth quarter. The ball floated through the rain and Sayers cradled it. Dashing through a mushy field that only kids would love to play on, he was off again, shedding and fooling 49ers tacklers. Next stop, the end zone, 85 yards away.

The punt return was Sayers's sixth touchdown of the day, tying Ernie Nevers of the old Chicago Cardinals and Dub Jones of the Cleveland Browns for a single-game league record that still stands. Then, before a seventh record-breaking touchdown could be scored, coach George Halas pulled Sayers from the game. Many thought Halas should

have given his running back the chance to go after a new record, but Sayers was not one of them. The self-effacing rookie said he had had a better day once in high school when he did score seven touchdowns.

Sayers said he was brought up not to focus on records and it made sense to take him out of play before the game's conclusion because the result was decided. Sayers said he has never regretted not staying in the lineup to pursue a seventh touchdown against the 49ers.

Sayers left it to others to praise him, which they did, rather loudly. Later, Halas said he felt Sayers could have scored one or two more touchdowns if he stayed in the lineup. It was very obvious in the late going that Sayers certainly would have had a heck of a shot at one more. The Bears had the ball on the 49ers' 2-yard line. Fans began chanting, "We want Sayers!" Halas did not put his swift runner back into the game; instead, backup halfback Jon Arnett plunged into the end zone for the Bears' final touchdown of the day.

If Halas had reinserted Sayers into the lineup, no doubt there would have been complaints from the San Francisco side of the field that the Bears were trying to run up the score. That hullabaloo would have blown over, but a Sayers seven-touchdown day would have endured.

Sayers gained 336 total yards and scored 36 points that soggy afternoon. Someone actually asked teammate Mike Ditka if the weather slowed Sayers. "Yeah, the mud affected the kid," the All-Pro tight end replied. "If it had been dry out there, he would have scored 10 touchdowns."

The 49ers on the other side of the field never forgot what they witnessed that day. They took it personally

GALE SAYERS

To a large extent, Gale Sayers barely scratched the surface of his football potential because of the many knee injuries that slowed him down. Sayers was the youngest man ever inducted into the Pro Football Hall of Fame at age 34.

However, an early retirement meant Sayers was forced into a different life. He became athletic director at Southern Illinois University, participated in the authorship of several books, and began a

> **I** wasn't concerned about records.
>
> —GALE SAYERS

very successful computer consulting business in the Chicago area.

Sayers also makes public appearances and speaks at events. In 2004, addressing a crowd at a College Football Hall of Fame luncheon, he said, "I don't care to be remembered as the man who scored six touchdowns in a game. I want to be remembered as a winner in life. Sure, I would have loved to have played 10 or 12 years of professional football. But the only things that would have happened were more touchdowns, more points, and probably more hurts. I got everything that pro football had to offer."

Gale Sayers is the youngest man ever inducted into the Pro Football Hall of Fame and had his number retired by the Bears in 1994. *(Photo courtesy of AP Images)*

GAME DETAILS

Bears 61 • 49ers 20

Location: Wrigley Field, Chicago

Attendance: 46,278

I was never involved in anything like that before or since.

—49ERS DEFENSIVE TACKLE CHARLIE KRUEGER

Box Score:

49ers	0	13	0	7	**20**
Bears	13	14	13	21	**61**

Scoring:

CHI Sayers 80-yard pass from Bukich (PAT failed)

CHI Ditka 29-yard pass from Bukich (Leclerc PAT)

SF Parks 9-yard pass from Brodie (Davis PAT)

CHI Sayers 21-yard run (Leclerc PAT)

SF Crow 15-yard pass from Brodie (PAT failed)

CHI Sayers 7-yard run (Leclerc PAT)

CHI Sayers 50-yard run (Leclerc PAT)

CHI Sayers 1-yard run (run failed)

SF Kopay 2-yard run (Davis PAT)

CHI Jones 8-yard pass from Bukich (Leclerc PAT)

CHI Sayers 85-yard punt return (Leclerc PAT)

CHI Arnett 2-yard run (Leclerc PAT)

the way Sayers ran roughshod over them despite their advance focus on corralling him.

"Great, damn, 'Chicago defense,'" linebacker Matt Hazeltine cursed at his coaches during the game.

Years later, Hazeltine said Sayers was so good he hated to play against the runner.

"You know what?" Hazeltine said. "Sayers was the only man I've ever been afraid to play. Not of contact, but afraid of being embarrassed."

Perhaps Sayers did not make too much of his legendary performance at the time because he was just starting out and expected there to be more days like it. However, Sayers's career was cut short because of severe knee injuries. By 1972 he had undergone four operations that affected both his left and right knees. Sayers's legendary wheels had become flat tires, and by age 29 he had retired from the NFL. If Sayers had come along 40 years later and had modern medical technology on his side, it's likely his career could have been salvaged. Five years after retirement, Sayers became the youngest man inducted into the Pro Football Hall of Fame in Canton, Ohio.

While still with the Bears, Sayers became the first African American professional athlete to room on the road with a white player. Sayers and running back Brian Piccolo, out of Wake Forest, became good friends and their relationship was spotlighted in newspapers and held up as an example of racial harmony in books and movies after Piccolo died of cancer.

Piccolo was in the hospital when Sayers was honored with a special award for courage based on his comeback from knee surgery. During his acceptance speech at a banquet, Sayers spoke eloquently of Piccolo's courage in battling the disease and asked those in attendance to pray for Piccolo. Then Sayers announced he was going directly to the hospital to give the award to Piccolo, the man who really deserved it.

December 18, 1932

BEARS CAPTURE "TOM THUMB GAME"

Bronko and Red Are Men of the Hour

The greatest play in Chicago Bears history was part of the drama of perhaps the strangest game in Chicago Bears history, known simply as the "Tom Thumb Game." In a game that had great plays, drama, and controversy to spare, it was fitting that it was decided on a play so spectacular that it resulted in National Football League rules changes.

As the 1932 season wound down it was apparent that the two best teams in the league were the Bears and the Portsmouth Spartans, the forerunners of the Detroit Lions. At that time the league was not separated into Eastern and Western conferences, so the teams with the top records met for a championship playoff. The Bears and Spartans posted the peculiar records of 7–1–6 and 6–2–4, respectively, that season. They twice played to ties of 7–7 and 13–13. It was surprising that sudden overtime was not adopted then given the frustrating lack of decisiveness in so many games, but that rule change didn't arrive for decades.

As one of the many side plots surrounding the game, the Bears' championship appearance represented the culmination of a promise from coach Ralph Jones. Jones filled in during one of Halas's leaves of absence as coach and said he would deliver a Bears title within three years. This was the third year.

With the Bears as hosts, normally a home game would be played at Wrigley Field. However, Chicago was suffering from a relentless blizzard that hammered the city, so in the dual interests of fan survival and prevention of player frostbite, the game was moved inside Chicago Stadium, home of the Chicago Blackhawks hockey team.

This was the first official game played indoors in NFL history, though the dimensions of the field had to be redrawn to an undersized 80-yards long and about 45-yards wide—hence, the "Tom Thumb" moniker. The Salvation Army had just sponsored a circus at the Stadium, leaving behind what Halas called "a swell brand of dirt." Kickoff was scheduled for 8:15 PM, making the title game likely the first NFL night game in history.

Pro football legends Red Grange (left) and Bronko Nagurski teamed up to lead the Bears to victory in the 1932 NFL Championship Game. *(Photo courtesy of AP Images)*

The venture proved entirely satisfactory to the spectators, who would have been forced to sit in subfreezing temperatures at Wrigley Field. It was not so popular with the players.

—*CHICAGO TRIBUNE* SPORTS EDITOR ARCH WARD

Weather forbidding, 11,198 fans, just about a full house, proved their devotion to the Bears by attending a contest that remained scoreless into the fourth period. The Spartans' best player, quarterback Earl "Dutch" Clark, was absent because of a conflict—his full-time job called for him to be coaching the Colorado College basketball team that night far, far away.

The Bears, on the other hand, were fully manned with fullback Bronko Nagurski and halfback Red Grange, two of the most famous players in the history of the sport.

Tales of the 6'2", 230-pound Nagurski's strength and power are legendary. Would-be tacklers often just bounced off his rock-hard, muscled body and it was only half-kiddingly joked that Nagurski didn't need blockers because he ran his own interference. The "Bronk" was also a fearsome tackle on defense.

Bronislau Nagurski was born on November 3, 1908, in Rainy River, Ontario, Canada, but grew up on a farm in International Falls, Minnesota. The origins of Nagurski mythology stem from a story told by University of Minnesota coaches. Legend has it that a Gophers coach looking for directions came upon a boy plowing a field. When the young man lifted the plow to point the way, Nagurski was signed on the spot. Nagurski's fame was well-established by the time he graduated from Minnesota and in an era when versatility was mandatory, it was believed he could play most any position.

Harold was the given name of Grange, born on June 13, 1903. His startling runs and multiple-touchdown games for the University of Illinois dazzled the Big Ten and the nation's football fans. Growing up in the Chicago suburb of Wheaton, Grange worked hauling ice to build stronger muscles and kept working at the job well beyond the days when he needed the money.

In a nothing-like-it-before-or-since roller-coaster ride in 1925, Grange single-handedly elevated the profile of professional football on a national tour. By then he possessed the most euphonious nickname in creation. "The Galloping Ghost" was a speedy and elusive runner, the perfect complement to Nagurski, and as a bonus was a sticky-fingered defensive back.

In the 1932 title game, the defenses seemed to quickly adapt to the strange playing conditions. Most of the championship game against Portsmouth was a defensive battle, with neither side able to outsmart the other. It would have taken some convincing to persuade anyone that decades later, an organization called the Arena Football League would thrive on a similarly small indoor field.

The Bears' fortunes were complicated when Grange was kicked in the head at the end of a 15-yard running play in the first quarter and was knocked unconscious. He went to the bench to clear his head and stayed there for most of the rest of the game. Throughout the first half and third quarter the score remained 0–0.

The turning point occurred when Bears safety Dick Nesbitt intercepted a Spartans pass and returned the ball to the Portsmouth 7-yard line. A now clear-headed Grange asked to be put back into the game.

One of the ground rules established before the game began was that a team's offense could choose to move the ball away from the sideline by forfeiting first down. The Bears did so, and on second down Nagurski lowered his shoulder and powered toward the goal line. He gained six yards, leaving the Bears a third-and-goal

GAME DETAILS

Bears 9 • Spartans 0

Location: Chicago Stadium, Chicago

Attendance: 11,198

Box Score:

Spartans	0	0	0	0	**0**
Bears	0	0	0	9	**9**

Scoring:
CHI Grange 1-yard pass from Nagurski (Engebretsen PAT)
CHI Safety, Wilson tackled in end zone

> **S**omeone had knocked me down, but I got the ball and hung onto it.
>
> —RED GRANGE

at the 1-yard line. The Portsmouth defenders formed an impenetrable wall on third down, and Nagurski was stopped for no gain.

On fourth down, the Bears might well have felt the law of averages favored Nagurski and repeated the previously stymied assault. But in reviewing a 10-man Portsmouth line, it seemed time to take a risk. The ball once again came into Nagurski's hands. The fullback ducked as if he was going to plunge forward, then abruptly faded back a few yards. Meanwhile, Grange vacated the backfield and sped into the end zone. Nagurski remembers his teammate being wide open; Grange said he was, but only after he fell flat on his back after being hit by a Spartan. Either way, Nagurski threw a jump pass into the end zone.

Touchdown! Enraged, Potsy Clark, Portsmouth's coach, protested that Nagurski was not five yards behind the line of scrimmage before throwing as the rules dictated at the time. Halas, whose temper was legendary when he was challenged, was breathing fire back at Clark. Oh, what Clark would have given for instant replay. The touchdown stood. The Bears kicked the extra point and added a safety for 9–0 final score. They were champions of the NFL.

Jones had made good on his pledge to deliver a champion to Halas and he returned to the college game for the rest of his career as Halas returned to the bench. The Bears adopted the jump pass over the charging line as a regular play in their repertoire.

Before the 1933 season, the league created hash marks to move the ball 10 yards in from the sideline and altered the rules to allow quarterbacks the freedom to throw from anywhere behind the line of scrimmage as a way to enhance the passing game. Also, league owners began to see the benefits of the passing game and footballs were reshaped to become more streamlined in order to aid their flight.

The greatest play in Bears history gave Chicago a championship and proved to be one of the most course-altering plays in NFL history. Without the changes that were implemented after this legendary game, pro football might never have become America's favorite sport.

Bronko's Flip to Red

The Portsmouth Spartans put forth a 10-man line to stymie the Chicago Bears on fourth down at the 1-yard line in the fourth quarter of the 1932 "Tom Thumb Game" for the NFL championship. Portsmouth anticipated that Bears fullback Bronko Nagurski would try to drive up the middle, but when the ball was snapped Nagurski faked toward the line, then took a few steps back and scanned the end zone. Halfback Red Grange was knocked to the ground by a Portsmouth defender, but managed to catch the jump pass from Nagurski for the touchdown.

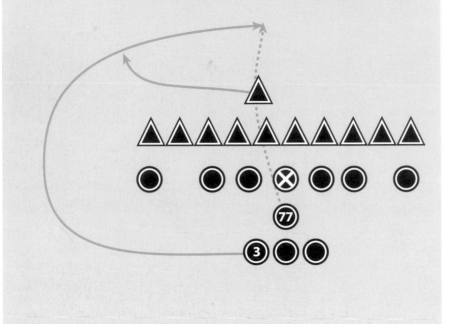

The view of the 80-yard field inside the Chicago Stadium, site of one of the most unusual games in NFL history.

Sources

BOOKS

Carroll, Bob, and Total Sports. *Total Football II: The Official Encyclopedia of the National Football League.* New York: Harper Collins Publishers, Inc., 1997, 1999.

Davis, Jeff. *Papa Bear: The Life and Legacy of George Halas.* New York: McGraw-Hill, 2005.

Dent, Jim. *Monster of the Midway: Bronko Nagurski, the 1943 Chicago Bears, and the Greatest Comeback Ever.* New York: St. Martin's Press, 2003.

Freedman, Lew. *Game of My Life: Chicago Bears.* Champaign, IL: Sports Publishing, LLC, 2006.

Grange, Red, with Ira Morton. *The Red Grange Story: An Autobiography As Told to Ira Morton.* Champaign, IL: Illini Books Edition, 1993.

Halas, George S., with Gwen Morgan and Arthur Veysey. *Halas by Halas: An Autobiography.* New York: McGraw-Hill, 1979.

McMahon, Jim, with Bob Verdi. *McMahon!* New York: Warner Books, 1987.

McMichael, Steve with Phil Arvia. *Steve McMichael's Tales from the Chicago Bears Sideline.* Champaign, IL: Sports Publishing, LLC, 2004.

Payton, Walter with Don Yaeger. *Never Die Easy: The Autobiography of Walter Payton.* New York: Random House, Inc., 2000.

Sayers, Gale with Fred Mitchell. *Sayers: My Life and Times.* Chicago: Triumph Books, 2007.

Wolfe, Rich. *Da Coach: Irreverent Stories from His Players, Coaches, and Friends.* Chicago: Triumph Books, 2001.

Youmans, Gary with Maury Youmans. *'63: The Story of the 1963 World Champion Chicago Bears.* Syracuse, NY: Syracuse University Press, 2004.

Ziemba, Joe. *When Football Was Football: The Chicago Cardinals and the Birth of the NFL.* Chicago: Triumph Books, 1999.

MEDIA GUIDES

1986 Chicago Bears
2007 Chicago Bears

NEWSPAPERS

The (Canton) *Repository*
Champaign News-Gazette
Chicago American
Chicago Tribune

Chicago Sun-Times
Los Angeles Times
New York Herald-Tribune
New York Journal-American
New York Sun
The New York Times
Washington Evening Star
The Washington Post
The Washington Times
USA Today
Unlabeled newspaper stories from Pro Football Hall of Fame Archives

OTHER PRINTED MATERIAL

Football Digest
NFL Game Day Programs
Pro Football Hall of Fame produced stories on individual Hall of Fame members
The Saturday Evening Post
Sport magazine
Sports Illustrated

PERSONAL INTERVIEWS

Doug Buffone
Harlon Hill
Richie Petitbon
Keith Van Horne
Bill Wade

WEBSITES

absoluteastastronomy.com
brokennewz.com
chicagobears.com
Answers.com
collegefootball.org

WIRE SERVICES

Associated Press
United Press International